Perennials

TIME
LIFE
BOOKS
®

Other Publications:

WORLD WAR II

THE GREAT CITIES

HOME REPAIR AND IMPROVEMENT

THE WORLD'S WILD PLACES

THE TIME-LIFE LIBRARY OF BOATING

HUMAN BEHAVIOR

THE ART OF SEWING

THE OLD WEST

THE EMERGENCE OF MAN

THE AMERICAN WILDERNESS

LIFE LIBRARY OF PHOTOGRAPHY

THIS FABULOUS CENTURY

FOODS OF THE WORLD

TIME-LIFE LIBRARY OF AMERICA

TIME-LIFE LIBRARY OF ART

GREAT AGES OF MAN

LIFE SCIENCE LIBRARY

THE LIFE HISTORY OF THE UNITED STATES

TIME READING PROGRAM

LIFE NATURE LIBRARY

LIFE WORLD LIBRARY

FAMILY LIBRARY:
    HOW THINGS WORK IN YOUR HOME
    THE TIME-LIFE BOOK OF THE FAMILY CAR
    THE TIME-LIFE FAMILY LEGAL GUIDE
    THE TIME-LIFE BOOK OF FAMILY FINANCE

Perennials

by
JAMES UNDERWOOD CROCKETT
and
the Editors of TIME-LIFE BOOKS

Watercolor Illustrations by
Allianora Rosse

TIME-LIFE BOOKS, ALEXANDRIA, VIRGINIA

THE AUTHOR: James Underwood Crockett, a graduate of the University of Massachusetts, received an Honorary Doctor of Science degree from that University and has been cited by the American Association of Nurserymen and the American Horticultural Society. He has worked with plants in California, New York, Texas and New England. He is the author of books on greenhouse, indoor and window-sill gardening, and has written a monthly column for *Horticulture* magazine and a monthly bulletin, *Flowery Talks,* for retail florists. His weekly television program, *Crockett's Victory Garden,* has been seen by more than three million viewers on 125 public broadcasting stations throughout the United States.

THE ILLUSTRATOR: Allianora Rosse, who provided the 148 delicate, precise watercolors of perennials beginning on page 90, is a specialist in flower painting. Trained at the Art Academy of The Hague in The Netherlands, Miss Rosse worked for 16 years as staff artist for *Flower Grower* magazine. Her illustrations of shrubs, trees and flowers have appeared in many gardening books. Miss Rosse lives in New Hampshire.

GENERAL CONSULTANTS: Dr. C. Gustav Hard, Associate Professor, University of Minnesota, St. Paul, Minn. Albert P. Nordheden, New York City. Staff of the Brooklyn Botanic Garden: Louis B. Martin, Director; Robert S. Tomson, Assistant Director; George A. Kalmbacher, Plant Taxonomist; Edmund O. Moulin, Horticulturist.

THE COVER: The late-summer colors of a perennial border make a striking combination: red, pink and yellow day lilies, deep lavender balloonflowers and at left the flat golden heads of achillea, or fern-leaved yarrow.

CORRESPONDENTS: Elisabeth Kraemer (Bonn); Margot Hapgood, Dorothy Bacon (London); Susan Jonas, Lucy T. Voulgaris (New York); Maria Vincenza Aloisi, Josephine du Brusle (Paris); Ann Natanson (Rome). Valuable assistance was also provided by the following individuals: Carolyn T. Chubet (New York); Jane Estes (Seattle).

CONTENTS

The flowers that bloom year after year 1

Among the most rewarding traits of perennials is the fact that they come up unprompted year after year to offer the garden masses and highlights of color in uninterrupted but ever-changing patterns from April to November. Perennials flower abundantly and multiply without being coaxed. Most of them are easy to grow. Some require spadework occasionally, but many will tolerate considerable neglect. In fact, I have seen long-abandoned farms in New England where gaping cellar holes and tumbled walls of old houses were adorned with great clumps of day lilies, thriving and spreading.

The perennials are numerous and diverse; they include such garden mainstays as delphiniums, columbines and daisies, and such oddities as cohosh bugbane, with its curious spike of white flowers that resembles a bottle brush. Some of the best of them appear at the very times that the garden needs them most. When the tulips and daffodils have faded and summer annuals still are seedlings, the bushy peony, the stately iris and the alluring hairy-leaved Oriental poppy rise to perform spectacularly. And when autumn frosts and gales have driven everything else off stage, chrysanthemums and hardy asters remain to flaunt their colors in a grand finale.

A perennial, in the broadest horticultural definition, is any plant that lives for three or more years. The definition covers a lot of ground, embracing both dandelions and giant redwoods and thousands of species in between. But when gardeners talk about perennials, they almost always mean—as does this book—flowering garden plants with stems that are herbaceous, i.e., fleshy rather than woody, and that usually die down to the soil's surface before winter, while the roots remain alive and ready to send up new growth the next season. (Technically, bulbous plants such as tulips and daffodils are perennials, but they generally are classified separately because of their method of storing food for next year's growth.)

What sets perennials apart from annuals and from biennials —which make good companions for perennials and which are also covered in this book—is the durability of their roots. Annuals

While his sweetheart holds a lantern, a Japanese gentleman plucks a chrysanthemum at night in a garden pavilion. Chrysanthemums have been raised in the Orient for 2,000 years.

sprout from seed, bloom, bear more seed with which to reproduce, and die—all in a single year. Biennials, which include sweet William, foxglove, Canterbury bell and wallflower, also sprout from seed, but spend their first year growing and their second year flowering and producing seed—and then die. Bearing seed is hard work for plants and in nature seed germination can be a chancy thing; the herbaceous perennials have found a more dependable way to survive and propagate. They have the same kinds of sex organs —pistils and stamens—as annuals and biennials and many of them do produce seeds annually. But others do so only sporadically; they concentrate their efforts toward survival in their roots, often spreading them through the soil to multiply the species.

A LONG-LIVED FAMILY However they multiply, flowering perennials are notably long-lived. Just the other day a friend recounted to me the history—insofar as it is known—of a dark red peony that has been in her husband's family for well over a century. It came to America from China, where peonies originated, perhaps in the cabin of a clipper ship's captain. How old it was then no one can say. Its first recorded appearance in this country dates back to 1846, when a young woman named Rebecca Bailey took the plant with her, via canal boat, when she moved from her birthplace in Dauphin County, Pennsylvania, to her new home in Jersey Shore, Pennsylvania. When she died in 1928 at the age of 96, the peony was still flourishing and her daughter Flora transplanted it to her own garden in Jersey Shore. Flora lived to be 83 but the peony outlasted her, and Flora's daughter Anna, who inherited it, shifted the plant to still another garden, in Du Bois, Pennsylvania, where it was blooming when Anna died at 94. A division of the plant then went to the Pittsburgh garden of Walter H. Stryker, Anna's son and Rebecca's great-grandson. And one of the plant's scions has been transplanted to the garden of Mr. Stryker's daughter, Judith French, in Forge Village, Massachusetts.

I suspect that Rebecca Bailey's peony has hundreds of equally venerable counterparts, the stories of which have been forgotten. All the attention that I give my own peonies is a handful of bone meal in the fall and perhaps another in the spring. Yet they bloom on and on. Not all perennials live as long as my friend's peony or those abandoned New England day lilies, however. Delphiniums, for example, may thrive for as long as eight years where winters and summers both are moderate, but survive only a year where the climate is hot. Still, most perennials grow well in most parts of the U.S.; even in Zones 9 and 10 *(map, page 151),* where the weather is too warm for some of them, others will flourish. On the warm and humid Gulf Coast, for example, day lilies do beautifully and some other perennials thrive, including coreopsis, acan-

8

thus, lavender cotton, Stokes's aster and false indigo. The dry, windy Plains States—the very opposite climatically of the Gulf Coast—do not lack for perennials either. It is true that such delicate little plants as primroses will not grow there, but peonies flourish. So do Oriental poppies, garden phlox, bearded irises, day lilies, chrysanthemums and many others.

Some perennials change their life styles to conform to their surroundings. Petunias and snapdragons are perennials in mild climates but in the North their roots perish in the cold. So Northern gardeners who cherish them—as I do—must treat them as annuals, planting their seeds anew each year. Conversely some annuals become biennials and some biennials become perennials in regions where winters are mild. In addition, different varieties of some plants, such as hollyhocks and forget-me-nots, may be annuals, biennials or perennials. Anomalies such as these make gardening more challenging and, to the dedicated gardener, more fun.

With perennials the challenges confront you early, despite the ease with which the flowers can be grown, for a perennial garden is a long-range and never static project that, ideally, incorporates both permanence and constant change. Its objective is to present a pleasant and even exalting array of color from early spring to late fall. But it is the rare perennial that blooms all of the growing season. That is the first challenge—to obtain continuity of color by planting different varieties to bloom harmoniously at different times.

Another challenge is to keep different types of perennials from overgrowing one another in the same beds and creating a horticultural slum. Some highly desirable perennials, notably chrysanthemums, spread so fast that their population explosion requires drastic control measures, including annual digging up and division of the roots. Other equally desirable perennials never outgrow their allotted space, providing they are given enough of it when they are planted. One such is the peony. Another is the gas plant, which, I must confess, gave me quite a start the first time I encountered it. The whole plant—dark green leaves and 1½ - to 2-foot spikes of rosy pink flowers—was suddenly enveloped in a flash of blue flame as I stood before it. I was a new 25-cents-an-hour helper in a nursery at Ward Hill, Massachusetts (this was in the early 1930s), and a more knowledgeable coworker had held a lighted match near the plant, igniting the highly flammable oil that the gas plant gives off. (If you decide to grow a gas plant, demonstrate its magic only in midsummer—it will not work at other times.)

Most gardeners can spare only a few hours a week for their plants—and therein lies a third challenge, to obtain maximum results with minimum work. Before you start to think of specific

SOME BASIC GOALS

plants, or even of the overall color and form that the garden will take, consider its potential sites from a purely practical standpoint. Good perennial gardens require free circulation of air; plant diseases thrive in stagnant air, particularly when the weather is humid. They require, for the most part, abundant sunshine; some perennials, such as day lilies, columbines and leopard's-bane, will tolerate shade and some, such as Japanese anemone, plantain lilies, yellow corydalis, western bleeding heart and Siberian bugloss, will thrive in it. But the majority will grow spindly stems with few flowers and fall victim to infections without ample sun. Finally, good perennial gardens require properly prepared soil—soil that is both well drained and sufficiently moisture retentive so that it will not bake hard; soil that is rich enough to withstand years of demand on its nutritive content and—most important of all—soil that is open and loose enough in structure to permit air as well as moisture to reach the roots. (Useful soil bacteria that assist the nutritional processes of plants cannot live without air.) Not all gardens offer such ideal conditions naturally, but given the air circulation and the sunshine, you can create the other essentials. (The preparation and maintenance of soil for perennials is discussed at length in Chapter 2.)

LOCATING YOUR BEDS

Once you know where you can grow perennials on your property, consider where you should grow them, that is, where they will look their best. They ought, if possible, to be visible from the house and perhaps from the patio or porch to lengthen your enjoyment of them. Because perennials bloom profusely and colorfully, the majority are most effective in masses, but they also serve very well when planted in small clumps to accent the hues of other flowers. They surpass themselves when they have a dark background that focuses attention on them rather than on a distant landscape or, more likely in these days of suburban living, the house next door. One of the finest plantings of Christmas roses that I have seen—a Christmas rose is a lovely little plant with evergreen leaves and 3-inch white blossoms that open in late fall or early spring—snuggles in a nook backed by the dark green of yews. Many other evergreens as well as deciduous hedges, vine-covered walls and fences make first-rate backgrounds for perennials.

In Victorian England it used to be considered akin to indecent exposure to plant perennials in anything but a long, straight border, 8 to 12 feet wide, or to mix perennials with other plants such as annuals and biennials. But you greatly increase your options if you plant perennials in various kinds of beds and if you mix them with other flowers, so I am for putting them wherever they will look good and grow well without getting in each other's way—beside the front door to add color to the all-green foundation planting, in a strip beside the garage, mingled with flowering shrubs or wherever else the conditions of sun, air and soil permit.

Most perennials, like other garden flowers, can also be grown in movable tubs and other containers, or in beds raised above the ground level. One gardener I know apparently took to heart the words attributed to a monk who lived 1,200 years ago: "Stooping is the worst thing for the aging gardener, and how can one escape the backache except by raising the beds?" My friend, who had retired and moved from New York to Cape Cod, built a bed of railroad ties rising 3 feet above his lawn, and he grows his perennials there. (Because it drains faster, such a bed has to be watered more often, but that doesn't require stooping and my friend has plenty of time.)

Certain perennials are natural plants for rock gardens and walls. A cousin of mine in Maine, who had no railroad ties but did have a stone retaining wall, made the wall and the space adjoining the top of it into a perennial garden. The wall is of fieldstone, laid without mortar, and she has set moss phlox and rock cress to grow between the stones and flow down the wall's face. A few of the larger perennials can be used in small groups or even standing alone, filling a spot that might otherwise be occupied by a flowering shrub or evergreen. In the Southwest I have seen a plume poppy—a plant that may grow 10 feet tall and bear huge plumes of small, feathery, creamy white blossoms—towering beside a wrought-iron gate. Its huge gray-green leaves and airy millinery made a striking complement to the tracery of the ironwork.

In planning any major planting of perennials, it is a good idea to work out its location, size, shape and combination of plants with pencil and paper first. Start conservatively. Grandiose dreams by a fireplace in midwinter do not realize themselves in easy upkeep, come spring, summer and fall, for even undemanding gardens need some weeding, some fertilizing and some scratching of the soil.

If you are planning a perennial bed that backs on a hedge, a wall or a fence, leave at least 3 feet of space between it and its backdrop, and make it from 6 to 8 feet wide. There are good reasons for both suggestions. Where the bed lies in front of a hedge, the space will prevent competition between the plants' roots and those of the shrubbery; it will also allow for circulation of air and will give you room to work at the bed's rear. In addition, it will help to preserve the hedge's looks, because if the hedge's lower branches are shaded all summer by tall perennials, they will eventually die, leaving ugly gaps that will prove all too noticeable in winter. This holds true for plants set in smaller clumps close to evergreens and shrubs; give them breathing space too. Walls and fences, of course, do not compete for soil nutrients or suffer from shading, but the 3-foot leeway

BEE BALM TEA

After the Boston Tea Party of 1773 discouraged the importation of tea into New England, the resourceful colonists took a leaf from the Oswego Indians and substituted for tea a perennial herb, bee balm (Monarda didyma), so named because its scarlet flowers are favorites of bees. A plant that grows from Quebec to Georgia, it is a relative of mint and has a similar fresh taste. The tea is easy to make if you follow the colonists' method, which they borrowed from the Indians: First dry the leaves by hanging them, still attached to the stems, in a cool dry place for about 10 days. Then remove the leaves and dice them into ¼-inch pieces. Brew as you would ordinary tea, using 1 teaspoon for each cup of freshly boiled water, plus 1 for the pot, and steeping for three to five minutes. The fresh leaves of bee balm, as the French have long known, also make a tasty addition to salads, wine and fruit punch.

PLANNING ON PAPER

is still a good idea because the plants need circulating air and room for their roots, and you need room to work in back of them. Remember too that brick, stone and concrete walls, particularly those facing south or west, will reflect or absorb and reradiate the heat of the sun. This may make conditions too warm for the plants. For one thing, the warmth can induce plants to sprout prematurely in spring, only to be nipped or even killed by late frosts.

The width of the bed from front to back is as important in your plan as the 3-foot breezeway behind it, because the ease with which one can obtain continuous color in a perennial bed increases in direct proportion to the width. Suppose you made the bed 3 feet wide. It could comfortably accommodate only two rows of plants, say low sweet Williams in front and taller chrysanthemums in back. The sweet Williams would cease flowering in July and the chrysanthemums would show only green foliage until early fall, leaving the bed colorless most of the summer. But a bed 6 to 8 feet wide will provide room for as many as six different kinds of plants from front to rear, and if you use early, midseason and late flowering varieties the bed can display color continuously.

At the same time you are planning the width of the bed and allowing for the needed open space in back, you should also consider the area in front. Perennials have a way of growing exuberantly—that is one of their charms—and frequently plants in the foreground will billow over the edges of the bed. If the bed is fronted by a lawn, as is often the case, mowing close to the bed becomes difficult or impossible and the grass grows up messily through the plants. The best solution is a broad edging or separating strip, over which the plants can spill with abandon without creating maintenance problems. This edging can be a garden path, or a single or double row of bricks laid flat and perpendicular to the line of the bed, or a 1- to 1½-foot strip of flagstones, or a heavy decorative mulch such as wood chips or rough bark. The irregular incursions of the plants onto this neat edging strip merely add to the natural informality of the garden; moreover, grass is easily mowed without hand edging if one wheel of the lawn mower is run along the strip.

CHOOSING PLANTS   Once you have determined the location and shape of your garden, you can start considering specific flowers. The illustrations and notes in the encyclopedia chapter (pages 91-150) will show you what they look like and how and where they can be grown, and the chart on pages 152-154 provides a ready reference to height, color, blossoming season and preferences in light. Choose your plants sparingly. In large gardens there is room for a great variety of plants, even those that bloom briefly, because they can be surrounded by others that will take over later. But the small garden cannot afford

PLANNING A PERENNIAL BORDER

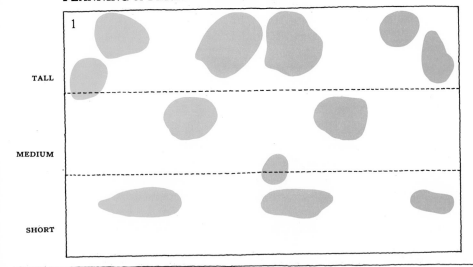

TALL

MEDIUM

SHORT

FALL

To make sure of an attractive combination of flowers blooming in a perennial border through spring, summer and fall, sketch the locations of plants on sheets of tracing paper laid over an outline of the bed. On the first sheet select tall fall-blooming varieties (see the encyclopedia, pages 91-150, and the chart on pages 152-154); draw these in as clumps (dark green) spaced along the back. Then add complementary fall plants (also indicated in dark green), placing medium-sized ones in the center and short ones toward the front.

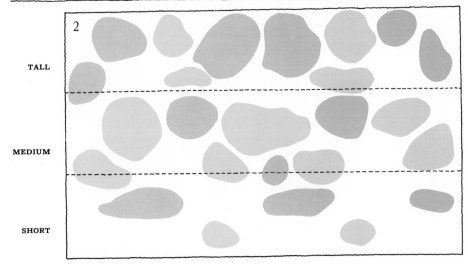

TALL

MEDIUM

SHORT

SUMMER

On a second sheet of tracing paper laid over the first, plan your midseason blooms. Since most plants that flower in summer are medium-sized, select these first as your main display; draw these in as clumps, concentrating them in the center of the bed and locating the plants (indicated in medium green) in some of the open areas not already occupied by the fall flowers. Then place in front and back a few tall and short summer-blooming varieties whose colors will complement the flowers you have chosen for the center.

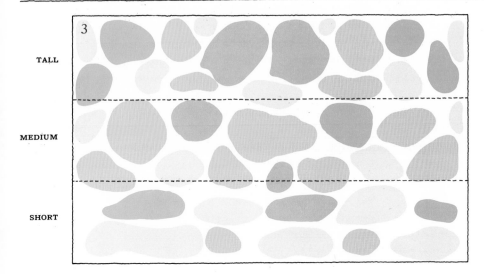

TALL

MEDIUM

SHORT

SPRING

On a third sheet of tracing paper laid over the other two, plan your spring-blooming plants (light green) in the remaining spaces. As most spring perennials are short, they naturally look best in the front of the bed. Some medium-sized and tall spring-flowering plants should be interspersed in the center and back. Now you can trace the outlines of your fall and summer displays through to the top sheet, or a fresh sheet, as a final buying and planting plan, filling in any remaining gaps with bulbs or annuals in desired quantities.

such luxury: every plant must pay its way by blooming long and by displaying ornamental foliage after the flowers fade.

The first step in laying out plants in a perennial bed is to try to think of them not as individual plants but as masses of shapes and colors, both of flowers and foliage, which, appearing at various seasons, allow you to paint an ever-changing garden picture. Simplicity should be the keynote; intricate designs usually fail to come off as well in reality as they do on paper, and they add measurably to maintenance. Color should be used in bold groups, not spotted here and there. Bright colors such as orange and red, however, have to be handled with some skill; most gardeners use them less lavishly than they do pastels, saving them as accent colors here and there to bring vibrancy to the more subtle shades.

DRAWING THE PLAN   In planning the garden's fine points, you must carry a number of different factors in your head simultaneously, so it is a good idea to use a sketch pad to help keep them straight. I find it useful to make three copies of my plan, each depicting the garden at a different peak season, to permit me to envision the changes that will take place as new flowers open and old ones fade (drawings, page 13). Some gardeners like to snip pictures from garden catalogues or magazines and move them about on their plans to give them a rough idea of various effects. Others use bits of colored paper, and some even fill in planting areas with children's colored crayons.

Whether or not you use such aids, I suggest you work backwards. It might seem logical to plan flowers first for spring, then for summer and fall, and to work from the front of the bed to the back. You can do this if you know your plants well, but I find it easier to work the other way round, going from October to May, and from the back of the bed to the front. The reason is fairly simple. In the most common kind of bed or border against the hedge or wall, the tallest plants (3 feet or more high) naturally go in the back (with a few placed forward here and there to dramatize them as accents and to avoid monotony). Since the majority of tall plants flower in late summer or fall, they are logically the backbone of the late-season garden. You will have a wide choice that includes hardy asters, tall chrysanthemums, sunflowers, Japanese anemones and boltonias. With the help of the encyclopedia, decide on a tall fall-flowering plant that particularly appeals to you and that will grow well in your climate and the sun and soil conditions of your bed. Working from left to right (simply because that is the way you read and write and is easiest for most people), place one group of this type of plant at the left rear of the bed, then establish a pattern by placing a second group of the same plant in the center rear and a third at the right rear. With fall color assured for the back of the bed, move to the center and select one or two types of middle-sized fall-blooming plants, in the 2- to 3-foot range, that will go well with those in the back row when both are in bloom; repeat these, too, at intervals. Two favorites here would be pompon chrysanthemums and mistflowers. In the front of the border, select one or two smaller fall-blooming plants such as dwarf-eared coreopsis or arctic chrysanthemum that will complement those in the middle and back rows.

Now move to summer-flowering plants. The emphasis here will probably be in the middle of the border, simply because the majority of the most spectacular plants that bloom in summer are in the middle height range of 2 to 3 feet—Shasta daisies, day lilies, foxgloves, Japanese irises and garden phloxes. Choose among these or others mentioned in the encyclopedia, setting groups of them at the left, center and right of the middle row. Then fill in your summer garden picture with some taller back-row accents such as the globe thistle and heliopsis and a few spots of color in the front row —lamb's ears and fleabane, for example.

Now move to spring-flowering plants. Here the emphasis will be on the front of the border, because the majority of plants that bloom at this season are low growing, under 2 feet. Try to choose plants that not only bloom early, but that either bloom over a long period or retain attractive foliage after the flowers have faded so that they will continue to adorn the garden; the front of a bed or border, after all, is a highly conspicuous part of the overall design. Hybrid bleeding hearts, for example, are a good choice because they start blooming early and continue to bloom most of the summer; many pinks not only flower a long time but keep their handsome gray-green leaves through the growing season. Having established the main spring blooming pattern at the front of the border, fill in the middle and back rows with other spring-flowering plants such as columbine.

After a certain amount of experimenting on paper to arrive at the best combination, you can draw up a master planting plan, indicating the names, quantities and placement of individual plants. From this you can make a buying list of the plants you need to start your garden before turning to your local nurseryman or to your mail-order catalogue. You may not want, or be able, to buy all of them at once, but with a plan as a guide you will at least be able to develop your plantings over a period of two or three years with some goal in mind, filling in bare spots with inexpensive annuals as the need arises, trying different combinations of colors and textures, making additions and corrections as you go. And that process of developing, experimenting and changing, in perennial gardens, can be half the fun.

WHERE TO SEE PERENNIALS

Home gardeners can see outstanding perennial collections—newly developed strains, prize winners, rarely grown types, arrangements of borders—at many gardens in the United States and Canada that are open to the public. Most of the perennial displays open in spring and close in fall when the flowers cease blooming. Among the finest are:

CALIFORNIA
Los Angeles State and County Arboretum, Arcadia; University of California Botanical Garden, Berkeley

MASSACHUSETTS
Berkshire Garden Center, Stockbridge

MISSOURI
Missouri Botanical Garden, St. Louis

NEW YORK
Brooklyn Botanic Garden, New York; Old Westbury Gardens, Old Westbury

NORTH CAROLINA
Sarah P. Duke Gardens, Duke University, Durham

OHIO
Kingwood Center, Mansfield

PENNSYLVANIA
Longwood Gardens, Kennett Square

WISCONSIN
Boerner Botanical Gardens, Hales Corners

TEXAS
Fort Worth Botanic Garden, Fort Worth

CANADA
BRITISH COLUMBIA
Butchart Gardens, Victoria

ONTARIO
Royal Botanical Gardens, Hamilton

QUEBEC
Montreal Botanical Garden, Montreal

The fine art of bordermaking

Among the most familiar garden sights are the beds of perennials that line the walks, lawns and patios of thousands of American homes, sending forth waves of color from early spring until the frosts of fall. As native as they might look in their surroundings, these plantings originated, surprisingly enough, during the 19th Century Victorian era in England. They were conceived by William Robinson, an influential gardening writer who felt that the ornate geometrical designs then in fashion, often filled with plants from distant lands, were unnatural and excessive. Instead, he championed the use of long straight-sided beds, which he called borders, planted with inexpensive and easy-to-grow perennials, many of them bred from native wild flowers like the common daisy and columbine. "There is no arrangement of flowers more graceful, varied, or capable of giving more delight, and none so easily adapted to almost every kind of garden," he wrote in 1883.

This free, informal credo was soon picked up by Gertrude Jekyll, a talented artist and gardener of the day who transformed bordermaking from a concept into a practical horticultural art. In some 350 borders that she designed around the turn of the century, Miss Jekyll perfected the technique of blending and contrasting many different types of flowers as well as foliage. She also advocated the practice of mixing into perennial gardens other kinds of flowers—bulbs, annuals and biennials—that she felt were "right in colour and that make a brave show where a brave show is wanted."

The American descendants of these English gardens make not only a brave but an extremely varied show. They generally follow Miss Jekyll's practices and aim to provide a succession of blooms from spring through fall. But no two borders are quite alike; the enormous diversity of sizes, shapes, colors, foliage and blooming cycles among perennials gives each gardener almost unlimited material with which to suit his own taste. Whatever his choice, the flowers he selects will have one thing in common: they will repeat their performance faithfully the next year, and the next, and the next.

The perennial borders of a garden path, seen in late summer, are dominated by plantings of pale pink and mauve phlox.

16

Planning a succession of bloom

By choosing perennials with an eye to their blooming times, a gardener can "program" his border to provide flowers whenever he wishes. He can, for example, plant a border that will bloom only in spring and autumn if he normally goes away during the summer—and at his vacation home he may enjoy another border planted only with summer-blooming perennials. Or if he is around home most of the summer he can plan a perennial border that will be filled with flowers from spring to fall, simply by selecting and locating plants—including some bulbs and annuals—to bloom in the desired succession. The four pictures below, each showing the same border in New York's Old Westbury Gardens, indicate how such planning produces a garden that changes strikingly with the seasons.

SPRING
Early-blooming irises, in purple, white, yellow and lavender, dominate the border, in front of the first red spikes of lupines. In the foreground are white petunias and marguerites (both grown as annuals in this northern garden).

EARLY SUMMER
The lupines and the blue spikes of delphiniums emerge from behind the foliage of the departed irises. In front of the border are white sweet Williams (foreground), pink border carnations and contrasting maroon sweet Williams.

MIDSUMMER
*The rear of the border blooms with tall
clumps of deep pink bee balm behind
pink and white phloxes. In the foreground
are clumps of white feverfew. Bright
colors are provided by such annuals as red
snapdragons and orange-red salvia.*

AUTUMN
*Clusters of low-growing late-blooming
chrysanthemums at the front lead
off the border's final show of the year.
Behind them and in the foreground
taller pink dahlias, growing from bulbs,
replace the midsummer annuals.*

Choosing shapes and colors

The huge family of perennials includes virtually every flower shape and color known; below are the delicate cuplike blossoms of pink Oriental poppies, on the page at right the bristly spheres of pale blue globe thistles, the daisylike rays of yellow rudbeckia and the flowering spikes of pinkish purple lythrum. But such a bonanza also can be a challenge for the gardener planning a perennial border. For while some shapes and colors go well together, others clash; some look best when massed, others when loosely grouped. In planning a border, many gardeners work much as a designer does, mixing and matching sizes, shapes and colors—and keeping in mind good combinations of flowers and foliage. Often the most effective combination turns out to be the simplest, like the understated but striking juxtaposition pictured on the following pages.

The spectacular but short-lived blooms of the Oriental poppy, seen here against a background of distinctively shaped irises, are often 8 inches or more in diameter; the plants should be widely spaced to provide the best effect.

The rudbeckia, or coneflower, with daisylike blossoms 3 to 4 inches across, is a relative of the wild black-eyed Susan. Planted in a mass, as seen here, it provides a brilliant splash of color.

The bright spikes of lythrums, which grow up to 4 feet tall, make a handsome display in small airy clusters. They look best when used as a background for short plants with rounded shapes.

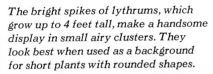

The globe thistle—whose botanical name Echinops means "hedgehoglike" —is an unusual midsummer perennial that grows about 3 to 4 feet tall. Planted in small groups, it provides a striking accent behind other border flowers.

The tiny-flowered plumes of astilbe, or false spirea, lend a pleasing counterpoint to the foliage of a perennial border in midsummer

Astilbe, which comes in many colors, also provides a lacy contrast to plants with larger individual blossoms such as Shasta daisies.

Starting with keynote flowers

SPRING	LATE SPRING	EARLY SUMMER

DOMINANT FLOWER

TALL BEARDED IRIS	CHINESE PEONY	COMMON FOXGLOVE

TALL (over 3 feet)

BLUE FALSE INDIGO COLUMBINE HYBRIDS	CAROLINA THERMOPSIS DELPHINIUM	BIG BETONY DUSTY MEADOW RUE
COLUMBINE MEADOW RUE ORIENTAL POPPY	ITALIAN BUGLOSS LUPINE	GOATSBEARD HOLLYHOCK
SHOWY LEOPARD'S-BANE	SALVIA HAEMATODES	PEACH-LEAVED BELLFLOWER

MEDIUM-SIZED (2 to 3 feet)

GEUM JACOB'S-LADDER	COMMON BLEEDING HEART DAY LILY	BIG-FLOWERED COREOPSIS CANTERBURY BEL
NAPSBURY ASTER SIBERIAN BUGLOSS	DAME'S ROCKET HONESTY	GOLDEN MARGUERITE PAINTED DAISY
SWEET WILLIAM	WONDER OF STAFA ASTER	PENSTEMON

SHORT (under 2 feet)

BORDER PINK FORGET-ME-NOT	CORAL-BELLS ENGLISH DAISY	BLUE FLAX CARPATHIAN HAREBELL
HYBRID BLEEDING HEART ICELAND POPPY	SWEET WOODRUFF WALLFLOWER	DWARF BLANKETFLOWER GERMAN CATCHFL
SEA PINK	WINE-CUP	WHITE CUPFLOWER

Probably the most popular way to plan a perennial border is to build the display for each season around a favorite flower. For early spring there are a few low-growing perennials such as polyanthus primroses and evergreen candytufts, but the great burst of color comes later with plants such as those shown here. Listed beneath each picture are plants that bloom at about the same time as the illustrated flower (for approximate dates of each season in your region, see page 151). Many perennials start earlier or remain in flower longer than the periods in which they are listed and a few, like coral-bells and forget-me-nots, will bloom all summer long.

MIDSUMMER	*LATE SUMMER*	*FALL*
RED-HOT POKER	**FERN-LEAVED YARROW**	**HARDY ASTER**

BEE BALM COMMON VALERIAN	AUTUMN MONKSHOOD BABIES'-BREATH	BLUE SAGE FALSE DRAGONHEAD
GLOBE THISTLE LYTHRUM	SIDALCEA HYBRIDS SNEEZEWEED	JAPANESE ANEMONE KAMCHATKA BUGBANE
ROUGH HELIOPSIS	SUMMER PHLOX	PINK BOLTONIA

ASTILBE FLEABANE	BORDER CARNATION	CONEFLOWER HARDY CHRYSANTHEMUM
MALTESE CROSS MOUNTAIN BLUET	GOLDFLOWER ST.-JOHN'S-WORT JUPITER'S-BEARD	NARROW-LEAVED PLANTAIN LILY
SHASTA DAISY	MISTFLOWER PINCUSHION FLOWER	PINK TURTLEHEAD THREAD-LEAVED COREOPSIS

CUPID'S-DART LILAC CRANE'S-BILL	BALLOONFLOWER SOLIDASTER	BLUE CUPFLOWER DWARF ASTER
SPIKE SPEEDWELL TRUE LAVENDER	STOKES'S ASTER WIDE-LEAVED SEA LAVENDER	DWARF HYBRID GOLDENROD LEADWORT
YELLOW CORYDALIS	WOOLLY BETONY	SEDUM

25

A plan comes to life

After selecting a succession of dominant and companion flowers, the gardener's next step in designing a perennial border is to draw up a plan like the one at left below (of the right-hand border in the photograph), indicating where each group of perennials, as well as some annuals and bulbs, will be planted. The photograph, taken in late spring, shows one seasonal combination of blossoms—white peonies, at left and right, with tall blue Italian buglosses behind them at right. The bladelike leaves of intermediate bearded irises, which were the keynote blooms of spring but by now have ceased flowering, can be seen in the right foreground. They were accompanied by white and pink sweet Williams, which continue to bloom along the front of both borders. Later the beds will be highlighted by phlox and globe thistle.

1 DAHLIA (bulb)

2 ITALIAN BUGLOSS

3 LANTANA (annual)

4 SWEET WILLIAM

5 GLOBE THISTLE

6 PEONY

7 PHLOX

8 IRIS

9 LEADWORT

10 HOLLYHOCK

11 BALLOONFLOWER

12 SHASTA DAISY

13 COLUMBINE

14 FOXGLOVE

15 ASTILBE

16 ORIENTAL POPPY

17 JACOB'S-LADDER

18 ASTER

19 BELLFLOWER

20 PANSY

21 CHRYSANTHEMUM

A double border on Long Island is dominated by tall blue Italian buglosses. Nearest the path are clusters of white and pink sweet Williams. The tall creamy white spikes of foxgloves have begun to bloom at the back of both borders.

When the border is a border

"Perennial border" has come to mean any long and narrow bed of blooms, but perhaps its most appealing form is still the original one: a band of flowers and foliage flanking a swath of lawn. Along the grassy path to the ivy-covered arcade of a Maine garden (*below, with planting diagrams*), an imaginative choice of plants—selected as much for their distinctive leaves as their blossoms—has produced a pleasant driftlike effect in muted tones of green, silver, lavender and white. Such a border is easily adapted to a garden area in which curves are more natural than straight lines—witness the curving border at right, which is set against a low wall to provide a flowery frame for the garden of another New England home. Its evergreen-punctuated symmetry forms a gay backdrop for green grass and white birch trees.

1 ARTEMISIA

2 SEA LAVENDER

3 IRIS

4 BLEEDING HEART

5 SUNDROP

6 DAHLIA (bulb)

7 BUTTERFLY WEED

8 PHLOX

9 PLUME POPPY

10 LILY (bulb)

11 GLOBE THISTLE

12 PEONY

13 MONKSHOOD

14 BUGBANE

15 MEADOW RUE

16 BEDSTRAW

17 BABIES'-BREATH

18 CANDYTUFT

19 ASTILBE

20 BLUE FALSE INDIGO

21 ALLIUM (bulb)

22 WOOLLY BETONY

23 PANSY

24 BROWALLIA (annual)

25 PENSTEMON

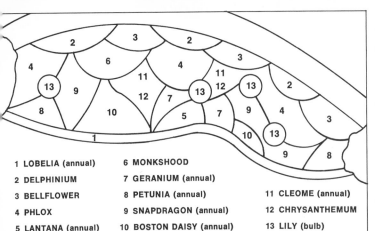

1 LOBELIA (annual)
2 DELPHINIUM
3 BELLFLOWER
4 PHLOX
5 LANTANA (annual)
6 MONKSHOOD
7 GERANIUM (annual)
8 PETUNIA (annual)
9 SNAPDRAGON (annual)
10 BOSTON DAISY (annual)
11 CLEOME (annual)
12 CHRYSANTHEMUM
13 LILY (bulb)

A curving border, effectively combining several perennials with a variety of annuals and bulbs, separates the small lawn from the hidden wall of this garden in Northeast Harbor, Maine. The tall blue and purple spikes of delphiniums and monkshoods rise above white and red phloxes in the center background. They will be replaced later by autumn-blooming chrysanthemums.

A muted blend of foliage and flowers lends subtle beauty to this double border in Bar Harbor, Maine. Contrasts of color are provided by plants like the pale lavender-and-white monkshood in the left foreground and clumps of silvery artemisias like the one in the right foreground. Adding bits of brightness to the right-hand border are the creamy plumes of astilbes, clumps of orange-flowered butterfly weeds and white garden phloxes. Seen in the far left background are tall sprays of lavender-pink meadow rues.

Perennials in a formal garden

While perennials are not usually associated with formal garden designs, it is possible to incorporate them quite effectively in formal beds and borders like the ones shown here. These beds are made up of a relatively small number of varieties that blend well with annuals and produce compact masses of flowers of uniform size and color. Notably absent are large and rampant types like hollyhocks and astilbes. Yet, despite their tidiness, these beds require no more attention than the informal designs shown on the previous pages; the dominant pink phlox is one of the longest blooming and most trouble free of the perennials. The accompanying plan for one of the beds (*right*) illustrates how a few well-chosen varieties of perennials and annuals can produce a rich blend of colors, shapes and textures in any garden.

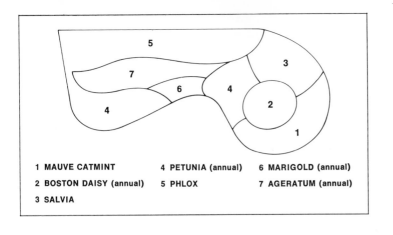

1 MAUVE CATMINT
2 BOSTON DAISY (annual)
3 SALVIA
4 PETUNIA (annual)
5 PHLOX
6 MARIGOLD (annual)
7 AGERATUM (annual)

A series of asymmetrical beds makes up the borders of this lawn. The view, from behind one of the phlox-dominated beds, shows yellow Boston daisies at right above mauve catmint in the opposite border.

Planting and caring for perennials 2

Because a perennial garden is a long-term project and because the soil for it must be prepared thoroughly enough to serve for a decade or more, I went to special pains a few years ago when my wife, Margaret, hinted that she wanted a small perennial garden of her own. I was determined to give her the best possible start, so when I had dug up the area I spread 4 inches of a very rich compost on top of it, instead of the usual 2, and worked it in well. Then my wife planted, among other perennials, a variety of white Siberian iris that normally grows 24 inches tall and a few bulbs of the gold-band lily that in most gardens rises 4 to 5 feet and bears blossoms 6 inches across. Because of my generous use of compost, though, my wife's irises soared to nearly 4 feet and the gold-band lilies to 8 feet, with blooms 12 inches across. They were spectacular, all right, but they were not quite what she expected.

I confess the incident only to emphasize how important soil preparation can be in starting a perennial garden—much more important than in preparing a bed for annuals, which blossom for a single season and die. Many perennials reach their peak only when they are three years old and may—as in the case of peonies and day lilies—flourish where you put them long beyond your own lifetime. All those years they use up nutrients from the soil. You can replenish the nutrients with fertilizers, of course, but once you have planted long-lived perennials you cannot change the structure of the soil—which is every bit as important to their well-being as fertility, for it controls both drainage and moisture retention. Soils that are heavy with clay tend to become compacted and this can mean death for perennials. Such soils must be opened and loosened so that air as well as moisture can reach the plants' roots. Light sandy soils, on the other hand, must be made spongy enough to trap and retain moisture and dissolved nutrients that otherwise would drain away.

Fortunately you can improve either type of soil by digging in a 2- to 4-inch layer of an organic material such as peat moss, compost, decayed cow manure, decayed sawdust or leaf mold, which

An array of vigorous perennials bears testimony to well-drained, well-prepared soil. Behind the mauve catmint in the foreground are yellow sundrops, purple salvia and creamy yellow thermopsis.

consists of rotting leaves. Any of these will do, but peat moss is the most generally sold at nurseries and garden centers around the country. It comes in several grades ranging from one that is finely ground to one that is made up of chunks ½ to ¾ inch in diameter. If it is available, I prefer the chunky kind—sometimes called poultry grade because it is used on the floors of henhouses and sometimes called nursery grade because it is widely used by professionals. In heavy soils the chunky peat moss promotes aeration and good drainage and in light soils its individual lumps act as reservoirs for water and nutrients. Unlike some of the other organic materials, notably decayed cow manure, peat moss provides no nutrients, but it does very well the job of moisture control for which it is intended.

So does compost—if you have space for a compost pile in your backyard. Making one *(drawings, below)* is not nearly the job that people thought it had to be when I was a boy—in those days it involved digging a deep pit. Through the alchemy of a compost pile, you can convert your leaves and other organic debris into clean, odorless, rich fertilizer with less effort and cost than it takes to stuff them into plastic bags for trash collection. Properly made compost is at least equivalent in plant food value to the best animal manure.

Compost-making speeds up the natural decay of organic materials by increasing the supply of nitrogen to the bacteria that at-

A COMPOST PILE FOR PERENNIALS

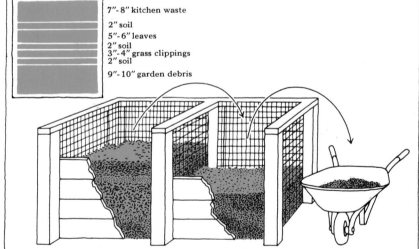

7"-8" kitchen waste
2" soil
5"-6" leaves
2" soil
3"-4" grass clippings
2" soil
9"-10" garden debris

An unending supply of compost is provided by twin bins, the backs and sides made of wire mesh to admit air, the fronts of removable boards to allow easy access. In the "brewing" bin, organic matter is alternated in layers (inset), each dusted with fertilizer, wetted and sealed with soil. As the material decays it is forked over; after three to six months it is transferred to the "use" bin, ready for the garden.

tack and digest the materials. It has been found that the addition of phosphorus and lime also speeds up the process. (Lime, in the form of ground limestone, needs to be added to correct the natural acidity of most organic matter, but should not be used if the compost is to be used for acid-loving plants.) To get the needed chemicals, simply use any ordinary lawn or garden fertilizer, organic or inorganic, plus a sprinkling of limestone.

Compost piles can be built in pits, on the open ground or within enclosures. I prefer enclosures because they hold the material in place and because they can be made attractive, or at least inoffensive—a consideration for both you and your neighbor if you live on a suburban lot. The material to be composted can consist of almost any nonwoody organic matter such as leaves, lawn clippings, old plant stems, pine needles, weeds, corn stalks, beet or carrot tops, spoiled fruit or vegetables, animal manure or even paper. All of these materials will decay much faster if they are put through a power shredder before being composted. (Shredders can be bought, or rented by the day, from garden-supply centers.) The usual way to build a compost pile is to put the material down in layers, the thickness depending on the coarseness or fineness of the material; leaves, for example, should be put in layers about 6 inches deep, grass clippings 3 or 4 inches deep. Spread out each layer on the pile, making sure the center is slightly concave to catch rain water, and sprinkle about a pint of fertilizer and a dusting of limestone on top. To make sure there is enough moisture to aid decomposition, dampen the pile for a few minutes with a hose, then top it off with a 2-inch layer of soil from your garden. This soil layer will help to settle the pile, seal in the heat generated during decomposition and add bacteria to speed decay. Continue sandwiching alternate layers of soil and organic material sprinkled with fertilizer and limestone until the pile is 3 to 4 feet high. It will take about three to six months for the composting process to be completed. If rainfall is light, hose down the pile from time to time to replace evaporated moisture. Turn the pile over with a spading fork after four to six weeks so that the outer material becomes incorporated into the center and has a chance to decay. A second turning in another four to six weeks will help to speed the process, but it is not mandatory. The compost will be ready to use when it is dark in color and the material from which it was made either loses its original form entirely or crumbles when touched. A 2-inch application of compost each year will make any soil enormously productive.

There is more to preparing the soil, of course, than the addition of organic material. But just what it will require in the way of extras can be determined only by a soil test. Your state or county agri-

ACID VERSUS ALKALINE SOIL

cultural extension office will give you an exact analysis for a nominal fee, or you can make one yourself, accurately enough for practical purposes, with an inexpensive soil-testing kit obtainable at garden centers. Such a kit will permit you to ascertain your soil's pH factor—that is, whether its chemical balance is acid, alkaline or neutral—and the availability in the soil of the essential nutrients, nitrogen, phosphorus and potassium.

The pH of your soil can make the difference between success and failure with perennials. It is measured on a scale that runs from 0, for extremely acid, to 14, for extremely alkaline. A pH of 7 is neutral. In those parts of the country that have abundant rainfall —most of the area east of the Mississippi and the coastal regions of the Pacific Northwest—soil is apt to be acid. In normally dry areas such as the Southwest it is usually alkaline, since the chemicals that make a soil alkaline are not leached away by rain. But you cannot rely on such generalizations. Areas that are broadly alkaline may have pockets of acidity, and vice versa.

Most perennials do best when the pH is around 6.5 (slightly acid) to 7.0 (neutral), but soils in various parts of the country range from 4.5 to 8.5, so some correction will most likely be needed in your garden. Only a soil analysis will tell for sure.

CORRECTING THE pH   The most effective and inexpensive material to raise the pH of an acid soil is ground limestone. I prefer dolomite limestone to other ground limestone because it also contains magnesium, a trace element that many soils lack. If your soil is too acid, and of medium consistency, you will need 5 pounds of limestone for every 100 square feet of area to raise the pH by ½ to 1 unit. If your soil is heavy with clay, or if you plan to add large quantities of an organic material that is acid—as most peat moss is—you will require one third more limestone.

To lower the pH of excessively alkaline soil, two materials are available, and your soil's special needs and the time you have before planting season will help you determine which to choose. One material is finely ground sulfur. It is slow acting but long lasting. The other is iron sulfate. It works quickly, but not over as long a period, for it washes out of the soil easily. Its merit is that it contains iron as well as sulfur; iron, deficient in many soils, encourages the production of healthy, deep green foliage and richly colored flowers. A half pound of ground sulfur, or 3 pounds of iron sulfate, will lower the pH of 100 square feet of area by ½ to 1 unit.

USING FERTILIZERS   At the same time you are considering the texture and acidity of your soil, you should consider its nutritive content. If you made a complete soil test, it probably showed your soil to be deficient in one or more of the three major fertilizer components: nitrogen, phosphorus (the phosphoric acid in packaged fertilizers) or potassium (potash). Labels on fertilizers use a numerical rating to identify the amounts of nitrogen, phosphoric acid and potash in the mixture and the sequence on the labels is always the same: 5-10-5 means the fertilizer contains 5 per cent nitrogen, 10 per cent phosphoric acid and 5 per cent potash. The balance, in inorganic fertilizers, is inert filler to dilute the chemicals (which would be too strong in their pure form) and to make them easier to spread.

Nitrogen stimulates rapid, lush green growth and a lot of it is essential, for example, in a lawn fertilizer. But perennials, which take their time about growing, need very little nitrogen; in fact, if they get too much they will produce weak, succulent stems and big, floppy leaves rather than flowers. The most important fertilizer element for perennials is phosphorus: it builds strong roots and stems, is important to the production of blossoms and provides both flowers and foliage with rich color. Potassium helps plants to resist diseases and cold—an important factor to any vegetation that lives for years in one place.

A good general fertilizer for perennials is 0-20-20, dug into the soil when the bed is prepared at the rate of 3 to 4 pounds per 100 square feet. As its rating indicates, it is devoid of the nitrogen that can harm them and rich in the phosphorus and potassium they need so much. If your soil requires only the addition of phosphorus, bone meal is an excellent source: spade in 3 to 6 pounds per 100 square feet. Wood ash from the fireplace and charcoal ash from the barbecue pit are rich in potassium and provide a good free supply of that vital element. A thin, even scattering of ashes, worked into the soil of the garden bed, will usually supply all the potassium that your plants need.

A friend of mine who, like so many of us, is concerned about ecology asked me the other day why I didn't recommend such natural, organic fertilizers as cow manure. Of course I do recommend them—well-rotted cow manure, at least one year old, is a splendid fertilizer; when I was a youngster on a New England farm I used nothing else on my plants. Such natural manures are not as concentrated as manufactured, inorganic fertilizers—they often have only a tenth or a fifth of the strength—but they work wonders because they contain microorganisms that release nutrients already in the soil and make them available to vegetation. But unless one lives near a dairy farm, natural stable manures are not easy to find. Dried cow manure, bone meal, cottonseed meal, blood meal and powdered fish fertilizer are much more easily obtained in garden centers and they are all the next best thing. Best of all is the compost from your own compost pile. I use a combination of natural

GOLDENROD: NOT GUILTY

The fall-blooming yellow goldenrod (Solidago), disdained by some gardeners as a weed although its hybrid forms are cultivated by others, is also blamed for causing the sneezing and suffering malady of hay fever. Allergists, however, point out that goldenrod's heavy, sticky pollen is insect-borne rather than airborne and only rarely causes an allergic reaction. The real villain, in most cases, is ragweed (Ambrosia artemisiifolia), whose flowers are loaded with light allergy-producing pollen. Goldenrod has not always been so maligned a plant. In other days its leaves were used fresh to help heal wounds and it was adopted by both Kentucky and Nebraska as their official state flower.

and chemical fertilizers in my own garden. The natural ones are the basic fertilizers I use year after year for long-range plant feeding. When a plant needs a quick pick-me-up I scatter a bit of quick-acting water-soluble chemical fertilizer around it.

PREPARING THE BED

A good time to get the basic soil-conditioning aids into the ground is several months before you plan to plant: summer digging is fine for fall planting, and fall digging for spring planting, to give the soil a chance to settle and the pH modifiers to become effective. If your soil is dry and heavy, as clay soils are, soak it thoroughly with a hose two days before you start to dig—the soaking will make it easier for you to work it. If the soil is light but dry, moisten it a day ahead of time, for the same reason.

Some gardeners insist that the only proper way to prepare a plant bed—for perennials, at least—is "double digging." This involves digging up the area to the full depth of a spade, removing and setting aside the sod as you go, and then digging some more until the hole goes down 2 feet. Sod is then tossed back into the bottom of the hole, too far down to sprout again—decaying, it provides organic matter and nutrients for the deep-ranging roots of the perennials. This school prevails in Great Britain, where gardeners apparently do not object to the tremendous labor involved in dig-

EDGING A BED OR BORDER

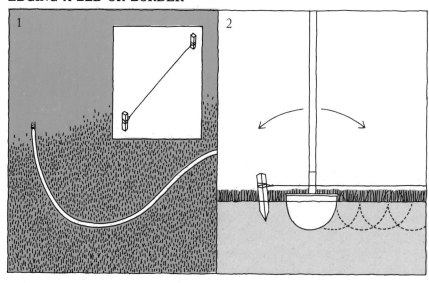

The easiest way to give a perennial bed a gracefully curved edge is to lay out the shape you want with a garden hose. To create a straight edge, simply stretch twine between stakes (inset) and tie it tautly at both ends.

Before preparing the bed (page 40), cut around the edge with a half-moon edging tool thrust vertically into the ground. Rock the edger from side to side (arrows) to drive it down all the way—4 inches. Overlap the cuts.

ging a border 100 feet long and 12 feet wide to a 2-foot depth. The method certainly works. The finest large perennial gardens I have ever seen are the botanical gardens in Edinburgh, and some of the best small ones are in the Cotswolds, where hollyhocks tower as high as the thatched roofs of the cottages. Presumably all of these beds were dug extra deep, English fashion.

I belong to the school of thought that believes digging a foot deep is enough. It is true that the roots of some perennials do reach down as far as 2 feet, but most of the feeding roots are in the top 12 inches of soil and, if drainage is adequate, the 1-foot depth suffices.

The easiest and most effective way to dig is with a rotary power tiller (I prefer the self-propelled type with tines mounted in a housing behind the wheels because it leaves the surface of the soil smooth as it digs). These can be rented from many garden supply stores or rental shops. Tillers can bite through sod and tough-rooted weeds, chopping them to bits as they go. But you had better not take advantage of that capability. Every little hunk of root from a dandelion, a milkweed and scores of other undesirables can reproduce another full-sized nuisance. So before you put the rotary tiller to use, strip the sod off your projected bed with a square-nosed nursery spade and put it on your compost pile. If you do not have a compost pile and do not want to start one, use the sod to fill in any bare patches in your lawn. If you are lucky enough not to need such patching, shake the soil loose from the sod to fall back on the bed, then discard the grass. Dig out every vestige of weed root with a spading fork. Whatever time you spend on the task will be short compared to the time it would take to uproot weeds once they and the perennials are full-grown.

USING A ROTARY TILLER

When you are satisfied that the site is weed free, make an initial pass over the bed with the tiller; this will break up the soil to a depth of 4 to 6 inches. Rake it over and pick out any weed roots you may have missed. Then spread your soil amendments—fertilizer, peat moss, lime or sulfur—over the surface and till again, mixing them all into a 12-inch depth.

Some spots in the garden—where, for example, you may plan to set a single clump of perennials in front of an evergreen—will prove too small to accommodate a tiller. There you will have to dig by hand. If the area has been covered by grass, remove the sod with a square-nosed nursery spade, which slices cleanly through the roots. Eliminate weed roots as you did in the big bed, then dig (drawings, page 40). If the area has been cultivated before, use a spading fork to turn the soil over to a depth of a foot, then dig in the 2 to 4 inches of peat moss or whatever other organic material you have chosen and any other soil amendments needed.

PREPARING THE SOIL FOR PLANTING

1. *To prepare a bed in a grassy area, strip off the sod with a sharp flat spade (either discard the sod or add it to your compost heap). Because the richest soil lies close to the surface, try not to take more than an inch of it with the sod.*

2. *With a spading fork, dig up and remove grass and weed roots so they will not sprout again. The likelihood of uncovering any large roots near the surface is slim if the bed is located properly— a minimum of 3 feet away from any shrubs, farther away from trees.*

3. *Use the spade to work the soil in small beds, but a rotary tiller is advisable for large beds. Turn over the soil to a depth of 8 to 12 inches, taking no more than a 4-inch-thick slice with each spadeful. Toss each slice beyond the hole from which it came and break it up with the spade.*

4. *When the entire bed has been spaded, work it again with a metal-pronged rake to level the top and pulverize the clods of soil on the surface. At the same time remove any remaining roots as well as any stones, sticks or other rubble.*

5. *With the spading fork, work into the soil a 2- to 4-inch layer of peat moss, 3 to 4 pounds per 100 square feet of fertilizer labeled 0-20-20, as well as any limestone or sulfur required to change the soil's pH factor (pages 35-36). Mix all of these with the soil down to a depth of 8 to 12 inches.*

6. *If the border is to be planted immediately, tamp the soil firm with your feet and smooth the surface with the back of your rake. If planting is to be delayed for several weeks, the soil will settle naturally without tamping.*

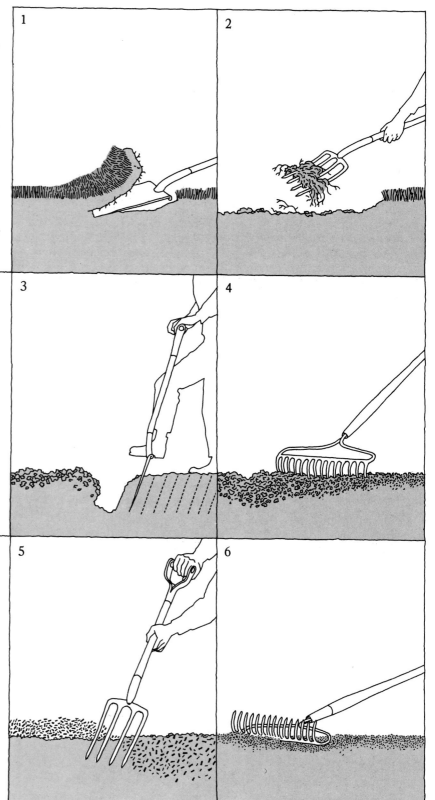

All the digging and the incorporation of organic matter will leave the soil too soft and loose for immediate planting. If you have prepared the bed well in advance, as you should, you do not have to do anything more about it for awhile. The soil will settle by itself with the help of occasional rain and, in the interim before planting, you will need only to pluck out an occasional weed. But if you are going to do any planting right away, you will have to firm the soil to eliminate air pockets in which roots would dry out. One way is to tramp back and forth on it, using a rake afterwards to smooth the surface. (Do not do this if the soil is wet or sticky, for it will become excessively compacted and negate the benefits of the organic matter; wait until it dries out.) A second way, which works well with light soils but not with heavy ones, consists of hosing the soil thoroughly to settle it and eliminate air pockets.

Regardless of when you prepare the bed—in summer for fall planting or in fall for spring planting—two factors determine the best planting time for perennials—the growth habits of each species and the region in which you live. The timing also depends on how you acquire your plants. Many garden centers stock perennials already growing in containers. These can be set out at any time they are available. But the same plants can often be bought as dormant bare roots. Nearly all perennials grow from crowns, which consist of a number of stems joined together at the base, sometimes in firm clumps, as in the case of garden phlox, and sometimes loosely, as in the case of chrysanthemums. The feeding roots extend below the stems. In the fall, when the plants approach dormancy, the stems die, but the crowns from which they rise begin to form small buds. During dormancy the buds remain inactive, becoming new stems in the next growing season. When you buy a bare-rooted perennial from a nursery, it may still have the stubs of the previous season's stems attached and the buds may or may not be discernible; in most cases they are less easy to see in the fall than in the spring. Many gardeners prefer to buy their perennials bare-rooted—they are less expensive than container plants, and dormant roots can be moved with virtually no risk of loss.

But bare-rooted perennials must be set out at the times the plants' growing habits and the climate dictate. In general, fall is the best planting time for bare-rooted perennials in Zones 6-10, and spring from Zone 5 north (map, page 151). But there are exceptions: bearded iris is best planted as soon as possible after flowering because that is the time when the old feeding roots die; about a month after flowering, new roots begin to grow, provided the plants are in moist earth. During that interval there is practically no risk involved in transplanting. Oriental poppies constitute another ex-

WHEN TO PLANT

41

DIVIDING AND PLANTING BEARDED IRIS

1. *Bearded irises need to be divided as shown here every four or five years to keep their vigor. Soon after the flowers fade, pry the entire clump gently out of the ground with a spading fork.*

2. *After washing the soil from the roots, trim the healthy leaves to a length of 4 to 6 inches; remove any shriveled leaves and dead flower stalks. If plants show any signs of iris borers or disease (pages 50-53), discard or burn the stalks and leaves; do not put them in a compost pile.*

3. *With a knife, cut off the fleshy outer roots as shown by the dashed line so that you get V-shaped pieces, each with two fans of leaves. Discard the old center root. If pieces contain borers, cut these out; dust the cuts with all-purpose fungicide to prevent rot.*

4. *Plant each root division in a hole made by plunging a trowel to its hilt into the soil, then pulling it up and toward you. Hold the division against the straight side of the hole, with the top of the roots just above the surface. Fill in and firm the soil until level.*

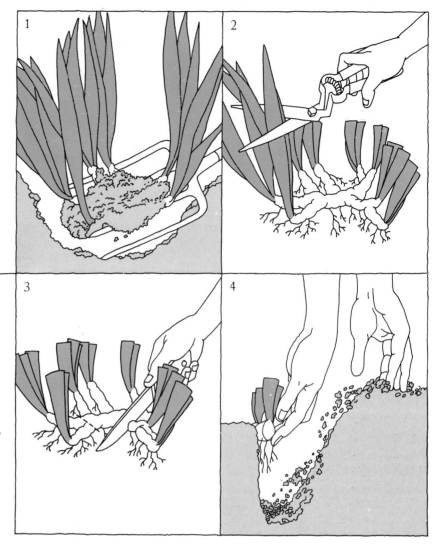

ception; they are unique in being extremely difficult to move when they are in active growth and nearly impossible to kill when they are dormant; dormancy comes in early summer when the tops die to the ground, and bare-rooted poppies can be moved at that time without loss. Peonies also have a special planting season; the best time to move peony roots is in September. By then the leaves will have nearly finished replenishing the strength in their roots for another year. Peony roots are long, slender and somewhat brittle; be especially careful not to break off the bright pink buds on the crown. Plant the roots so the tips of these buds are no more than 2 inches below the surface of the soil. No part of peony culture is more important than the depth of planting. Whenever anyone tells me his peonies don't blossom, I immediately suspect that they were planted too deeply, and this generally proves to be the case. There are some other exceptions to the general rule on planting time—spring north of Zone 5, and fall in Zones 6-10—and these exceptions can be found in the encyclopedia section (pages 92-150).

How you plant is as important as when you plant. Three factors are critical to good planting. One of them is space for the roots. Don't dig tiny holes and try to cram the roots into them. If you have prepared the bed properly, the soil will be soft and it will be easy to scoop holes big enough to accommodate the roots without crowding. Spread the roots outward as well as downward so that they can begin to establish themselves and take up nourishment immediately. If a crown is large, build a little mound of firm soil in the center of the hole, set the crown on it, and drape the roots over the edges; this prevents the possibility of having an air pocket underneath the crown.

A second and equally critical factor is depth of planting. If you buy perennials growing in containers, you have no problem; simply set them at the same depth at which they were growing. If you buy them as dormant plants, place them at the depth at which the plant grew the previous season. You can determine this easily on crowns that still have old stems because the soil will have left its mark on them; on crowns that have started new growth, the new shoots will be lighter in color below the old soil level than above it. But some dormant plants, such as those of Oriental poppies, have no such guiding marks because they have neither old nor new stems at planting time. Consult the encyclopedia for their proper planting depths. (Proper depth of planting is so important for two perennials that are basic to perennial gardens, bearded irises and peonies, that drawings are devoted to them on pages 42 and 44.) A third critical factor in planting is the firmness of the soil. There must be no pockets of air in which roots can dry out, for dried roots die. After you have set the crowns in the ground with the roots spread and the tops at the proper depth, firm the soil by tramping on it. Pressing it with your hands is not enough: you cannot apply enough pressure to eliminate air pockets.

Precautions against drying out are particularly necessary when you are transplanting. Mark the new site for each plant in advance with a stake and dig your new holes before you dig up your old plants. If you have to keep the plants out of the ground for any length of time, moisten the roots and keep them covered with damp burlap until you can plant them again.

Whether you plant your perennials in the fall or in the spring, mark every site where you have set a plant. If you trust your memory, you may find yourself digging into and ruining some slow starters when you are hoeing weeds or starting other plants. For plant markers, I generally use 8-inch redwood stakes stuck 3 or 4 inches deep in the soil beside each plant. In addition, I identify each group of plants with a stake bearing an indelible label.

CARING FOR PERENNIALS   Perennials, whether they are old plants or young, respond well to shallow cultivation in early spring; cultivated plants grow faster than uncultivated ones. Use a tined cultivator with three or four prongs set at right angles to the handle, and work over the entire surface of the bed to a depth of an inch or two, between groups of plants and between individual plants. This will uproot weeds and allow air to get into the soil, essential for healthy growth. (Many people cultivate with a hoe, but they risk injuring shallow roots with the sharp cutting edge.) Unless the bed is a new one and already fertilized, work in fertilizer containing nitrogen, phosphorus and potassium around each plant (from year to year the soil's natural nitrogen content is depleted so some should be added). If you are using 5-10-5, a level tablespoonful suffices for an initial spring feeding of a small clump. Older and larger plants may need more fertilizer—the amount depends on the size of the plant and the strength of the fertilizer, but it is better to err on the side of caution. Give a well-established phlox, for example, no more than a handful of 5-10-5. Scatter the fertilizer on the soil's surface, keep-

DIVIDING AND PLANTING PEONIES

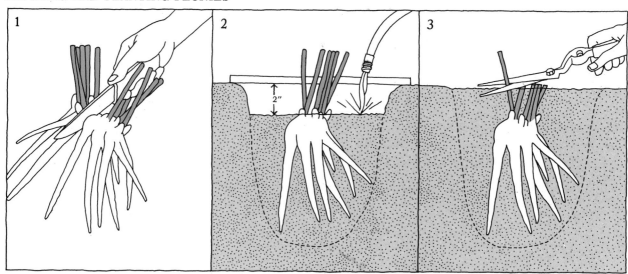

1

2

3

To propagate a peony, dig up and cut apart the clump in early fall, taking care not to break its roots. After washing, the roots should be divided so that three to five prominent buds remain on each of the new divisions.

Using a board as a guide to get the buds about 2 inches below ground level, set each division into a hole containing prepared soil (page 40). Then fill the hole to the level of the buds and water the plant thoroughly.

When the water has drained away, firm the soil with your hands to press out any air pockets that may remain under the plant, then fill the hole to ground level. Cut off the peony stems close to the surface of the soil.

ing it off the leaves and crowns so it cannot burn them, and work it into the soil with the cultivator.

Four to six weeks after this first cultivating and fertilizing, do it again. This time it will be a little more difficult because the plants will be bigger and you will have less room in which to work. Do it anyway. It will be the last time that season.

Two other jobs remain to be done immediately after the second fertilizing and cultivating. One is mulching to conserve moisture and keep down weeds. The other is staking to support those plants that might be blown over or snapped off by the wind or splattered with mud when they bend too low. I detest the appearance of stakes, and I cherish the grace of a hollyhock stalk that grows in a natural curve. But I fear the havoc that a summer thunderstorm can wreak, and I recognize that staking is unavoidable. So I keep it to a minimum and do it as inconspicuously as possible. I don't do any staking until the plants have filled out sufficiently to conceal the stakes, at least in part (drawings, page 46).

A clump of hybrid delphiniums may be as much as 5 feet high when its blossoms open, but I wait to stake it until the mass of foliage at the base has grown nearly to its full height and the flower spikes have begun to stretch upward. Then I choose slender green stakes of bamboo or reed that are long enough to reach about three quarters of the way up the ultimate height of the plant, and about halfway up the expected height of the flower spikes. I insert three or four stakes in the ground, concealing them among the plant's leaves as best I can. I weave soft green twine into a sort of cat's cradle from stake to stake about a foot above the soil and repeat the weaving a foot higher; individual stems are not tied but are allowed to grow up between the strands of twine. This allows them to sway in a breeze, but restrains and protects them in a strong wind. As the flower spikes lengthen and approach the top of the stakes, I weave more twine as high up as I can for the stems to grow through; the growing plants will soon conceal the twine. This kind of staking suits any tall plants. Different staking works better for lilies, young delphiniums and young monkshoods that send up only one or a few flowering stalks. Each of these stalks needs its own bamboo stake, about three fourths as long as the plant is tall and set at an angle to follow the natural bend of the stem. For tying the stem to the stake, I use green or tan twine or raffia fiber. Be careful not to constrict the stems in tying them to the stakes, or to force them into unnatural positions. Tie the twine or raffia securely to the stake but loosely around the stems.

The best staking for peonies is a ring of heavy wire on legs that rise 15 to 18 inches above ground. Such supports can be pur-

STAKING FOR SUPPORT

chased at garden centers as well as from garden supply mail-order houses. The elevated ring holds the center stems of the peony upright and allows the outer stems to bend naturally and gracefully, but keeps the heavy blossoms from touching the ground and becoming splattered with mud.

For weak-stemmed plants such as gaillardia, coreopsis, hardy aster, sneezeweed and lupine, all of which tend to flop over in wind and rain, the best support consists of stout, twiggy branches. They should be set around the plants when the stems are still quite low, so that the foliage can grow around and through them.

MULCHING AND WATERING

Whether or not your plants need staking, they will benefit from a mulch, applied immediately after the second fertilizer application, to conserve moisture and discourage weeds. There are many mulch-

FOUR WAYS TO STAKE PERENNIALS

1. *Tall floppy perennials such as lupine and coreopsis can be held upright by sticking twiggy branches into the ground around them. Foliage will hide the branches before the flowers open.*

2. *Clumps of spiky perennials such as delphiniums are best supported by green garden twine wound around stakes three fourths as tall as the plants' expected height; set four stakes around each clump. When the blossoms begin to appear, weave the twine between the stems at 1-foot intervals.*

3. *If a perennial has only a few slim stalks, as does this young monkshood, tie each of them to a reed or bamboo stake three fourths the height of a fully grown plant. Loop soft twine or raffia loosely around the stalk, but tie it tightly to the stake (inset).*

4. *To restrain thick bushy clumps of perennials such as peonies, use a three-legged circular wire stand, available at many garden stores. Place the stand around the plants when they are about a foot tall and press the legs about 8 inches into the ground to anchor them.*

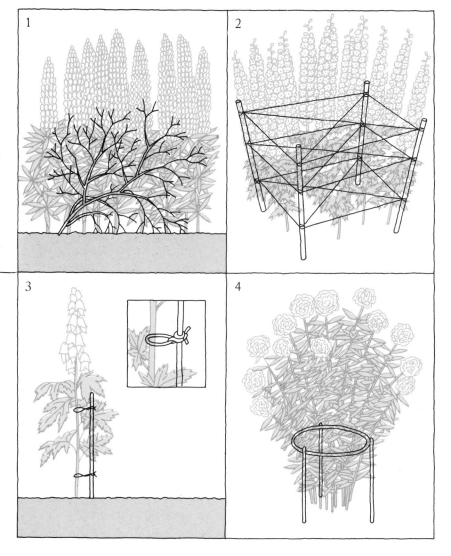

ing materials that will do this job satisfactorily, but I prefer those that gradually disintegrate during a season and by the following spring can be easily worked into the soil during the first cultivation and application of fertilizer. For that reason I do not use such long-lasting mulches as wood chips, ground bark or pine needles. I prefer mulches that include partly decayed sawdust, buckwheat hulls, ground corncobs, grass clippings, coarse peat moss, leaf mold and compost. Sawdust, leaf mold, compost or grass clippings, being relatively heavy and compact, should be spread about an inch thick in the areas between plants; buckwheat hulls, ground corncobs or peat moss, being light and loose, should be 1½ to 2 inches thick. The thickness should taper off close to the stems of the plants so that the crowns do not rot after a rain. Use most of the mulch on the ground between the plants, where weeds are most likely to appear (*drawing, right*).

Mulch will help keep your perennial garden moist in mid-summer, but it cannot do the job alone. So many plants growing in such close proximity use enormous quantities of water, and if nature does not supply it, you must. Without an adequate supply of water, perennials cannot mature and flower properly because their stems become woody and stunted.

Watering should be done so that it goes to the roots rather than onto the foliage. Regular wetting of the foliage makes the plants vulnerable to fungus diseases such as mildew that mar their appearance and sap their strength. If you spray your garden with a hose give it a thorough soaking, and do it early enough in the day so the water dries off the foliage before nightfall. I water my perennial garden with a porous canvas hose that soaks the soil slowly or with a sprinkler hose that has pin-point holes; I keep the holes aimed down at the ground and the pressure low so that the water just seeps into the earth. Your plants will indicate when they need water by wilting—be sure to water them immediately when this happens. Garden phlox is so sensitive to drought that you can use it the way coal miners used canaries to indicate the presence of gas in a mine. If the lower leaves of your garden phlox wilt, water the whole garden right away—even if all the other plants look fine.

With such basic care, your perennials should flower bountifully. But you can control the size and production of blooms by several methods illustrated on page 49. First of all, you can double or even triple the number of flowers that appear by pinching back the growing stems of certain plants, forcing them to send out three or four stems where there was only one before. The stems will be shorter and the flowers will be smaller, but both will be far more numerous than without the pinching. This procedure is especially advanta-

MULCHING FOR SUMMER

To hold the moisture that plants need, to protect shallow roots from sun and to keep down weeds that might compete for nourishment, mulch the perennial bed in late spring following the last application of fertilizer. Lightweight organic materials work best: chunky peat moss, leaf mold, compost or grass clippings. Spread the mulch about ½ inch deep directly beneath the plants and cover the spaces between them —where the sun hits the ground—with a layer 1 to 2 inches thick. The mulch will gradually disintegrate over winter; in spring work it into the soil around the plants with the first application of fertilizer—replace the mulch later in the season by spreading a fresh layer.

PINCHING AND THINNING

geous with fall-blooming plants such as chrysanthemums, sneeze-weed, hardy asters and boltonias that have a long growing season to develop many stems and buds. In lowering the height of plants, pinching back makes them less vulnerable to wind, so they may not have to be staked for support.

To obtain large flowers rather than many smaller ones, thin out the stems rather than pinching them back; by restricting each plant to only a few stems, you force it to produce fewer but bigger blossoms. The common garden phlox, which blooms in midsummer, is often treated this way. Ordinarily a clump two years old or older sends up at least a dozen stems, each bearing a 3- to 4-inch flower cluster. But gardeners who want to make their phlox resemble the magnificent specimens pictured in garden catalogues remove all but four or five stems per clump early in spring. The results are large individual blossoms growing in impressive clusters, which may develop a breadth as great as 10 inches.

DISBUDDING FOR BIG BLOOMS

There is a special kind of thinning that is called disbudding: instead of eliminating entire stalks, you remove only the side buds in order to concentrate all of the strength of each stem into producing a single magnificent flower. Disbudding is often practiced with peonies, and the solitary blossom that develops could win a blue ribbon at an agricultural fair. But for each splendid bloom, two potential flowers—at least—have been sacrificed. Each plant produces only a few flowers, and most of them open and fade about the same time. In the interest of continuing color in the garden, I prefer not to disbud, but to snip out the central flower as soon as it fades and to let the side buds develop into smaller—but no less lovely—blooms that will prolong the plant's flowering season.

PROLONGING THE BLOOM

The obvious reason for removing faded flowers is that it improves the appearance of the garden. But there are other less obvious and equally important reasons. One of them is that by removing the waning blooms before seed is produced, you almost always can obtain a second crop of flowers from such perennials as delphiniums, lupines and garden phlox, all of which otherwise would have only one flowering period in a season.

It works this way: when these flowers fade, they go to seed, and with the production of seed, the plant completes its life cycle for the season. If you remove the flowers before the seeds form, the plant tries again, bearing new flowers to make seed. But the timing of the flower plucking must be precise—after the flowers have faded and before they have produced any seed. The method also must be precise, and it varies for different plants. With phlox, coreopsis and anthemis, snip off only the top one third of the stalk from which

(continued on page 54)

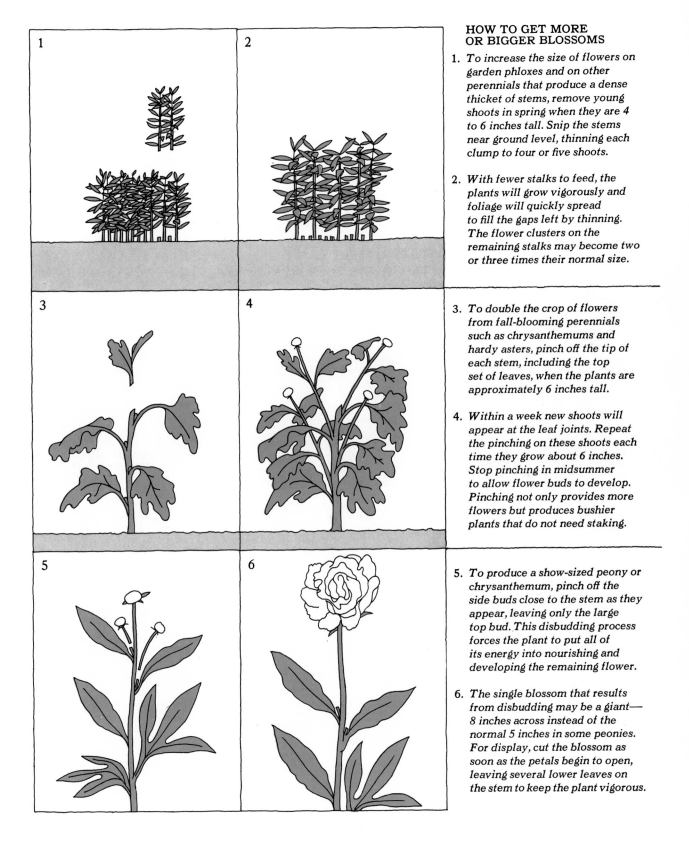

HOW TO GET MORE OR BIGGER BLOSSOMS

1. *To increase the size of flowers on garden phloxes and on other perennials that produce a dense thicket of stems, remove young shoots in spring when they are 4 to 6 inches tall. Snip the stems near ground level, thinning each clump to four or five shoots.*

2. *With fewer stalks to feed, the plants will grow vigorously and foliage will quickly spread to fill the gaps left by thinning. The flower clusters on the remaining stalks may become two or three times their normal size.*

3. *To double the crop of flowers from fall-blooming perennials such as chrysanthemums and hardy asters, pinch off the tip of each stem, including the top set of leaves, when the plants are approximately 6 inches tall.*

4. *Within a week new shoots will appear at the leaf joints. Repeat the pinching on these shoots each time they grow about 6 inches. Stop pinching in midsummer to allow flower buds to develop. Pinching not only provides more flowers but produces bushier plants that do not need staking.*

5. *To produce a show-sized peony or chrysanthemum, pinch off the side buds close to the stem as they appear, leaving only the large top bud. This disbudding process forces the plant to put all of its energy into nourishing and developing the remaining flower.*

6. *The single blossom that results from disbudding may be a giant— 8 inches across instead of the normal 5 inches in some peonies. For display, cut the blossom as soon as the petals begin to open, leaving several lower leaves on the stem to keep the plant vigorous.*

Controlling pests and diseases

Although perennials are among the healthiest of garden plants, some types are susceptible to disease and to damage by various pests. In combating such threats, an ounce of prevention is worth more than a pound of chemicals. Regular clearing of accumulated weeds and dead stalks robs pests of their favorite breeding places, and well-drained plant beds eliminate the moist conditions favored by fungi.

When plants first show signs of damage, simple measures are often effective: knocking insects off

PEST	DESCRIPTION	METHODS OF CONTROL
	APHIDS Among the most familiar of garden pests, aphids are tiny plant lice, 1/16 to 1/18 inch long, yellowish green to black in color, that are usually found clustered on tender new shoots. They suck a plant's juices, stunt its growth and cause deformities like curling leaves, and they also secrete a sticky fluid called honeydew on which a fungus called sooty mold thrives. If no control measures are undertaken, aphids may produce several generations of young in a single growing season. SUSCEPTIBLE PLANTS: CHRYSANTHEMUM, COLUMBINE, GLOBE THISTLE, HOLLYHOCK, SUNFLOWER	A stream of water from a garden hose will knock aphids off plants and may discourage them from returning. If the problem persists, a thorough spraying with malathion or dimethoate is effective.
	JAPANESE BEETLES The most destructive of a large family of pests that also includes the black blister beetle and June beetle, the Japanese beetle is an Oriental import readily identified by its metallic bronze wing covers. About 1/2 inch long, it is voracious in hot weather, chewing foliage and flowers alike. Clusters of Japanese beetles destroy a plant by reducing its leaves to skeletons. SUSCEPTIBLE PLANTS: ASTILBE, FOXGLOVE, HOLLYHOCK, ROSE MALLOW	If there are only a small number of beetles, pick them off with your fingers and toss them into a can of water topped with a film of oil or kerosene. Heavy infestations should be sprayed with carbaryl, malathion or methoxychlor. Larvae are effectively controlled by means of milky disease spores (*page 53*).
	LEAF HOPPERS Wedge-shaped insects 1/16 to 1/4 inch long, leaf hoppers damage foliage by sucking sap from the leaves. Their presence is signaled by a white stippled effect on the leaf surface or a burned look around the edges. Some leaf hoppers transmit virus diseases such as aster yellows. The insects get their name from their habit of jumping away quickly when disturbed. SUSCEPTIBLE PLANTS: BABIES'-BREATH, CATMINT, CHRYSANTHEMUM, COREOPSIS, ITALIAN BUGLOSS	Spray with water to knock exposed leaf hoppers off plants. If infestation is severe, spray weekly with malathion or carbaryl, particularly the undersides of leaves.
	IRIS BORERS These moth larvae, hatched from eggs laid in old iris stalks and garden debris in late autumn, emerge in the spring as tiny caterpillars. They bore into new iris leaves and eat the soft interior tissue, gradually working their way down into the roots. The borers not only damage the plants with their chewing but carry the bacteria that produce foul-smelling soft rot, one of the serious diseases that affect irises. SUSCEPTIBLE PLANTS: IRIS, ESPECIALLY BEARDED VARIETIES	Clear iris beds of old leaves and stems, where borers lay their eggs in the fall. Spray young plants with carbaryl, dimethoate or malathion in early spring, before the borers enter the leaves.

plants with water from a garden hose or snipping off diseased leaves. The wise gardener avoids powerful broad-spectrum insecticides that can eliminate both beneficial and harmful insects and leave residues that may eventually affect animals and even humans. Formulas compounded to control specific pests and diseases, available under various brand names, are preferable. In many cases it is possible to control pests by introducing into your garden their natural enemies, such as those shown on page 53.

PEST	DESCRIPTION	METHODS OF CONTROL
	SNAILS AND SLUGS The chief differences between these two members of the mollusk family are size and shell—snails are usually ½ to 1½ inches long and have complete shells while slugs are about twice as large and have only slight humps. Both are usually concealed by day but emerge at night to feed on low-hanging leaves. Leaving a telltale slimy trail behind them, they chew large holes and may completely devour young shoots. SUSCEPTIBLE PLANTS: BELLFLOWER, DELPHINIUM, HOLLYHOCK, TUFTED PANSY	Because slugs and snails find it difficult to crawl over rough surfaces, lay protective strips of coarse sand or cinders around plant beds. The pests can be lured to a drowning death by placing shallow bowls of beer or grape juice near plants. When there is heavy damage, use metaldehyde in spray, dust or pellet form.
	SPIDER MITES Tiny members of the spider family, barely visible to the naked eye, spider mites are ubiquitous hot-weather pests that build small webs on the undersides of leaves. By sucking sap from the leaves, they stunt growth and cause yellow, gray or brown discolorations. An even smaller family member, the cyclamen mite, is one of the principal pests that attack delphinium plants. SUSCEPTIBLE PLANTS: CLEMATIS, CONEFLOWER, HOLLYHOCK, PHLOX, PRIMROSE	Destroy spider-mite webs with strong jets of water from a garden hose. If this treatment proves ineffective, spray weekly for several weeks with a miticide such as dicofol or chlorobenzilate.
	LEAF MINERS These tiny (less than 1/16 inch) larvae of certain flies, moths or beetles are hatched from eggs laid inside the leaves of plants. The larvae consume the tender interior of the leaves, leaving behind serpentine trails of blistered tissue called mines. When damage is severe, the mines sometimes form a single large blotch and eventually the leaves shrivel and drop off. The plant may die if such defoliation is unchecked. SUSCEPTIBLE PLANTS: CHRYSANTHEMUM, COLUMBINE, MONKSHOOD, SHASTA DAISY	Spray new leaves with malathion, diazinon, dimethoate or carbaryl once a week for three weeks. This kills off adult insects before they can lay eggs. Once the eggs hatch, the larvae are relatively immune to most sprays because they are protected by the leaf surfaces.
	THRIPS These barely visible winged insects, about 1/20 inch long, scrape open the tissue of leaves and buds and drink the sap, causing discolorations and deformities and leaving behind distinctive brown or silvery streaks on the outside of leaves. Thrips tend to remain on the same plant, producing several generations each season. SUSCEPTIBLE PLANTS: BELLFLOWER, BLANKETFLOWER, DAY LILY, DELPHINIUM, FOXGLOVE, GOLDENROD, PINK	Unlike many pests, thrips infest gardens unpredictably, sometimes appearing one year and not the next. Infestations can be readily controlled by spraying with malathion or dimethoate, repeating at two-week intervals if necessary.

DISEASE	DESCRIPTION	METHODS OF CONTROL
	LEAF SPOT Also called leaf blight, black spot, tar spot, shot hole and anthracnose, this disease produces dark spots on leaves; the spots often join to produce large irregular blotches. Infected leaves wither and die, and extensive defoliation can damage or kill a plant. The disease is caused by bacteria and fungi that generally attack plants in the spring and when humidity is high. SUSCEPTIBLE PLANTS: CHINESE LANTERN PLANT, CHRYSANTHEMUM, DELPHINIUM, MONKSHOOD, SUNFLOWER	Remove old leaves, stems and other plant debris in which fungi and bacteria thrive. Cut off and remove infected leaves. Like most diseases, leaf spot is best controlled by preventive spraying. Apply captan, ferbam, folpet, maneb or zineb at the beginning of the growing season and repeat every two weeks until the plants bloom.
	BOTRYTIS BLIGHT Like most fungus diseases, botrytis blight can become a severe problem during protracted periods of humid, sunless weather. Soft blotches of discoloration appear on leaves, stems, flowers and bulbs, eventually running together to form a grayish fuzzy mold. This mold, which kills young plants and injures older ones, produces microscopic spores that can be carried by the wind to spread the infection. The blight survives the winter in the form of hard black blisters *(inset)*. SUSCEPTIBLE PLANTS: ANEMONE, CHRYSANTHEMUM, GERBERA DAISY, LUPINE, PEONY	Cut away and remove diseased portions. Avoid overwatering. Thin out plants so they get more light and air or transplant them to a dry, sunny location. Spray every two weeks throughout the growing season with zineb, phaltan, thiram or captan.
	POWDERY MILDEW This fungus, usually more unsightly than harmful, coats leaves with a white or pale gray powder. The infection eventually causes the leaves to yellow and wither and it may inhibit growth, but only rarely does it kill a plant. The disease is common in late summer and early fall, when cool nights follow warm days. It also occurs frequently when plants are overcrowded or are located in damp, shady spots. SUSCEPTIBLE PLANTS: BOLTONIA, CLEMATIS, DELPHINIUM, FALL ASTER, PHLOX	Plant mildew-resistant varieties whenever possible. Avoid late-afternoon sprinklings. Spray weekly, starting in midseason, with dinocap, sulfur or folpet.
	DAMPING OFF This fungus, often found in damp soil, attacks young seedlings at the ground line, causing apparently healthy new plants to topple and die suddenly as the disease rots their stems through. When it attacks the roots of older plants the fungus is called root rot. SUSCEPTIBLE PLANTS: SEEDLINGS OF MOST PERENNIALS	Avoid overwatering seedbeds and seedlings. Preventive measures before planting include treating seeds with captan, phygon or spergon and drenching the soil with captan.
	RUST The appearance of raised spots called pustules marks the onset of the fungus disease called rust. The pustules are often reddish in color but may range from bright yellow to black. They are usually found on the undersides of leaves and stems. In severe cases the pustules become enlarged and grow together, destroying leaves and occasionally entire plants. SUSCEPTIBLE PLANTS: ACHILLEA, GAY-FEATHER, HOLLYHOCK, LUPINE, MEADOWSWEET, SEA LAVENDER	Buy rust-resistant varieties whenever possible. Remove and destroy rust-infected leaves. Spray every two weeks throughout the growing season with sulfur, ferbam, zineb or maneb. When the flowering season is over, cut infected plants to the ground and remove the stalks at once. Do not use them in compost.

Using nature's pest killers

An increasingly attractive alternative to chemical spraying and dusting—and one that avoids their possibly harmful side effects—is the introduction into the garden of certain insects and disease-carrying bacteria that prey almost exclusively on pests. Some of the natural controls listed below provide broad protection—ladybugs devour any number of different plant-eating pests—while others are more specific. Milky disease spores, for example, single out the larvae of the Japanese beetle for slow but certain death.

NATURAL CONTROL	DESCRIPTION	GARDEN APPLICATION
	LADYBUGS Also known as the lady beetle and ladybird, the ladybug can be any of hundreds of different beetles, the most familiar of which is the spotted *Hippodamia convergens* illustrated. Prodigious predators even in the larval stage, when they devour as many as 20 or 30 aphids a day apiece, ladybugs eat twice as much when adults. They are most active in hot weather and will reproduce several times in a single growing season if there are enough pests to feed them all. INSECT VICTIMS: APHIDS, LEAF WORMS, MEALY BUGS, MITES, SCALE INSECTS	Ladybugs are sold in packages of 10,000 adults, enough for a small garden. Because they migrate freely when food sources are exhausted, it is best to store the package in the refrigerator and release them in small groups at the base of infested plants over a period of from three to four weeks.
	LACEWING LARVAE The adult lacewing is rather handsome, about ½ to ¾ inch long with gauzelike wings and large glittering eyes. But it is the ugly little larvae, called aphid lions, that are most useful as pest killers. In their two-week larval period they feed almost constantly on aphids and other insects—including other lacewing larvae—by seizing them in tong-shaped jaws and sucking out their body fluids. As adult lacewings, only a few varieties continue to eat insects. The rest subsist on a bland diet of aphid honeydew and flower nectar. INSECT VICTIMS: APHIDS, LEAF HOPPERS, MITES, THRIPS, WHITE FLIES	Lacewing eggs are sold in vials by insect farms, which mail them anywhere in the country. The sticky eggs should be scattered on a number of infested plants, so that the larvae, which hatch a few days later, will attack the nearest pests instead of each other.
	PRAYING MANTISES A relative of the grasshopper, the praying mantis gets its name from the way it sits with front legs held up as if in prayer. Actually the powerful legs are used to seize and hold unwary insects that pass by. The mantis is a predator from birth, feeding almost immediately on aphids and small flies. The adults, up to 5 inches long in some species, are indiscriminate gluttons that tackle the largest insects—including each other—and have been known to attack frogs and lizards. INSECT VICTIMS: APHIDS, BEETLES, CATERPILLARS	Praying mantises are sold in their egg cases, the size of golf balls, which may hatch as many as 400 insects each a few days after being fastened to a sturdy plant. Two or three cases are enough for an average-sized garden.
	MILKY DISEASE This slow-working bacterial disease attacks the larvae, or grubs, of Japanese beetles, turning their normally clear blood to milky white and halting their development into adult beetles. Death may take weeks or months, however. The disease is introduced by a dust containing spores of either *Bacillus popilliae* or *Bacillus lentimorbus* mixed with talc and chalk to prevent the spores from being killed by sunlight. INSECT VICTIMS: LARVAE OF JAPANESE BEETLES	The dust, available in garden centers, is applied in spring and fall at a rate of 1 teaspoonful per 4-foot interval on lawns near perennial beds, where the grubs thrive eating grass and plant roots just below the surface. The spores remain in the ground and multiply to attack successive generations of grubs.

the flowers grew. Side branches will develop below the cut and will form new flowers. With delphiniums and lupines, first cut off the stalks just below the faded flowers, leaving as much of their foliage as possible. In a few weeks, new stalks will rise from the soil. Then you can cut off the old stalks at ground level as shown in the drawings below. (If you cut the old stalks to the ground before the new ones have appeared, the plant will probably die.) The new stalks will produce a new crop of flowers.

Even if a plant will not flower a second time, faded blooms should be removed. Producing seed taxes the strength of a plant and unless seeds are needed, it is better to channel the plant's energy into building a stronger root system for the following year. Unwanted seeds that are allowed to ripen fall to the ground, where they may sprout like weeds and eventually compete with the parent plant for food and moisture. Worse, many such seedlings —particularly those of the brilliantly colored garden phlox—bear little resemblance to the lovely flowers whence they came, reverting instead to the muddier colors of their ancestors.

PERENNIALS AS CUT FLOWERS One way you can multiply the pleasure of perennials is to harvest some of them for use indoors, both as fresh cut flowers and in dried arrangements. Many gardeners raise peonies, delphiniums, chrysan-

MAKING DELPHINIUMS AND LUPINES BLOOM IN FALL

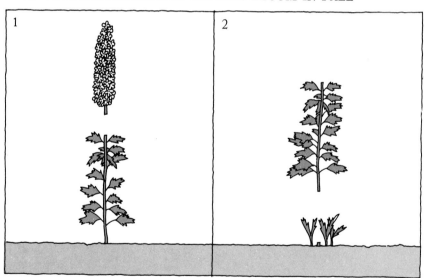

For a fall crop of delphiniums and lupines, remove spring flower spikes as soon as they fade. Cut just below the spike base. Scratch fertilizer around the roots to encourage new stalks, but leave old foliage intact.

When the new growth has reached a height of about 6 inches, cut the old foliage stalks to the ground. The new stalks will produce flowers—smaller than previously, yet nonetheless welcome—within about two months.

themums and pyrethrums in cutting gardens just for that purpose, but the list of perennials that will survive well in vases indoors is a gratifyingly long one. It includes, to name only a few, lupines, Oriental poppies, salvias, Japanese anemones, artemisias, yarrows, monkshoods, centaureas, globe thistles and coreopsises.

Cut flowers are not dead flowers—they continue to live and grow for a while; how long depends in part on the treatment they get. Their chief requirement is water, which not only carries food to their cells but also fills the cells, keeping the stems sturdy and the blossoms upright. The best time of the day for cutting flowers is in the late afternoon, after the plants' store of energy has been built up during several hours of daylight. Use a sharp knife or garden shears and choose stems with buds that are half or three quarters open; full-blown blossoms will not last long. Strip off the stems' lower leaves—plants give off moisture through their leaves and removal of some of the leaves will help to conserve it. When I step into the garden to cut flowers, I always carry a broad-mouthed vase three quarters full of water from the hot-water tap (100° or 110°) and plunge each stem into it immediately after I have severed it. I do not use cold water; plants, like other living things, are stimulated by warmth and slowed down by cold. When the vase is full, but not to the point of crowding, I take it indoors and put it in the coolest place in the house for a couple of hours. Only after that do I begin to arrange the flowers. At this point, I remove any remaining leaves that would be below the water level in the vase, because they would decay and foul the water with bacteria. Then I trim the stems to the desired length, and it does not matter a bit whether the cut is straight across or slanting. What does matter is that the cut should be a clean one, made with extra-sharp scissors and without squeezing the stems—that could impede the intake of moisture. Some plants, such as poppies, ooze a substance that tends to clog the stems; in such cases, the stems should be seared for an instant over a lighted match, a candle or a gas-stove burner; this searing will prevent clogging.

Many gardeners believe that the lives of cut flowers can be lengthened by the addition of aspirin or sugar or even copper pennies to the water. Aspirin and pennies do neither good nor harm, but sugar used alone actually is harmful: it stimulates the growth of bacteria, which clog the open cells at the ends of the cut stems. Most of the commercial cut-flower foods, however, do work. They contain sugar to provide quick energy, but they also contain substances that inhibit the growth of bacteria, maintain color in the petals and slow the flowers' metabolism so that they will survive longer. If you use a material of this kind, put it in the vase before you go out into the garden, so that the flowers can start benefiting from it immediately. With a cut-flower food it is necessary only to add fresh warm water daily to replace what the flowers have consumed. When it is not used, you should remove the flowers from the vase daily, rinse the vase clean and refill it with warm water.

HOW TO DRY FLOWERS   For centuries, gardeners have been extending their enjoyment of certain perennials—babies'-breath, sea lavender and Cupid's-dart, to name a few—by turning them into permanent dried arrangements. The usual methods were hanging the cut flowers in a dry place or burying them in sand or borax to absorb their moisture. In the last decade, a faster and more reliable method has been developed, one that also preserves the true color of flowers that cannot be dried successfully by the old methods. It involves the use of silica gel, a substance widely employed in industry to protect dehydrated foods and sensitive instruments from dampness. You can buy it at any flower shop. Silica gel looks like sugar and can absorb water equivalent to 40 per cent of its own weight. Ordinarily blue, it turns pink when it is saturated, but dries out again and reverts to blue after half an hour's warming in a 250° oven. When the silica gel is not in use, it must be stored in an airtight container to keep it dry; you will find that the tins that Christmas fruitcakes come in are ideal for such storage, for they can do double duty and serve again in the flower-drying process itself.

Flowers that are to be dried should first be stripped of foliage and fragile stems. The heads of the flowers are then placed, facing up, on a layer of silica gel about 1½ inches deep on the bottom of the tin, and more silica gel is sprinkled over them until they are covered. The tin's lid is put on and sealed with masking tape. Within four to seven days the flowers have dried and can be gently removed from the gel. (If you lose a petal, stick it back on, using a toothpick to apply transparent glue.) Blossoms that are not going to be made into bouquets immediately can be stored in a tightly covered glass jar with a teaspoon or two of silica gel to keep them dry. When you are ready to do your dried flower arranging you can mount the flower heads on stems made of green florists' wire. First run a length of wire up through the head of each flower, then bend the top of the wire to make a small hook and, finally, pull the bent wire down into the flower head so that the hook is concealed.

WINTER PROTECTION   Perennials have little trouble surviving winter where snows start early and stay late, or where the climate is mild all year. But they need some special care in areas where wind and cold arrive when the ground is still bare and where winter thaws may be followed by sudden freezes that can push the roots out of the ground and damage them. When the leaves have withered in fall, I cut down all the old stalks right to the ground and put them on the compost heap. At this time it is easy to discern which plants are encroaching on their neighbors and should therefore be divided. A few that are cold resistant can be divided right then and there *(Chapter 3); the* others should wait until spring.

Next, I replace missing stakes and labels to avoid mistakes and lapses of memory next season. Then I scatter a handful of bonemeal around the patriarchs such as peonies and gas plants that are not scheduled to be dug up, divided and replanted in newly fertilized soil. The phosphoric acid it contains will strengthen their roots. Then I wait for the ground to freeze.

In cold weather zones, perennials do best when they are frozen solid and remain completely dormant all winter. So where there is danger of alternate freezing and thawing, they should be covered, not to keep them warm, but to keep them cold; for this reason the perennial bed should be mulched after the ground has frozen —never before it has frozen. By then any mice that might have been tempted to nest in the mulch will have found homes elsewhere and will be less likely to gnaw the roots. The ideal mulch is light enough to permit air to penetrate, but substantial enough to shade the soil and keep it from thawing every time the sun shines on it. My favorite mulch for this purpose is salt, or marsh, hay. Ordinary hay will not do—it mats, keeping out air, and it is full of weed seeds that will sprout the next spring. Salt hay, on the other hand, is wiry and does not absorb moisture; it does not mat and it does permit the passage of air. Moreover, its seeds sprout only in salt marshes, so they do not become a problem in the perennial garden. A layer of salt hay 6 to 8 inches thick suffices. Another good mulch, more easily available in some regions, consists of evergreen boughs. Some gardeners buy up leftover Christmas trees from corner lots, cut off their springy branches and lay them over the perennial bed. Two layers of boughs, crisscrossed, should suffice. They admit air to the ground but keep out the sun. If neither of these mulching materials is available, you can use an 8-inch blanket of straw to cover your dormant plants.

In the spring I remove my winter mulch in two stages, three or four days apart, just as the first new sprouts appear; this permits the tender new growth to become gradually acclimatized to the chill spring air. I use a long-handled fork to lift the hay or the boughs rather than pulling them off with a rake, whose tines might damage the tender growth that has already started to push up through the surface of the ground. Then my perennials are almost ready to reward me with lovely blossoms that, with only a little more effort on my part, will multiply and fill my garden— and the gardens of my friends as well.

THE PEONY'S MAGICAL PAST

The offhand way modern gardeners cut peonies for indoor bouquets would have shocked the ancients, who endowed the plant with magical powers. To the Greeks, the flower was a charm against evil spirits and had to be plucked with care: It was thought to be watched over by a woodpecker; if it was taken in daylight, the woodpecker would peck out the eyes of the gardener. The Greeks consequently picked peonies in the middle of the night, when any sensible woodpecker is sound asleep. The Romans were even more cautious in handling peonies. They thought that the plant emitted a soft groan as it emerged from the earth, and that anyone close enough to hear the groan would die. To pull up a peony, a dog was tied to the plant. Enticed with meat, the animal pulled up the plant as humans stayed out of earshot.

Four all-time favorites

Every perennial has its devotees, but in the world of the specialty gardener—the dedicated amateur who devotes himself to the loving cultivation of one or two flowers and their varieties—four favorites stand out: the iris, the day lily, the primrose and the chrysanthemum. Because they have been extensively hybridized, each is available in a stunning range of forms and hues. Each is relatively easy to grow and each lends itself readily to further hybridization, enabling the enthusiast to produce new and unusual varieties of his own.

Such concentration on the cultivation of one kind of flower was once the prestigious avocation of the rich and fashionable. The late stripteaser and actress Gypsy Rose Lee took great pride in her excellent collection of day lilies. Mary Pickford, America's sweetheart of the silent screen, lavished her affection on irises. Rex Stout, the mystery-story writer whose hero Nero Wolfe spent his nondetecting time raising orchids, concentrated on both day lilies and irises in his own spare time. Today, however, specialists come from all walks of life, and some of the finest gardens are tended by housewives, teachers and businessmen. All of the perennials on the following pages were grown by gardeners like Mrs. Lewis Mack *(right)*, of New Canaan, Connecticut, who began specializing in chrysanthemums 20 years ago.

Many of these flower growers share membership in one of the national societies that exist for each of the four major perennial specialties. These societies provide information, assist in the sale and exchange of plants and organize flower shows. But perhaps their most important function is that of standardizing the nomenclature. They assign designations to colors, shapes and sizes and to new types of flowers. These designations, used on the following pages, do not follow the scientific system universally used by botanists; they may vary from one society to the next. But for the specialist they provide a simple and convenient means for identifying the different types of his favorite perennial, for exchanging information about them and for placing his orders with commercial growers.

Outfitted with magnifying lenses and pollen-dusting brushes, Mrs. Lewis Mack displays a hybrid she created.

Iris: rainbow flower

The ancient Greeks, dazzled by its colors, named it the iris, the "eye of heaven," which was also their word for the rainbow. It was also a favorite in the royal gardens of Europe as early as the Ninth Century. Today the multihued iris continues to fascinate gardeners everywhere. Among the more than 20,000 varieties are flowers that do indeed match every shade of the rainbow except bright green—and that color too may yet emerge among the 700 or more new varieties that are introduced each year. Many varieties, like the ones that are shown here, are hybrids of the popular spring-blooming tall bearded iris prized as much for the beauty of their upright and drooping petal formations as for the array of colors that first attracted gardeners of the past.

WHITE SELF
Meadow Snow

VIOLET SELF
Blue Mountain

PLICATA
Space Ship

RUFFLED YELLOW SELF
Tropic Sun

BLACK SELF
Quiet Night

BI-COLOR
Ballyhoo

ORANGE SELF
Orange Beauty

The tall bearded irises shown below in a kaleidoscope of hues and shapes are divided by the American Iris Society into seven categories. A self is a flower of a single color. A bi-color has upright petals, called standards, of one color and drooping petals, called falls, of another color. A plicata's petal colors contrast with a base tone. A bi-tone has two shades of the same color, and a blend shows subtle variations of a single color. The variegata is a brown and yellow combination, while the amoena has petals of two colors, one always white. Within the seven categories are types like the ruffed, a flower bred for its deeply rippled petals. The names given below the category designations identify the specific variety of each flower.

RED VIOLET SELF
Sorcerer's Apprentice

BLUE SELF
Sky Harbor

YELLOW SELF
Radiente Sun

RED SELF
Caliente

VARIEGATA
Samurai

AMOENA
Talent Show

BI-TONE
Wine and Roses

BLEND
Louise Watts

Mr. and Mrs. George Watts, pictured at left in their quarter acre of irises in Armonk, New York, grow 320 varieties of this one flower. One of their favorite irises, bred by a friend, is the red-violet blend held by Mrs. Watts and named for her: Louise Watts.

A second Watts specialty is revealed in two views of their garden. The top picture, taken in June, shows some of their large iris collection. The bottom, taken only a month later, is filled with day lilies (overleaf), which bloom toward the end of the brief iris season.

Day lily: beauty for a day

Although the Chinese long cultivated day lilies—both for their beauty and as an ingredient in some of their dishes—only three varieties hybridized from this ubiquitous wild flower were widely grown in American gardens before World War II. Today there are more than 12,000, most of them bred and collected by enthusiasts undeterred by the day lily's unusual blooming pattern. The typical plant produces 50 or more flowers during its blossoming season, which can occur as early as spring or as late as early fall. But each blossom lasts only a day, accounting for the plant's common as well as its botanical name, *Hemerocallis,* "beauty for a day." The newer varieties, shown here and on the following pages, offer a choice of colors, sizes and shapes.

YELLOW
Martin Viette

MELON
Abalone

RED
Oriental Ruby

ORANGE
Inca Treasure

POLYCHROME
Titan

PINK
Edna Spaulding

PURPLE
Emperor's Robe

EYED
Oriental Mist

BI-COLOR
Howdy

These day lilies represent the major categories established by the American Hemerocallis Society. They include six basic color classifications—orange, pink, red, purple, yellow and melon—as well as the polychrome, a blend of shades of one color. The bi-color has contrasting colors in its petals, while the eyed lily is a single-colored flower with an "eye" of another color. The tetraploid is a genetic variation with thick petals and deep colors. The flaring spider has large gaps between its six narrow petals, while the similarly shaped double has twice as many petals. The recurved type has deeply curled petals. Low-growing day lilies are shorter than 20 inches. Small ones have flower diameters between 3 and 4½ inches; anything smaller is a miniature.

SPIDER
Grand Parade

RECURVED SEPALS
Rondo

TETRAPLOID
Twilight Sky

RECURVED
Ribbon Curls

MINIATURE
Kewpie Doll

SMALL
Little Rainbow

DOUBLE
Beauty Medley

LOW GROWING
Chateaugay

Mrs. Irving Fraim of Waltham, Massachusetts, who has been raising day lilies for more than 25 years, holds a few of the 300-odd varieties that flourish in her garden. Her basket of cut flowers includes many of the basic day lily colors in her favorite pastels.

An unusual day lily named Aabachee, shown below in close-up, represents a 20-year hybridizing effort by Raymond Cheetham of Kent, Ohio. He crossed and recrossed seven different flowers and scores of their offspring to produce this unusual purple spider type.

Primrose: gem of the rock garden

The tiny primrose requires little space; the 25 varieties pictured here could all be grown together in a modest rock garden wherever the climate is suitably cool and moist. All are descended from wild primroses *(Primula)* that grow in mountains and meadows from the Alps to the Himalayas. The enormous diversity of primroses can be judged from the sampling of categories below, established by the American Primrose Society. The listed varieties include species primroses, little changed from their wildflower ancestors, as well as the eye-catching auriculas, first bred from alpine flowers more than 400 years ago. The acaulis, or English primrose, bears a single flower on a short stem; the polyanthus has clusters of flowers on a longer stem. The garryarde is a short-stemmed polyanthus hybrid from Ireland with unusual dark foliage, while the juliana is a creeper that thrives in rocky crevices.

SHOW AURICULA
1 *Dunder's Red*
2 *Snow Lady*
3 *Etha Tate*

BORDER ALPINE AURICULA
4 *unnamed seedling*

EXHIBITION ALPINE AURICULA
5 *unnamed seedling*

GARDEN AURICULA
6 *Denna White*

DOUBLE AURICULA
7 *unnamed seedling*

GARRYARDE
8 *Guinevere*

SPECIES PRIMROSE
9 *Primula kisoana*
10 *Primula denticulata*
11 *Primula sieboldii*
12 *Primula elatior*

POLYANTHUS
13-19 *unnamed seedlings of various types*

JULIANA
20 *Kay*
21 *Jay Jay*
22 *Marguerite*

ACAULIS
23 *unnamed seedling*
24 *unnamed seedling*
25 *Quaker's Bonnet*

A close-up of blossoms of an auricula primrose reveals the dustlike particles called farina, here scattered thinly over the fronts of the petals and thickly on the backs. Such particles are found on many primroses and are believed to protect them from excessive sunlight.

Cyrus Happy, a photographer-editor of industrial publications who lives in Tacoma, Washington, displays some of his prized collection of auriculas on a wrought-iron stand that is a relic of the Victorian period in England, when primrose gardens were fashionable.

71

Chrysanthemum: the queen

The chrysanthemum, elegant botanical cousin of the common daisy, was cultivated by Oriental specialists for more than 2,000 years before reaching Europe in the 17th Century. By that time the Orient had already produced most of the basic types shown here, and the Japanese were venerating the flower as Ki-Ku—the Queen of the East—the personal emblem of the emperor. European botanists named it chrysanthemum, which means "golden flower." Today there are more than 1,000 varieties of chrysanthemums in dozens of shades. Normally the plant blooms in handsome autumn clusters (*pages 76-77*) but, by using a technique called disbudding (*drawings, page 49*), specialists can produce single oversized flowers like those shown below.

1 SPOON	2 REFLEXING INCURVE	3 SEMI-DOUBLE	4 DECORATIVE	5 ANEMONE	6 SPIDER	7 SINGLE
Alabama	*Dark Bronze Indianapolis*	*Edwin Painter*	*Otome Pink*	*Daybreak*	*Miss Atlanta*	*Marguerita*

The flowers shown here represent the 13 categories established by the National Chrysanthemum Society. The spoon and the quill types take their names from the shapes of their petals. The petals of the laciniated type have fringed tips and those of the reflex twist into tiny tubes. The spider has slender, drooping petals. The anemone's petals radiate outward, as do the thistle's. The single has one row of petals; the semi-double may have as many as five rows. The petals of the incurve type curl inward to form a round head, as do the petals of the reflexing incurve, the decorative and the pompon types.

8 REFLEX
Yellow Symbol

9 POMPON
Luna

10 THISTLE
Yellow Saga

11 LACINIATED
Miss Olympia

12 QUILL
Peggy Ann Hoover

13 INCURVE
White Pocket

In a shaded corner of her Bethesda, Maryland, garden, Dr. Gwendolyn Wood examines some of the spider chrysanthemums that have won her a number of awards. She is particularly fond of Miss Atlanta, a spider type shown at the upper left-hand corner.

A distinguished pioneer among West Coast chrysanthemum fanciers, Dr. Ira Cross casts an affectionate eye over the small garden he has tended for more than 30 years in Berkeley, California. He bred the anemone types at lower left, named Lady Blanche for his wife.

A bright blanket of autumn colors formed by chrysanthemums of the decorative category fills the Maryland garden of Isabel Chappell (seated) and Gladys Guinn, retired teachers.

Propagating new plants for your garden 3

Perennials proliferate like kittens and, as with kittens, some people always have too many and are eager to find good homes for them. In the Massachusetts town where I live, and in other communities, that circumstance is put to work for the benefit of all concerned. Every spring, and sometimes in late summer as well, the good ladies of the four or five garden clubs in town donate their surplus primroses, chrysanthemums and the like for public sale on a church lawn, or the town common, or somebody's front yard. Other amateur gardeners can stock up at little cost, and the garden clubbers can use the proceeds of the sale to pay for such civic beautification projects as flower boxes along the business streets or plantings outside the railroad station. Many friends of mine, and I myself, find such sales a great help in keeping their gardens young. And many a beginning gardener, once he realizes that most of the plants that he has purchased or has seen on sale were produced from someone's existing garden plants, decides to try propagating his own. In this way he can not only enlarge his garden but also replace old overgrown specimens with vigorous free-flowering ones at little or no expense.

Once you decide to try your hand at propagation, you have a choice of several different methods. In the case of some plants, such as delphiniums and perennial peas *(encyclopedia)*, you can get excellent results if you propagate biologically, that is, by means of seed from one plant that has been fertilized by pollen from another. However, you must buy seed properly produced by seedsmen to breed true; there is no predictability in propagation by seed taken from flowers in your garden. The offspring may display undesirable characteristics of one or more forebears. More reliable results, however, can be depended upon if plants are propagated vegetatively, that is, produced from pieces taken from a single parent plant. Vegetative propagation ensures that the offspring will inherit all of the traits of its single parent plant. This is particularly helpful in expanding or rejuvenating a perennial border, for ex-

This 50-foot border of plantain lilies, prized as much for their foliage as for their lilylike flowers, grew in eight years from just four plants. Divided and replanted, they spread to form the impressive display shown.

ample, since the gardener can be certain that his new plants will duplicate precisely the color patterns, sizes and heights of the old plants from which they come.

The commonest method of vegetative propagation, and the one most amateurs start with, is division, which is simply breaking up a large plant into several smaller ones. This operation does not harm the plants; in fact, most perennials will stay healthier if they are dug up, divided and replanted periodically. An old, and still good, rule of thumb is to divide plants every third flowering season. There are exceptions: peonies and gas plants, for example, which are slow spreading and slow to reestablish themselves after division, should remain undisturbed as long as they thrive; chrysanthemums, on the other hand, spread so fast that they should be divided every year (how often to divide each type of plant is noted in the encyclopedia section). It may take a good deal of will power, I know, to dig up a clump of flowers that appears just at its prime, but that is the way to keep your garden young and at its best over a period of years.

The reasons for digging and dividing are twofold. First, fast-growing perennials overrun and crowd out their neighbors, so they must be kept under control for the sake of the garden as a whole. Equally important is the need for growing space for all parts of each plant. As a plant spreads, the new roots and stems on the clump's periphery thrive in the fresh soil and breathing space, but in the center, competition for nutrients, water, light and circulating air becomes increasingly intense and roots and stems weaken. The result is a ring of healthy flowers around a dying heart. Wise gardeners avoid this unsightly result by dividing the old clump and leaving in its location only as many vigorous roots and stems as the available space can support in good health. The remaining healthy parts of the clump can be immediately replanted; the dying center of the clump should be discarded.

The best time to divide depends on the kind of plant and where you live. Generally, spring-blooming plants such as primroses and moss phloxes should be divided in early summer after they have flowered. Summer-blooming plants such as sea pinks and garden phloxes do well when they are divided in late summer or early fall. Fall-blooming plants such as chrysanthemums, mistflowers and sneezeweed should be divided in spring when they will have a whole growing season ahead.

However, this rule has its exceptions: from Zone 5 north (map, page 151), where winters are severe, it is advisable to divide most plants in very early spring before they begin to produce new growth. They are then sure to have enough time to develop a strong root system and anchor themselves firmly in the earth before cold weather arrives. If they are divided and replanted later in the year, they may be forced out of the ground to die in the alternate freezing and thawing of the soil in late winter and early spring.

With plants such as bee balm, sneezeweed or fall aster, which have relatively shallow roots that may be reached and lifted with little difficulty, the easiest way to divide a clump is to dig with a sharp spade at the clump's periphery, using the spade to cut away outer sections of the plant and as much soil as will adhere to them (drawings, below). Most perennials have eyes, or buds, in their upper roots that are easily visible in spring and often visible in fall. With such plants, cut each section, called a division, to include two to four eyes; from them stems eventually will grow. The rest of the clump should then be dug up and the old center discarded.

To replant a division where the old plant was growing, do not simply stick it back in the hole. Spade the spot thoroughly to a depth of at least a foot, and work into the soil a 2- to 4-inch layer of peat moss and a dusting of fertilizer labeled 0-20-20. Then set the division in the hole at the same depth that its parent was, spreading the roots loosely; cover them with soil, firm the soil with your feet and water thoroughly. If you are doing the job in late summer or early fall, the plant being divided will have live stems and leaves.

HOW TO DIVIDE PLANTS

REVITALIZING OLD CLUMPS OF PERENNIALS

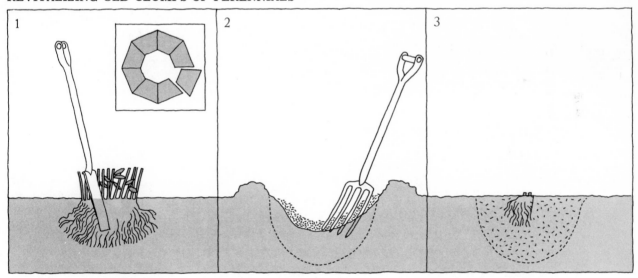

To revitalize a sneezeweed, hardy aster or any other perennial that spreads to form a large clump surrounding a dying center, cut the clump into segments (inset) with a sharp spade. Discard the old center.

With a spading fork, loosen the soil in the bottom of the original hole and drop in a couple of inches of peat moss and a light dusting of 0-20-20 fertilizer. Mix the fertilizer and peat moss thoroughly with loose soil.

Replant one segment, or division, in the old hole, other divisions elsewhere in the garden. Cut off the old stems close to ground level and water well. Each division should soon fill the space allotted to it.

Cut the stems halfway back before you plant; the new roots could not support full-sized stems. Plants that are divided in early spring, when their top growth is still only an inch or two in height, do not require any cutting back.

The method of division that you use will be dictated in part by the plants. The roots of day lilies, for example, are so intertwined that it requires two spading forks back to back *(drawings, below)* to pry them into segments after they are out of the ground. But primroses come apart easily and their roots can be separated gently with the fingers. In every case, though, prepare the soil properly and water the plants thoroughly after planting.

TAKING STEM CUTTINGS Propagation by division serves the garden well when a clump has outlived, or is about to outlive, its usefulness. But occasionally you will want to multiply an attractive still-young clump that is doing so well where it is that you hesitate to dig it up and divide it, or one that should be left alone and never divided. In either case you can create new plants by cutting segments of stems from the plant and inducing them to produce roots of their own *(drawings, page 84)*. Stem cuttings, like plant divisions, produce young perennials that duplicate their parents precisely in both the color and shape of their blossoms. This is an important consideration in modern hy-

THREE WAYS TO DIVIDE PERENNIAL CLUMPS

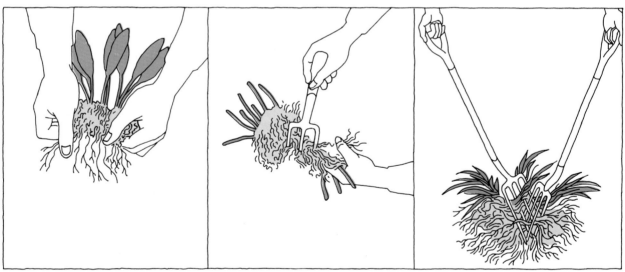

Shallow-rooted plants such as primroses are easy to pull apart by hand. After digging them up, shake off the soil and gently separate the clump into small plant segments, each with a few leaves intact.

Long whiskery roots like those of phlox may be pried apart with a hand fork. Replant only those segments with strong roots; shriveled pieces from the center of the clump must be thrown away.

Thickly intertwined roots such as those of day lilies must be forcibly separated. Thrust two spading forks, back to back, into the clump and, using the handles of the forks as levers, pry the roots apart.

brid perennials, which are often erratic in producing seed—and the seeds, when they do appear, produce plants that may revert to the less desirable shape and color of an ancestor. Unlike plant divisions, stem cuttings allow you to have your clump of prized flowers and multiply it too, with barely visible and only temporary damage to the parent. This method works especially well with lavenders, pinks, solidasters and evergreen candytufts.

The best season to take stem cuttings, sometimes referred to as "slips," is generally spring or early summer. To make a cutting, choose a stem that is mature and firm but not yet hardened and woody. Use a sharp knife or pruning shears to slice off a 2- to 6-inch segment of the tip at a point ¼ inch below the joint, called a node, where a leaf sprouts from the stem. If the tip of the cutting has buds or flowers, pinch the tip off; this operation forces the cutting to concentrate on root production rather than on top growth. Strip off the lower leaves of the cutting so that about an inch of bare stem will go below the surface of the ground when you plant, but do not remove the upper leaves—the cutting will need them as a source of energy while it continues its growth processes. Fresh cuttings tend to wilt quickly when the weather is warm and they should be planted immediately. If you cannot do so speedily, moisten them slightly and keep them in a plastic bag in a cool place.

Do not attempt to plant a stem cutting in the garden; it must be started in a container where you can provide conditions conducive to rooting. For a few cuttings, a 4-inch flowerpot will serve. For a large number, you can use a bigger pot or any container—such as a shallow box or a gardener's flat—that is at least 4 inches deep and has provision for drainage. Fill the pot or flat to within ½ inch of its top with a porous rooting medium such as coarse builders' sand, vermiculite, perlite or shredded sphagnum moss that will admit plenty of moisture and air. Moisten the rooting medium thoroughly. Sand should be wet, tamped, and wet again before the cuttings are set; the alternative materials should be wet but not firmed before the cuttings are inserted.

When you have the rooting medium and the container ready, dip each cutting's bottom ½ inch into water and then into powdered rooting hormone, a root-stimulating chemical available at garden centers and nurseries. Shake the cuttings to remove excess powder. Use the blunt end of a pencil, a stick or a finger to poke holes an inch deep in the rooting medium; insert the cuttings in the hole, firm the rooting medium around them and water well. To conserve moisture and keep the cuttings from wilting, cover the box or flat with a sheet of clear plastic (a plastic food bag serves well for pots and small boxes), seal it by folding the plastic under the container and set it in a bright spot out of direct sunlight (the sun's

THE MEASURE OF LOVE

An old name for bellis perennis, the familiar English daisy, is "measure of love," a tribute to generations of lovelorn maidens who plucked the petals of the daisy one by one to the rhythmic chant of "he loves me, he loves me not." To make it come out right, the trick is to begin with "he loves me" on the first petal—for reasons botanical and mathematical. Since virtually all daisies have an odd number of petals, the words "he loves me" will almost invariably coincide with the tearing-off of the last petal if they are also used for the first.

rays would build up excess heat beneath the plastic covering and cook the cuttings). The plastic—in effect a tiny greenhouse —should keep the cuttings and their rooting medium adequately moist, but check them daily and sprinkle the rooting medium sparingly with tepid water if it becomes dry. In most cases, rooting occurs in about two to four weeks.

When the cuttings show small new leaves, an indication that roots have developed, open the plastic to let in fresh air; in this way the new plants become acclimated before the bag is completely removed. Gently pry a cutting or two from the rooting medium; if new roots are ½ to 1 inch long, the cuttings are ready to move to the garden. I put mine first in a reserve garden, a small home nursery that I keep right beside my vegetable garden. There the young plants can be spaced out in easy-to-tend rows to continue their

STARTING NEW PLANTS FROM STEM CUTTINGS

1. *To propagate perennials from stem cuttings, take 2- to 6-inch segments from the tips of stems, cutting about ¼ inch below a leaf joint. Remove the lower leaves. To prevent wilting, sprinkle the cuttings with water, place them in a plastic bag and set them in a cool place.*

2. *Stimulate root growth by dipping the bottom ½ inch of each stem in rooting powder; tap off the excess. Do not dip the stem in the container; if diseased it might contaminate the remaining powder.*

3. *Using a small dowel or a pencil, make 1-inch-deep holes 1 to 2 inches apart in a flat or pot with a 4-inch bed of moist vermiculite, perlite or sphagnum moss. Insert cuttings, then firm the rooting medium and water thoroughly.*

4. *Cover the flat with clear plastic stretched over wire hoops and tucked under the flat. (If you use pots, fit a plastic bag over each.) Set the cuttings in a bright but not sunny place. When new growth appears, open the plastic to admit air. Transplant the cuttings when the roots are ½ to 1 inch long.*

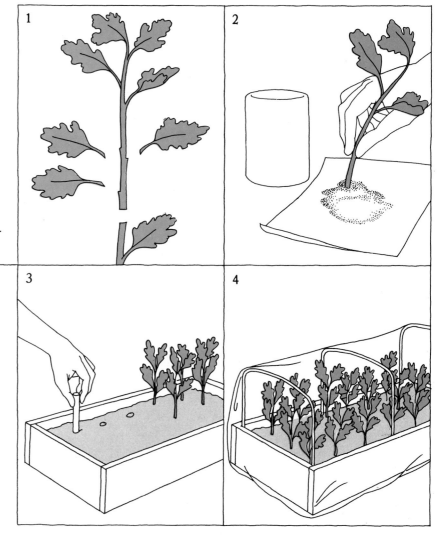

growth without being overwhelmed by larger, older plants. When they have become big enough to hold their own in the main garden, they are transplanted to go on display there.

Another way to increase some of your cherished plants is to make cuttings from roots rather than stems. Nature uses this technique on occasion, as I learned back in 1934 when I was working for a nurseryman who specialized in perennials. It was an exceptionally cold winter and there was no snow on the ground to act as insulation for the nursery's plants; many hardy species were killed outright. Even the garden phlox, normally extremely tough, suffered disaster—all the buds (the point at which stem and root merge) and center crowns perished, and the nurseryman wrote them off as a total loss. But late in spring, a circle of tiny new plants appeared around each dead crown. The tiny roots farthest from the crowns, although cut off by the cold, had survived on their own, and where each large plant had stood there were now dozens of small ones.

Horticulturists employ this regenerating characteristic of tiny roots to reproduce such plants as Japanese anemone, butterfly weed, Siberian bugloss and blanketflower. They snip off bits of roots, usually in the fall, either when they have lifted plants for division or by digging into the ground around them. If you try this method *(drawings, page 86)*, use a sharp knife or scissors to cut off tips of the roots. The size of the root pieces and the manner of replanting them differ with various plants. For most species, pieces of root 1 to 2 inches long will be big enough; such pieces should be laid on their sides in light soil or coarse builders' sand in a wooden gardener's flat or other shallow box with drainage holes. Cover them with ½ inch of sand; firm the sand thoroughly over the root cuttings and moisten it. Finally, put the box in a cold frame for the winter. A cold frame is nothing more than an outdoor box that is heated by the sun and protects young plants from extreme cold and wind. It can be easily made out of boards of decay-resistant wood such as redwood or cypress to enclose an area about 3 by 6 feet. The back of the box, facing north, should be 18 to 30 inches high; the front, facing south, should be 12 to 24 inches high. The sides should slope slightly, and the entire frame should be topped with glass or heavy-gauge clear plastic. The sloped cover allows the rain to run off. Root cuttings, protected in such a structure, will send up shoots in spring. When they do, move them to a nursery bed; they will eventually become big enough for the flower garden.

Some plants—Oriental poppy, bleeding heart and a few others specified in the encyclopedia—require special treatment when roots are cut *(drawings, page 87)*. Their root pieces should be longer—3 to 4 inches—and each segment should be potted separately and upright, in potting soil or in a mixture composed of ⅓ sand, ⅓ garden soil and ⅓ peat moss or compost. Put the mixture into 5- or 6-inch pots and bury each root so the tip is ½ to 1 inch below the surface. Be sure that the root is right side up; the end of the root that was closest to the crown of the parent plant must be at the top. Moisten the soil thoroughly and then put the pots in a cold frame for the winter. The roots will develop growth buds at their tops and in the spring the new plants will begin to grow. But in most cases they will not flower until their second season, so they too should go into the nursery bed until they are ready.

PROPAGATING FROM SEEDS

Seeds, of course, are much less expensive than nursery-grown plants but they can tax the gardener's patience—it takes from two to three years, for example, to bring a balloonflower into bloom from seed.

MAKING CUTTINGS FROM SLENDER ROOTS

1. *To propagate phloxes, Japanese anemones and other perennials that have roots no thicker than ¼ inch, first slice off the outer ends of the roots in the fall with a sharp spade, starting about 6 inches from the clumps. Root pieces can also be taken while the plants are being lifted for division (drawings, page 82).*

2. *After cleaning the roots by hosing them down, cut off and discard the thin ends of the roots and cut the remaining healthy middle sections into 1- to 2-inch lengths.*

3. *Lay the root cuttings horizontally an inch or so apart in a gardener's flat filled with light soil or sand and cover them with ½ inch of sand. Firm the sand well and water thoroughly until the water seeps out the bottom of the flat. Then set the flat in a cold frame (opposite) for the winter.*

4. *Remove the flat from the cold frame the following spring. When the new plants are about 3 inches tall, transplant them to a nursery bed, then in fall transplant them again to selected locations in your display bed or border.*

Even peonies, normally grown from divisions of named varieties, can be raised to maturity from seed, but it takes five to seven years for a peony seedling to blossom. Nevertheless, there is an immense satisfaction in seeing plants that you yourself have raised from seed come into blossom for the first time, and I am confident you will find it well worthwhile to try this method of propagation with at least some of your perennials.

Neither divisions nor stem or root cuttings will work for multiplying biennials such as Canterbury bells, common foxgloves and wallflowers, which so often supplement perennials in the garden. You have to start them from seed. Many perennials also may be grown from seed, among them gas plants, columbines, lupines and delphiniums. There are, however, many pitfalls in such an endeavor. Home-grown seed can reflect selective breeding only rarely—the

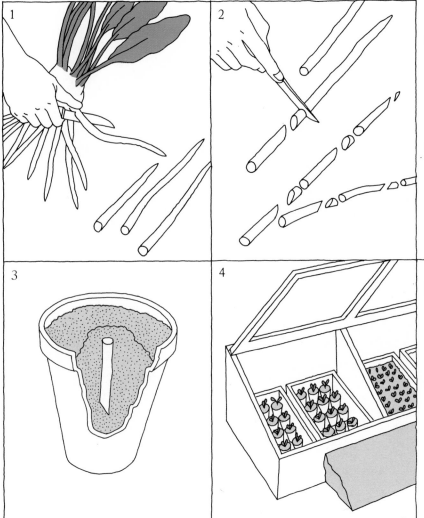

MAKING CUTTINGS FROM THICK ROOTS

1. *To propagate plants with roots ½ inch or so in diameter —Siberian bugloss and common bleeding heart, for example—dig them up in spring and slice off a few healthy outer roots with a sharp knife or pruning shears.*

2. *Cut the roots into 3- to 4-inch pieces in such a way that you can keep track of the top and bottom of each cutting. The easiest way is to make a flat cut at the end nearest the plant and a slanting cut toward the tapered root end from which new roots will grow.*

3. *Plant each cutting with its top flat end up in a pot or box 5 to 6 inches deep filled with potting soil obtainable from any garden center. Cover with ½ inch of soil and water thoroughly.*

4. *Stored over winter in a cold frame, the cuttings will start sending up shoots and leaves when spring arrives. Leave them in the frame until they are about 3 inches high. Then transfer them to a nursery bed to continue growing until their next dormant season, when they will be ready for permanent planting.*

IMPERIAL CHRYSANTHEMUM

The Chinese introduced the chrysanthemum to Japan in the Fourth Century, and the Japanese were instantly captivated by the erect, elegant flower, upon which honors were heaped. Made an imperial emblem in 797, the flower has been celebrated down the ages in Japan by exquisite pen-and-ink renderings, celebratory poems and annual festivals. To this day, the Emperor is said to sit on the Chrysanthemum Throne. The imperial standard remains a stylized chrysanthemum of 16 petals, a motif reflected in the ensign flown by Japanese naval forces, which shows a red ball with 16 rays radiating from it—neatly combining the imperial chrysanthemum with the national sobriquet, "Land of the Rising Sun."

bees in your garden are not choosy and pollinate both good and poor plants. Few home gardeners can ever hope to produce seeds with the noble pedigrees achieved by professional seedsmen. Moreover, many perennials are hybrids whose seeds cannot be relied upon to breed true.

As I suggested at the beginning of this chapter, there is a way around the problem. The answer lies in buying seeds of named varieties or strains that have been scientifically developed over a period of years. By using these you can be sure that the flowers you choose will perform in the way you wish. They offer far more than exciting colors; different ones often have different times of bloom and are available in varying heights. Delphiniums are a good example: rather than having only the familiar blue ones, the gardener can select strains that produce purple, lavender, pink or white flowers as well as specific shades of blue. By choosing a number of strains he can have delphiniums that bloom from late spring through most of the summer and that grow anywhere from 1 to 6 feet tall.

For both biennials and perennials the techniques of reproducing plants from seed are the same, but the time for sowing them varies with the species. The seeds of biennials generally should be planted in midsummer so that the seedlings will have time to make strong growth before winter. (A few species such as pansies and English daisies as well as so-called annual strains of foxgloves, Canterbury bells and sweet Williams will bloom their first year if their seeds are sown early indoors; but plants grown in this way do not usually produce as large or as many flowers as do those grown from seed sown the previous summer.)

Some perennials, such as pinks and hollyhocks, germinate quickly and are up and growing in a matter of days. Others, such as gas plants and primroses, may lie dormant for six months or more before sprouting. The seeds of some plants, such as delphiniums, should be sown immediately after their seed pods ripen, for their fresh seeds germinate more dependably than do old ones. The normal germination period for perennials is from 10 days to a month.

Unlike annuals, many of which can be permanently damaged by frost, perennials often grow better in very early spring than at any other time of the year. Since they do not need frost protection, there is no advantage to growing them indoors; in fact, indoor temperatures are usually too warm for them. Therefore the best way to start perennials, and biennials, from seed is outdoors. Preferably, the seeds should be sown within the protected environs of a cold frame, not to protect the seedlings from cold so much as from too-strong summer sun and drying winds. For this purpose all you need is a simple temporary structure of boards with a piece of muslin tacked across the top. An alternative is an open flower bed about 3 feet wide (which is a convenient width to work) with its soil raised about 2 inches above the surrounding ground to provide good drainage. Seeds sown in such a bed will do well, but will need more attention to watering while they are germinating and when the plants are small and young.

Whether you use a cold frame or an open bed, prepare the soil carefully. Dig it about 6 to 8 inches deep, rid it of weeds and stones and break up lumps with a garden rake until the soil looks as though it had been pulverized. Add about 1 part peat moss to each 2 parts of soil, then dig the bed over again and rake it smooth. Do not add fertilizer; it would stimulate the seedlings to send up fast, very tender growth.

Plant your seeds in separate rows spaced about 6 to 8 inches apart; to make rows, use the edge of a yardstick or a thin board to press shallow furrows into the ground across the bed. This will make each row about 3 feet long and should give you space for as many seedlings of a particular variety as you could possibly want. For fine seeds, first fill the furrows with vermiculite and then sow the seeds sparingly on top; they will sift down slightly into the vermiculite. Sow larger seeds about ½ to ¾ inch apart in the furrows and cover them with about ¼ inch of vermiculite. Moisten the seedbed with a fine mist, then cover it with a piece of damp burlap to keep the soil moist. After four or five days lift a corner of the covering daily and peep under it for signs of green; some germinate faster than the average. On the day the seedlings first appear, remove the burlap; bare the seedlings late in the afternoon so that they will have overnight to adjust to their new conditions and to the gradual appearance of light the next morning. The seedlings will need protection from strong sun until they have developed two or three true leaves (which, unlike the initial seedling leaves, are recognizably like those of the mature species). To provide temporary shade, fix a piece of plastic window screening or a section of slatted snow fencing a few inches above the seedlings on stakes set into the corners of the bed. During the seedlings' early growth the seedbed should be kept lightly moistened by sprinkling, but should never be allowed to become soggy, for fungus diseases fatal to seedlings thrive in excessive dampness. When the seedlings have three to four true leaves, they can be dug up gently with a little stick such as a plant label and reset in a nursery bed; space them 6 to 10 inches apart, depending on the size of the species. When the young plants have become large enough to begin flowering, you can move them to the display bed that will become their permanent home. Like any plants you have propagated yourself—whether by seed, cuttings or divisions—they will give you a special thrill as you watch them grow up to add beauty to your garden year after year.

An encyclopedia of perennials and biennials

Perennials and their frequent companions, the biennials, are available in such a wealth of colors, sizes and flowering seasons that choosing the best ones for your garden might appear overwhelming. The following encyclopedia of 126 genera of plants, which include the outstanding perennials and biennials, should help to narrow the field. In addition to providing information about the plants—the regions in which they grow and the soil, light and moisture conditions they require—the entries indicate any unusual characteristics. There are, for example, several colorful varieties that can be planted in wooded, even swampy, areas and left untended to bloom indefinitely. There are perennials whose foliage is so distinctive they are grown more for this reason than for their flowers. Many perennials can be enjoyed indoors as cut flowers.

Once you have made your selections, how do you begin in your garden? Most perennials are sold by nurserymen as container-grown or bare-rooted plants. Container-grown plants, which are sold actively growing in their own soil, can be planted at any time; bare-rooted plants, which are sold while dormant, are generally set out in fall in Zones 6-10, and in spring from Zone 5 north. For those gardeners who want to propagate their own plants from existing ones in their garden, the encyclopedia entries note which of the methods described in Chapter 3 are best for each plant. The most common method is the dividing of mature clumps; this is generally done after the plants flower: in summer for spring-flowering plants, fall for summer-flowering plants, and spring for fall-flowering plants. From Zone 5 north, plants that flower from midsummer on should be divided in early spring.

Plants are listed by their Latin names. In the case of white perennial flax *(Linum perenne album),* the genus name, *Linum,* is followed by the species, *perenne;* the third name, *album,* indicates a white-flowered variety. Common names are cross-referenced to Latin ones. A chart on pages 152-154 gives characteristics of species to which each illustrated plant belongs.

The bounty of a perennial garden, drawn by Allianora Rosse, includes the large daisylike flowers of a lavender aster and a yellow leopard's-bane (center), tiny clusters of coral-bells (right) and pink dianthus (bottom).

A

ACANTHUS

A. mollis (soft acanthus), *A. mollis latifolius* (broad-leaved acanthus), *A. spinosus* (spiny acanthus). (All also called bear's-breech)

Although the flowers of acanthuses are handsome, some gardeners remove the flower stalks as soon as they appear and grow the plants solely for their distinctive foliage, which was immortalized in the Fifth Century B.C. in the design for the capital of the classic Greek Corinthian column. The shiny dark green deeply lobed leaves rise directly from the ground and may be 2 feet long and 1 foot wide; those of the spiny acanthus are tipped with stout thorns and must be handled with gloves. In early summer flower stalks 2 to 4 feet tall bear 18-inch spikes of 1-inch tubular white, rose or lavender flowers with broadly flaring lips. Small leaves along the spikes and leaflike bracts just under the flowers are often tinged with purple. The flowering season lasts about two months; spikes may be cut for indoor arrangements or dried for winter bouquets, although the original colors tend to fade.

HOW TO GROW. Acanthuses grow well in Zones 8-10 and do best in very well-drained locations (too much moisture in winter can be fatal). In hot parts of the Southwest they need light shade but elsewhere they flourish in full sun. Set plants about 3 feet apart. The stout, drought-resistant roots range far in good soil, so it is advisable to plant acanthuses where the roots will be confined, as between a walk and a wall. New plants may be grown from seeds sown in spring but usually take three years to blossom; they may also be started in fall from root cuttings, which often take two years to flower. Dig up and divide after three to five flowering seasons, in spring or in fall.

BEAR'S-BREECH
Acanthus mollis

ACHILLEA

A. filipendulina, also called *A. eupatorium* (fern-leaved yarrow); *A. millefolium* (common yarrow, milfoil); *A. ptarmica* (sneezewort); *A. tomentosa* (woolly yarrow)

Yarrows are easy-to-grow perennials that vary in size from creeping kinds suitable for rock gardens to 3- to 4½-foot-tall types for the back of a border. Most bear fernlike foliage that has a pungent fragrance. Recommended varieties of the showy fern-leaved yarrow, which blossoms from early summer to early fall, are Coronation Gold, 3 feet tall with flat-topped 3-inch clusters of mustard-yellow flowers; Gold Plate, 4 to 4½ feet tall with 6-inch clusters of deep yellow flowers; and Parker's Variety, 3½ to 4 feet tall with 3- to 4-inch clusters of deep yellow flowers. The blossoms are excellent for cutting and may be dried for winter decoration. The common yarrow, a European wild flower, has muddy white flowers, but the varieties Fire King and Crimson Beauty bear 2- to 3-inch clusters of bright red blossoms on 18-inch stems from midsummer through fall. Sneezewort, so named because its dried roots were once ground and used as snuff, is a white-flowered perennial that bears 3- to 6-inch clusters of small fluffy ball-shaped flowers in summer. The flowers, held high above shiny dark green willowlike leaves, are dramatic in a border and excellent for cutting. Notable varieties are Angel's Breath, Perry's Giant White and The Pearl, all of which grow about 2 feet tall, and Snowball, which grows about 15 inches tall. The woolly yarrow has fernlike gray-green leaves and creeping stems, from which 6- to 12-inch flower stalks rise, bearing 1½- to 2-inch flat-topped clusters of bright yellow flowers from early summer to early fall. The variety Moonlight has pale yellow blossoms.

HOW TO GROW. Yarrows thrive in Zones 3-10, in full sun and well-drained soil, and will tolerate drought, though in

FERN-LEAVED YARROW
Achillea filipendulina
'Coronation Gold'

COMMON YARROW
Achillea millefolium 'Fire King'

windy places tall varieties may need staking. Set plants 1 to 2 feet apart. Propagate by dividing clumps; this should be done every two to four years to prevent overcrowding.

ACONITE, AUTUMN See *Aconitum*

ACONITUM

A. autumnale, also called *A. henryi* (autumn monkshood, autumn aconite); *A. cammarum sparkianum* (Spark's Variety monkshood); *A. carmichaelii,* also called *A. fischeri* (azure monkshood); *A. lycoctonum,* also called *A. vulparia* (wolfsbane); *A. napellus* (English monkshood); *A. uncinatum* (clambering monkshood)

The showy, helmetlike flowers of monkshoods, borne on tall spikes, are usually blue or purple, but white- and yellow-flowered varieties are also available. Their glossy dark green deeply cut leaves are decorative all summer. Valuable in perennial gardens, generally as tall accent plants, monkshoods also make ideal informal plantings in moist, lightly shaded woodlands. The flowers are excellent for cutting. The roots, leaves and seeds are poisonous and very dangerous if eaten or if their juices get into scratches.

The autumn monkshood grows 4 to 5 feet tall and bears navy-blue flowers from midsummer until early fall. The azure monkshood grows 2½ to 3 feet tall and bears pale blue flowers in fall; a selection called Barker's Variety grows 5 to 6 feet tall and has dark amethyst-blue flowers; and another, known as Wilson's azure monkshood (*A. carmichaelii wilsonii* or *A. wilsonii*), grows 5 to 8 feet tall and has amethyst-blue flowers. A selection of *A. cammarum* known as Spark's Variety, or sometimes as *A. cammarum sparkianum,* grows 5 to 6 feet tall and has deep violet-blue flowers. Wolfsbane grows 3 to 4 feet tall and bears yellow flowers in early to midsummer. English monkshood grows 4 to 6 feet tall and bears blue-to-purple flowers from mid- to late summer; a white-flowered variety, *A. napellus album,* grows 4 to 5 feet tall, and bicolored monkshood (*A. napellus bicolor,* also called *A. bicolor* and *A. cammarum bicolor*) grows 4 to 5 feet tall and has white flowers edged with blue. Clambering monkshood grows 3 to 5 feet tall and bears blue flowers in summer.

HOW TO GROW. Monkshoods do best in Zones 3-8 in partial shade and a cool, moist soil enriched with compost or leaf mold, but will thrive in full sun if the soil is moist enough. Space plants 12 to 18 inches apart with the crowns, or tops of the root structure, just beneath the surface. Plants set out in fall should be protected with a winter mulch of salt hay, straw or evergreen boughs during their first winter. New plants can be started from seeds sown as soon as possible after they ripen; germination periods vary and seedlings take two to three years to produce their first flowers. Monkshoods suffer severely when their roots are disturbed, and should not be divided and reset.

ADONIS

A. amurensis (Amur adonis), *A. vernalis* (spring adonis)

Rising from the earth as soon as the frost leaves the ground, adonises brighten the garden with a two-month display of flowers. The 2- to 3-inch blossoms of Amur adonis, which blooms very early in spring, come in shades of yellow, pink, orange and copper as well as in white; plants frequently bear more than one flower to a stem, and their deeply divided leaves have three distinct segments. The spring adonis, which usually blooms two to three weeks after the Amur adonis, bears a single buttercup-yellow or white flower on each stem; the stems are lightly clothed with finely divided, feathery foliage.

The first flowers of both adonises appear when the stems

SPARK'S VARIETY MONKSHOOD
Aconitum cammarum sparkianum

SPRING ADONIS
Adonis vernalis

For climate zones and months of flowering, see page 151.

are only 3 to 4 inches tall, but the plants continue to grow, reaching 9 to 15 inches during the peak of the blooming season. After the seeds ripen in late spring, the leaves shrivel and disappear, and the plants rest beneath the soil until the following spring. Adonises are best grown in generous clumps near the front of a border or in a rock garden. Set them beside such plants as creeping babies'-breath or Carpathian bellflower, which develop enough summer foliage to carpet the ground when the adonises are dormant.

HOW TO GROW. Adonises grow in Zones 3-7 in any well-drained garden soil in full sun or light shade. Set plants 6 to 10 inches apart. New plants can be started from seeds sown in summer; if home-grown seeds are to be used, plant them as soon as possible after they ripen. Seedlings usually require two years to reach flowering size. Clumps may be divided for propagation at any time the plants do not have foliage, that is, from late spring until very early the following spring, but most gardeners dig up and reset adonises in early fall. Otherwise, clumps should be allowed to remain undisturbed for at least three to five years.

AGATHAEA COELESTIS See *Felicia*
AGERATUM, HARDY See *Eupatorium*
AGROSTEMMA CORONARIA See *Lychnis*
ALKANET See *Anchusa*

ALTHAEA
A. rosea (hollyhock)

Although associated with Elizabethan gardens and English cottages, hollyhocks are native to China and were first brought West in the 16th Century. They quickly won favor because of their long blooming period, from midsummer to early fall. The flowers are borne on long wandlike stems; blossoming begins at the bottom of the stems and moves progressively upward so that 1½ to 2 feet of each stem is covered with flowers throughout the season. Plants usually grow 5 to 9 feet tall from low clumps of hairy leaves 6 to 8 inches across; each clump sends out three to six stems. The blossoms are 3 to 5 inches across and range in color from white through every shade of yellow, pink, lavender and red to nearly black. In addition to the old-fashioned cup-shaped single flowers, there are spectacular new strains whose petals are fringed, ruffled or doubled. Because of their height, hollyhocks look best at the back of a border or against a fence or wall.

HOW TO GROW. Hollyhocks grow as short-lived perennials in Zones 3-8 and as biennials in Zones 9 and 10. They need full sun, moist but well-drained soil and staking to support the fragile stems in windy locations. New plants are best started from seeds sown in summer for flowering the following year. Once established in a garden, hollyhocks often grow spontaneously from seeds dropped during the summer, and these seedlings are worth transplanting. Hollyhocks may live and blossom several years in Zones 3-8 if their stalks are cut off at their bases after the blossoms fade, but these old plants will rarely flower as freely as husky young ones started from seeds each year. Varieties of annual hollyhocks are also available; started from seeds indoors or in greenhouses in midwinter, they will blossom the following summer.

ALUMROOT See *Heuchera*

ANAPHALIS
A. margaritacea (pearly everlasting), *A. yedoensis* (Japanese pearly everlasting)

The name pearly everlasting is appropriate for these species of *Anaphalis:* the buttonlike flowers, which grow in

HOLLYHOCK
Althaea rosea

JAPANESE PEARLY EVERLASTING
Anaphalis yedoensis

94

clusters 2 or more inches wide, are composed of tiny silvery white petals that retain their color and texture when dried. Clumps of pearly everlastings grow 1 to 2 feet tall and blossom from midsummer to fall. Because their slender 2- to 4-inch leaves are heavily coated with white hairs, the plants look silvery gray, a useful color to contrast with other plants having darker foliage and flowers of brighter hues. Pearly everlastings are wild flowers of the fields and meadows in much of North America and Asia.

HOW TO GROW. Pearly everlastings grow in Zones 3-6 in full sun or light shade. They do well in almost any well-drained soil and will tolerate poor, dry soil. Set plants 12 to 15 inches apart. New plants can be started from seeds sown in summer to blossom the following year. Dig up, divide and replant when the clumps become overcrowded, usually after three or four years of flowering.

ANCHUSA
A. azurea, also called *A. italica* (Italian bugloss, alkanet)

The bright blue blossoms of Italian bugloss are about an inch across and from early to midsummer are borne in clusters on stems that reach a height of 3 to 6 feet. The leaves are large—the lower ones may be a foot or more in length —rough and tongue-shaped (the name bugloss is Greek for "oxtongue"). Varieties such as Dropmore, Morning Glory and Opal grow 5 to 6 feet tall and are well suited to the back of a border. The Loddon Royalist and Royal Blue varieties rarely exceed 3 feet.

HOW TO GROW. Italian bugloss thrives in Zones 3-10 except in Florida and along the Gulf Coast. It grows in full sun or light shade and well-drained soil. Set plants 1½ to 2 feet apart. Late in the fall mound 2 to 3 inches of soil directly over the newly set plants to divert moisture from them during the winter. If planted in soil that drains poorly —such as moist clay—plants may die in winter because their fleshy roots have a tendency to rot. Roots should be dug up and potted in late fall and kept in a cold frame. The foliage of Italian bugloss becomes floppy and unattractive after the flowers fade. If leaves and stalks are cut to the ground at that time the plants will shoot up and blossom again, but less generously, in early fall. In windy locations the stalks may need staking to keep them from being blown over or snapped off. New plants can be grown from seeds sown in spring or early summer, but will not be of the same quality as named varieties produced from root cuttings or clump divisions started in spring or fall. Plants started by any one of these methods will blossom the next year. Plants rarely bloom well for more than two seasons without being dug up, divided and replanted; this can be done in spring or fall.

ANCHUSA MYOSOTIDIFLORA See *Brunnera*

ANEMONE
A. hybrida, including plants derived from or sold as
A. hupehensis japonica, *A. japonica* (Japanese anemone);
A. vitifolia robustissima (grape-leaved anemone)

Both the Japanese anemone and the grape-leaved anemone bear their handsome 2- to 3-inch pink or white flowers from late summer to midfall, when relatively few flowers like them are blooming. Their deeply lobed dark green leaves make a thick 12-inch mound from which the slender many-branched flower stalks rise to a height of 2 to 3 feet. Anemone hybrids, developed from Chinese and Japanese species, include Alba, also known as Honorine Jobert, which bears single white flowers, with only one ring of petals; Kriemhilde, blush-pink semidouble flowers, with more than one ring of petals; Margarette, double rose-pink flow-

ITALIAN BUGLOSS
Anchusa azurea 'Loddon Royalist'

JAPANESE ANEMONE
Anemone hybrida

For climate zones and months of flowering, see page 151.

GOLDEN MARGUERITE
Anthemis tinctoria 'Moonlight'

ers, with many overlapping rings of petals; Profusion, single deep rose-pink flowers; and September Charm, single silvery pink flowers. The grape-leaved anemone, native to the Himalayas, bears single deep pink flowers.

HOW TO GROW. Japanese and grape-leaved anemones grow in Zones 5-10 except in Florida and along the Gulf Coast. They do best in light shade and a well-drained soil that has been liberally supplemented with peat moss; they will tolerate sun if there is ample moisture during the growing season. Set plants about 18 inches apart. In Zones 5 and 6 protect plants in winter with a 6-inch mulch of salt hay, straw or other light organic material. Anemones become more beautiful as the plants increase in size, so do not disturb the roots except for purposes of propagation. New plants started from root cuttings or clump divisions made in early spring will bloom the same year.

ANTHEMIS
A. tinctoria (golden marguerite, yellow camomile)

Hybrid varieties of golden marguerites are prolific and easy to grow, bearing yellow daisylike blossoms about 2 inches across all summer and into early fall. Most varieties grow 2 to 2½ feet tall and have dense fernlike foliage, pungent when crushed. They provide good cut flowers, and insects infrequently bother them. Some recommended varieties are Beauty of Grallagh, deep yellow flowers; Grallagh Gold, orange-tinged yellow flowers; and Moonlight, a soft primrose-yellow variety.

HOW TO GROW. Golden marguerites grow in Zones 3-10 except in Florida and along the Gulf Coast, in full sun and almost any well-drained soil. Set plants about a foot apart. Because the plants bear so many flowers, it is almost impossible to prevent some from dropping seeds, but any seedlings are apt to be inferior to their hybrid parents and should be discarded. Plants can be started from clump divisions or from stem cuttings taken in spring; they should flower the same year. Divide clumps in spring after two years of flowering.

AQUILEGIA
A. caerulea (Rocky Mountain columbine), *A. canadensis* (American columbine), *A. chrysantha* (golden columbine), *A. hybrida* (hybrid columbine)

Columbines blossom in mid- and late spring, bearing their airy, distinctive flowers high above clumps of deeply lobed dark green or blue-green leaves. Blossoms are 1½ to 4 inches across; their colors, mostly pastel, include many tones of red, pink, yellow, blue and lavender as well as white. The flowers usually are made up of five petallike sepals set on top of the petals, which may be the same or a different color. The back of each true petal is elongated into a peculiar appendage called a spur, which varies in length from ½ inch to as much as 6 inches. (The botanical name of the genus *Aquilegia* comes from the Latin *aquila*, meaning "eagle," and alludes to the clawlike curve at the end of each spur.) Hummingbirds are frequent visitors to columbines, seeking nectar in the spurs. Because the flowering season ends early, columbines should be planted where their fading leaves will be camouflaged by the developing foliage of other plants. Columbine flowers are excellent for cutting.

The Rocky Mountain columbine grows 1½ to 2½ feet tall and has 2- to 3-inch blue and white flowers. The American columbine, one of the parents of modern hybrids, grows 3 to 4 feet tall and has yellow blossoms 2 to 3 inches across. Hybrid columbines offer 3- to 4-inch blossoms in a full range of colors and a wide selection of plant sizes. Seeds are usually sold both in color mixtures and in

COLUMBINE
Aquilegia hybrida 'Spring Song'

shades of a single color. Typical of today's improved strains are Dragon Fly Hybrids, which grow 15 to 18 inches tall; Spring Song, which grows 2 to 2½ feet tall and whose flowers sometimes have more than a single ring of petals; and McKana's Giant Hybrids, McKana Improved and Mrs. Scott Elliott Hybrids, all of which grow 2½ to 3 feet tall.

HOW TO GROW. Columbines do well in Zones 3-10 except in Florida and along the Gulf Coast. They grow best in moist but well-drained soil in very light shade, but will tolerate full sun except in hot dry areas. Set plants 10 to 15 inches apart. In Zones 4 and 5 mulch columbines in late fall with salt hay, straw or other light organic material to keep the plants from heaving out of the ground during alternate thaws and freezes. Plants are best started from seeds purchased from a commercial grower—seeds from the garden are likely to revert to a less desirable variety. Seeds sown in summer will produce flowering-sized plants the next spring. Since columbines usually lose their vitality after three years, they should be replaced at that time.

ARMERIA

A. maritima; A. plantaginea; A. pseudoarmeria, also called *A. cephalotes, A. formosa; A.* hybrids. (All called sea pink, thrift, armeria)

From late spring to midsummer, and occasionally until the end of summer, sea pinks send up 1- to 1½-foot stems topped with 1-inch globelike clusters of pink, lilac, white or red flowers that are excellent for cutting. In the temperate climate of the Pacific Coast, plants may bloom all year. Wherever they grow, their 6- to 10-inch tufts of grasslike bluish foliage stay green the year round and always look neat. The size of sea pinks makes them suitable for planting in a rock garden, along a path or at the front of a border. *A. maritima* is the most common sea pink; its variety Vindictive is an especially fine deep pink. A cherry-pink variety of *A. plantaginea* called Bees' Ruby is also widely grown. An excellent variety of *A. pseudoarmeria* is the bright pink Glory of Holland. Other outstanding sea pink hybrids include Royal Rose, with bright pink flowers, and Ruby Glow, with deep rose blossoms.

HOW TO GROW. Sea pinks can be grown in Zones 4-10 except in Florida and along the Gulf Coast. They require full sun and excellent drainage, and do best in rather poor, dry soil; too much moisture and fertilizer diminish flower production. Set plants 9 to 12 inches apart. Common types are often grown from seeds sown in spring to blossom the same year, but seeds of named varieties may not produce plants resembling their parents. These varieties are best propagated by clump division in early spring or early fall. Because old clumps tend to die out in the middle, all sea pinks should be divided after three years of flowering.

ARTEMISIA

A. albula 'Silver King' (Silver King artemisia), *A. lactiflora* (white mugwort), *A. schmidtiana* 'Silver Mound' (Silver Mound artemisia). (All called wormwood)

Artemisias are valued more for their feathery aromatic leaves than for flowers. Silver King, which grows about 3 feet tall and produces unobtrusive white flowers in late summer, has silvery white foliage excellent for fresh and dried bouquets. White mugwort grows 4 to 5 feet tall and has dark green leaves, silvery underneath; from mid- to late summer it abounds in tiny fragrant creamy flowers along its upper branches. Silver Mound has silvery leaves and slender stems that form dense mounds about a foot high with an equal spread; in late summer it bears inconspicuous white flowers.

HOW TO GROW. Artemisias grow well in Zones 4-10 ex-

SEA PINK
Armeria plantaginea 'Bees' Ruby'

WORMWOOD
Artemisia albula 'Silver King'

For climate zones and months of flowering, see page 151.

97

GOATSBEARD
Aruncus sylvester

BUTTERFLY WEED
Asclepias tuberosa

SWEET WOODRUFF
Asperula odorata

cept in Florida and along the Gulf Coast, thriving even in poor soil, in full sun or light shade. Moisture is important in the growing season, but excellent drainage is essential; wet soil in winter is often fatal. Plant artemisias 12 to 18 inches apart. Propagate Silver King and white mugwort from clump divisions; the plants grow rapidly and usually should be divided every spring or fall. Silver Mound should be propagated from stem cuttings in spring or summer. Clumps rarely spread and are best left undisturbed.

ARUNCUS
A. sylvester, also called *A. dioicus, Spiraea aruncus* (goatsbeard)

For two weeks in early summer, each 4- to 6-foot stalk of goatsbeard is crowned with a 6- to 10-inch plume of tiny blossoms. Because the flowering season is relatively short and the foliage is tall, goatsbeard is generally placed at the back of a border, but it is also dramatic when massed alone as a separate planting. Its tolerance for partial shade and wet soil makes it popular in woodland gardens.

HOW TO GROW. Goatsbeard does well in Zones 4-9 in almost any soil, in sun or light shade. Set plants 18 to 24 inches apart. To get new plants, divide clumps in spring or fall; otherwise clumps can remain undisturbed indefinitely.

ASCLEPIAS
A. tuberosa (butterfly weed, pleurisy root)

Too beautiful to be called a weed, butterfly weed probably got its name because it is a common wild flower in most parts of the U.S. and southern Canada; its second name, pleurisy root, recalls its use as a medicine by the Indians. A single plant may send up 5 to 10 flower stalks 1 to 2 feet tall, lined with slender 2- to 4-inch hairy leaves and topped by several 2-inch clusters of small, fragrant, vivid orange blossoms, which bloom from midsummer to early fall. In fall the 2- to 3-inch canoe-shaped seed pods open to disperse clouds of silky seeds. The flowers are excellent for cutting and the pods are attractive in dried bouquets.

HOW TO GROW. Butterfly weed grows in Zones 4-10 in the sun, in well-drained sandy soil. Because its taproot reaches deep into the ground, it can withstand drought. Set butterfly weeds 8 to 12 inches apart. Since the plants sprout in late spring it is wise to mark their locations with stakes so that the buds, which start underground, are not damaged when the soil is cultivated early in the season. New plants can be grown easily from seeds sown in spring or summer to blossom in two years. The long taproots make these plants difficult to divide, and clumps should remain undisturbed indefinitely.

ASPERULA
A. odorata (sweet woodruff)

Sweet woodruff, often used in rock gardens and as a ground cover in shady areas, bears an abundance of tiny fragrant white flowers in late spring and early summer that are excellent for cutting; the dense mound of foliage 6 to 8 inches high is attractive all summer. Fresh leaves are used to flavor May wine; dried leaves are used in sachets.

HOW TO GROW. Sweet woodruff grows in Zones 4-9 except in Florida and along the Gulf Coast. It does best in light shade and moist, acid soil (pH 4.5 to 5.5) liberally supplemented with leaf mold or peat moss. Set plants 10 to 12 inches apart. New plants can be started from clump divisions in early fall or spring. They rarely need dividing.

ASTER
A. amellus (Italian aster); *A. frikartii* 'Wonder of Stafa'; *A. hybridus* (Oregon aster); *A. novae-angliae* (New Eng-

land aster), *A. novi-belgii* (New York aster), both also called hardy aster, Michaelmas daisy; *A. yunnanensis* 'Napsbury' (Napsbury aster)

Perennial asters range in height from less than a foot to 6 feet. The predominant colors are blue, lavender and purple, but among the hybrids are white varieties and every shade of red from pink to crimson. The Italian aster grows 18 to 24 inches tall and produces many 2-inch blossoms from mid- to late summer. In addition to the basic species, which has purple flowers, there are such fine varieties as Blue King and King George, both bright blue, and Sonia, clear pink; all have bright yellow centers and are fragrant. Wonder of Stafa, a hybrid that may become 2½ to 3 feet tall, produces 2½-inch lavender-blue yellow-centered flowers. In most of the country it blossoms from spring to fall, but in frost-free climates bears occasional flowers throughout the year. Oregon asters are 9- to 15-inch-tall plants that are covered with 1½- to 2-inch blossoms from late summer to fall; excellent varieties include Bonny Blue, medium blue; Pink Bouquet, rose pink; Snowball, white; and Twilight, deep violet.

The most important selections of the New England aster, which produces masses of 1½- to 2-inch flowers from late summer to early fall, are Harrington's Pink, clear pink, and September Glow, ruby red; both become 4 to 5 feet tall. The flowers of all New England asters close at night. New York asters, which produce 1½- to 2-inch flowers from late summer to early fall, include Autumn Glory, 3 to 4 feet tall, claret red; Crimson Brocade, 3 feet tall, bright red; Eventide, 3 to 4 feet tall, purple; Marie Ballard, 3 to 4 feet tall, pale blue; Patricia Ballard, 3 feet tall, pink; and White Lady, 5 to 6 feet tall, white. The Napsbury aster, a variety of a Chinese species, grows about 2½ feet tall from an 8- to 12-inch mound of dark green leaves and produces 3-inch orange-centered bright blue flowers, one to a stem, from midspring to early summer.

HOW TO GROW. Italian, Napsbury and Wonder of Stafa asters grow in Zones 5-10; the other species and hybrids survive winter as far north as Zone 4. None are recommended for Florida or the Gulf Coast. All grow well in full sun in ordinary well-drained garden soil. Set tall-growing asters about 2 to 2½ feet apart, low-growing ones 12 to 18 inches apart. To stimulate flowering, encourage branching and strengthen the tall, late-blooming varieties so that they stand without staking, cut off the tips of the canes in late spring and again a month later in early summer.

Propagate asters by digging up and dividing clumps. Oregon, New York and New England asters multiply rapidly and should be divided and reset in fall or spring every other year; Italian, Napsbury and Wonder of Stafa asters grow at a more moderate rate and should be divided in spring after about three years of flowering.

ASTER, CORNFLOWER See *Stokesia*
ASTER, STOKES'S See *Stokesia*
ASTER HYBRIDUS LUTEUS See *Solidaster*
ASTER ROTUNDIFOLIUS See *Felicia*
ASTERAGO LUTEA See *Solidaster*

ASTILBE
A. arendsii (astilbe, false spirea)

For two months in midsummer, astilbes bear on their 2- to 3-foot stalks spectacular spirelike plumes 8 to 12 inches tall that are composed of myriads of tiny flowers. The flowers are good for cutting if they are allowed to open fully before being picked. The fernlike leaves, deep green to bronze in color, make handsome mounds 12 to 18 inches tall. Outstanding hybrid varieties include Bridal Veil and Deutsch-

ASTER
Aster frikartii

MICHAELMAS DAISY
Aster novi-belgii

ASTILBE
Astilbe arendsii 'Rosy Veil'

For climate zones and months of flowering, see page 151.

BLUE FALSE INDIGO
Baptisia australis

ENGLISH DAISY
Bellis perennis

land, white flowers; Fanal and Red Sentinel, deep red blossoms and bronzy foliage; Rosy Veil and Peach Blossom, pink flowers; and Hyacinth, lavender flowers.

HOW TO GROW. Astilbes can be grown in Zones 4-8 in moist soil supplemented with peat moss or leaf mold. Though they will get along in full sun, it is easier to grow them in light shade so they do not dry out rapidly in summer. They require well-drained soil, particularly during the winter months, when the plants are resting. Plant astilbes 15 to 18 inches apart. Astilbes are what are called "gross feeders." They multiply rapidly and exhaust the soil around them, then become unkempt and produce few flowers. For this reason, the clumps should be dug up and divided in spring or fall after every two or three years of flowering. Before resetting the plants, replenish the soil with peat moss or leaf mold and a dusting of fertilizer of 0-20-20 composition. Many florists force astilbes into flower in the spring; after such plants have finished blooming, they can be set outdoors and will flower the following year.

AVENS See *Geum*

B

BABIES'-BREATH See *Gypsophila*
BACHELOR'S-BUTTON See *Centaurea*
BALLOONFLOWER See *Platycodon*

BAPTISIA
B. australis (blue false or wild indigo),
B. tinctoria (yellow false or wild indigo)

Blue false indigo grows 3 to 5 feet tall and from midspring to early summer sends out 9- to 12-inch spikes of purplish blue 1-inch flowers, followed by fat 2- to 3-inch seed pods; it has blue-green cloverlike leaves composed of three 2- to 3-inch-long segments. Yellow false indigo grows 2 to 3 feet tall and from midspring to fall bears 1½- to 3-inch spikes of bright yellow ½-inch flowers; the silvery green leaves have segments only ½ inch long. Both species make unusual-looking cut flowers. The woody stem of false indigo makes a weak but usable blue dye.

HOW TO GROW. False indigos grow in Zones 3-10 in almost any soil in full sun or very light shade. They grow best if started from seeds sown in fall or spring; the plants begin to blossom when they are two or three years old. Space flowering-sized plants 18 to 30 inches apart. To encourage blue false indigos to send out more blooms, pinch off faded flowers before they form new seeds. False indigos almost never need dividing, for though the clumps increase in size, the long taproots reach deep and do not spread to encroach upon other plants.

BEARDTONGUE See *Penstemon*
BEAR'S-BREECH See *Acanthus*
BEE BALM See *Monarda*
BELLFLOWER See *Campanula*
BELLFLOWER, CHINESE See *Platycodon*

BELLIS
B. perennis (English daisy, true daisy)

The English daisy, immortalized by poets, is a delightful 6-inch-tall plant with red, pink or white flowers 1 to 2 inches across. The yellow centers stand out on varieties with a single ring of petals and those with more than one ring (semidouble), but are obscured by the numerous overlapping petals on double varieties. On most plants one blossom adorns each stem, which rises from a low clump of 2- to 3-inch dark green leaves. English daisies generally bloom from early spring to early summer and produce a few flowers in the fall, but in cool coastal areas of California they may blossom all year. Although the species name *perennis* means "perennial," English daisies are usually grown as biennials, and sometimes even as annuals.

HOW TO GROW. English daisies grow throughout Zones 3-10 in full sun or light shade in moist soil that has been well supplemented with peat moss. Set plants 8 to 9 inches apart. In Zones 3-5 plants require special care to help them survive the winters. They should be dug up in fall with clumps of soil clinging to their roots, set snugly together in a cold frame and mulched after the ground freezes with a 4- to 6-inch covering of straw or salt hay. New plants can be grown from seeds. In Zones 3-7 sow seeds in the spring or summer to flower the following spring; in fall in Zones 3-5 move the seedlings to a cold frame for the winter, then into the main garden in spring. In Zones 8-10 sow seeds in late summer or early fall for early spring blossoms. If heavily petaled double flowers are wanted, buy fresh seeds of double-flowered strains; seeds from home-grown plants usually produce single-flowered seedlings even though the parent plants had double blossoms. New plants can also be propagated when dividing the clumps, which should be done every year to prevent overcrowding.

BERGAMOT, SWEET See *Monarda*

BERGENIA

B. cordifolia (heart-leaved bergenia), *B. crassifolia* (leather bergenia). (Both formerly classified in the genera *Megasea* and *Saxifraga*)

Bergenias appeal to gardeners because of their large handsome leaves and their 3- to 6-inch clusters of delicate flowers, which appear in spring. Colors range from deep purplish pink to pale pink and occasionally white. The leaves of the heart-leaved bergenia are 8 to 10 inches across with sawtoothed edges; flowers are borne on nodding stems that extend barely above the foliage. The leather bergenia has oval leaves of similar size; its flowers bloom on stout stems 12 inches or more above the foliage. Because the leaves are attractive even after the flowers fade—they remain green throughout the year in southern regions and turn a handsome bronze in fall in cold areas—the plants are often used near the front of a border or along a path.

HOW TO GROW. Bergenias can be grown in Zones 4-10 except in Florida and along the Gulf Coast; they thrive in almost any soil in full sun or light shade, although they prefer light shade in hot areas. They tolerate a wide range of moisture conditions, growing slowly in dry areas and rapidly in constantly wet spots, such as beside a brook or pool. Set plants 12 to 15 inches apart. In Zones 4-6 cover the plants with a mulch of salt hay or straw to shade the leaves from winter sun. New plants can be started by dividing and resetting clumps when they become overcrowded, usually after three or four years of flowering.

BETONICA See *Stachys*
BETONY See *Stachys*
BISHOP'S-HAT See *Epimedium*
BLADDER CHERRY See *Physalis*
BLANKETFLOWER See *Gaillardia*
BLEEDING HEART See *Dicentra*
BLUEBELL, TUSSOCK See *Campanula*
BOCCONIA See *Macleaya*

BOLTONIA

B. asteroides (white boltonia),
B. latisquama (pink or violet boltonia)

Clouds of starlike 1-inch blossoms in pink, lavender or

HEART-LEAVED BERGENIA
Bergenia cordifolia

PINK BOLTONIA
Boltonia latisquama

For climate zones and months of flowering, see page 151.

SIBERIAN BUGLOSS
Brunnera macrophylla

white top the willowy stems of boltonias from midsummer to early fall, rising above smooth, narrow gray-green leaves 1 to 3 inches long. Snowbank, an excellent white variety, grows about 4 feet tall. Dwarf pink boltonia, *B. latisquama nana*, grows 2½ to 3 feet tall.

HOW TO GROW. Boltonias grow in Zones 3-10 in almost any soil in full sun or light shade. Space plants 18 to 24 inches apart. New plants can be started from divisions of clumps in spring. Boltonias increase rapidly; to prevent overcrowding, clumps should be divided every other year.

BRUNNERA
B. macrophylla, also called *Anchusa myosotidiflora, Myosotis macrophylla* (Siberian bugloss)

Siberian bugloss is a relative of the forget-me-not, as is apparent from its ¼-inch yellow-centered blue flowers, which bloom on 12- to 18-inch stems from early spring to early summer. The long-stalked leaves are 4 to 5 inches across in spring, increasing to about 8 inches wide by midsummer. Siberian bugloss is a good choice for the middle of a shaded border, and it is also often planted to grow untended, as if wild, in wooded areas.

HOW TO GROW. Siberian bugloss grows in Zones 3-10 except in Florida and along the Gulf Coast; it does best in light shade in soil that has been well supplemented with peat moss or leaf mold and is kept constantly moist. Set new plants 12 to 15 inches apart. Siberian bugloss is best propagated from root cuttings taken in early spring or from seeds sown in fall to blossom the following year. To prevent overcrowding, divide clumps after every two or three years of flowering.

BUGBANE See *Cimicifuga*
BUGLOSS, ITALIAN See *Anchusa*
BUGLOSS, SIBERIAN See *Brunnera*
BURNING BUSH See *Dictamnus*
BUTTERFLY WEED See *Asclepias*

C

CALLIRHOË
C. digitata (finger poppy mallow), *C. involucrata* (low poppy mallow). (Both also called wine-cup)

Poppy mallows bear 2-inch blossoms from late spring to late summer and occasionally even until frost; the slender flower stalks, about 1 foot tall, rise from sprawling stems that become as long as 3 feet. The blossoms of the two species are almost identical, but their foliage differs: the finger poppy mallow has smooth, deeply cleft leaves while the leaves of the low poppy mallow are hairy and less deeply notched. Since both poppy mallows have heavy, carrotlike roots that tend to rot if planted in poorly drained locations, they are best suited to the crevices of a rock wall or for carpeting a dry bank.

HOW TO GROW. Poppy mallows grow in Zones 3-10 in full sun and almost any well-drained soil; because they have deep roots they can tolerate dry locations. Set plants about 18 inches apart. New plants may be grown from stem cuttings started in early summer or from seeds sown in early spring; flowers will bloom late the same year. Poppy mallow should remain undisturbed indefinitely.

CAMOMILE, YELLOW See *Anthemis*

CAMPANULA
C. carpatica (Carpathian harebell, tussock bluebell), *C. glomerata* (clustered bellflower), *C. medium* (Canterbury bells), *C. persicifolia* (peach-leaved bellflower). (All also called bellflower)

LOW POPPY MALLOW
Callirhoë involucrata

CANTERBURY BELL
Campanula medium

Bellflowers of both the perennial and biennial species are among the mainstays of a flower garden. All are undemanding in their care and reliable and prodigious in their blossoming.

The Carpathian harebell is one of the most dependable and delightful species of bellflowers. It forms neat clumps of foliage 4 to 6 inches tall. Wiry 6- to 8-inch stems rise from the clumps and are topped by 2-inch flat-cupped blue or white flowers from early summer into late fall. Among the better varieties are Blue Carpet, clear medium blue; Cobalt, deep blue; Wedgewood, pale blue; and White Wedgewood, white.

The clustered bellflower grows 1 to 2 feet tall and bears dense clusters of 1-inch upward-facing white, blue or purple bell-shaped flowers from late spring to early summer. Joan Elliott is a handsome variety with deep violet flowers; Alba is a variety with white blossoms.

Canterbury bells are biennial species of bellflower. During the second year of its life cycle, it sends up flowering stalks 1½ to 3 feet tall, bearing bell-shaped flowers about 2 inches long. The flowers come in white or shades of pink or purplish blue, and bloom from late spring to midsummer. Some strains of Canterbury bells have one bell set within another; this type of flower is called hose-in-hose. Still another blossom type, often listed as *C. medium calycanthema* is called cup-and-saucer, an apt description of the shape of its blossoms.

The peach-leaved bellflower is a particularly durable species. The variety Telham Beauty has 2- to 3-inch porcelain-blue bells that bloom along the top half of the 4-foot flower stalks in summer; Grandiflora Alba is an excellent similar variety that bears white flowers.

HOW TO GROW. Bellflowers grow in Zones 4-10 in full sun or light shade in almost any well-drained garden soil. Set bellflowers 12 to 18 inches apart. New plants of the perennial types may be started from clump divisions in early spring. The biennial Canterbury bells should be started from seeds sown in early summer to bloom the following year; some perennial varieties will blossom the first year from seeds sown indoors about six months before the flowering season, but they do not approach the magnificence of the biennial strains.

Carpathian harebells and peach-leaved bellflowers are slow to spread and should ordinarily be divided after three to five years of flowering. The clustered bellflower spreads more rapidly, however, and may need to be divided after every two or three years.

CANDYTUFT See *Iberis*
CANTERBURY BELL See *Campanula*
CARNATION See *Dianthus*

CASSIA

C. marilandica (wild senna)

Wild senna is a striking 4- to 7-foot plant that blooms in late summer. The 1- to 3-inch clusters of ½-inch bright yellow blossoms have conspicuous, chocolate-colored, pollen-bearing anthers. The fernlike light green leaves are 6 to 10 inches long, and the foliage is so attractive that the species would be worth growing even if it had no flowers. The height of wild senna makes it especially suitable for the backs of borders; it may also be made to look as if it were growing wild by planting it randomly and leaving it untended in lightly shaded grassy or wooded areas.

HOW TO GROW. Wild senna grows in Zones 4-10 in full sun or light shade in any well-drained soil. Set plants about 2 feet apart. New plants are easy to grow from seeds, which are produced abundantly in long flat pods in late summer

PEACH-LEAVED BELLFLOWER
Campanula persicifolia

WILD SENNA
Cassia marilandica

For climate zones and months of flowering, see page 151.

CUPID'S-DART
Catananche caerulea

MOUNTAIN BLUET
Centaurea montana

DUSTY MILLER
Centaurea rutifolia

and should be sown directly in the garden in fall to flower the following year. Clumps of wild senna can remain undisturbed indefinitely.

CATANANCHE
C. caerulea (Cupid's-dart, blue cupidone, blue succory)

The 2-inch flowers of Cupid's-dart are highly unusual; they look as if the ends of the petals have been clipped with pinking shears. The flowers bloom atop 2-foot wiry stalks in mid- to late summer and occasionally later, and are excellent for cutting and in dried winter bouquets. The low, attractive clumps of foliage, with leaves 8 to 12 inches long, make the plants particularly suitable for use at the front of a border. Some of the recommended varieties of Cupid's-dart are Blue Giant, blue; Alba and Perry's White, white; and *C. caerulea bicolor,* whose blue-centered petals are tipped with white.

HOW TO GROW. Cupid's-dart does well in Zones 4-10 in almost any soil, but requires full sun and excellent drainage —especially in winter. Space plants 8 to 10 inches apart. Start new plants of named varieties from divisions of clumps in spring or from root cuttings taken in the fall to blossom the following year. Other Cupid's-darts may also be grown from seeds sown early in spring to produce flowers in summer, but seed-grown flowers vary greatly in color and many are unattractively pale.

CATCHFLY, GERMAN See *Lychnis*
CATMINT, MAUVE See *Nepeta*

CENTAUREA
C. dealbata (Persian centaurea); *C. gymnocarpa* (dusty miller, velvet centaurea); *C. macrocephala* (globe centaurea); *C. montana* (mountain bluet, perennial bachelor's-button); *C. rutifolia,* also called *C. cineraria, C. candidissima* (dusty miller)

The several species of centaureas include widely different plants whose foliage color, flowers and hardiness have little in common.

The Persian centaurea grows 1½ to 3 feet tall and bears 2-inch feathery-petaled flowers from midsummer to early fall or even later into the fall. The flowers are lilac to purple in color and are excellent for cutting. The fern-shaped foliage is smooth on top and covered with silvery hairs underneath.

The dusty millers, both *C. gymnocarpa* and *C. rutifolia,* grow 1 to 2 feet tall and are so admired for their spectacular silvery white foliage, which is also fernlike and covered with soft velvety hairs, that many gardeners cut off the small yellow or purple flowers even before they open in summer to focus attention on the dramatic leaves.

The globe centaurea sends out 3-inch bright yellow flowers above sparse foliage on stiff 3- to 4-foot stems in early summer to midsummer. The mountain bluet looks like an annual bachelor's-button or cornflower except that its flowers are twice as large, about 3 inches across. The plants grow about 2 feet tall on weak stems that need staking. They blossom from early summer to early fall and are excellent for cutting.

HOW TO GROW. Persian and globe centaureas and mountain bluets thrive in Zones 4-8; dusty millers, though useful as annuals anywhere, can be grown as perennials only in Zones 9 and 10. All need sun and well-drained soil. Set plants 12 to 18 inches apart. New plants can be started from clump divisions or from seeds sown in spring or summer to bloom the second summer. To prevent overcrowding, most centaureas should be dug up and divided every two to four years; the mountain bluet, a particularly rapid grower in good soil, may have to be divided and reset every other year.

CENTRANTHUS
C. ruber (Jupiter's-beard, red valerian)

Jupiter's-beard, a dependable plant even for gardeners who claim to have a brown thumb, almost never fails to put forth great clusters of tiny red, pink or white flowers high on its 2- to 3-foot stems from early summer to midfall. So eager is this European wild flower to grow that it sometimes escapes from gardens and flourishes by the wayside. Its fragrant blossoms are excellent for cutting; the more they are picked, the more blossoms appear.

HOW TO GROW. Jupiter's-beard grows well in Zones 4-10, in full sun or light shade in almost any well-drained soil. Space plants 12 to 15 inches apart. New plants can be started from seeds sown in spring to flower the following year or from clump divisions in spring. To prevent overcrowding, divide clumps every three or four years.

CERATOSTIGMA
C. plumbaginoides, also called *Plumbago larpentae* (leadwort)

Leadwort grows 9 to 12 inches tall; its clusters of small flowers, less than an inch across, bloom from midsummer into early fall and often later. At the end of the blooming season, the upper leaves turn reddish bronze. Leadwort makes a fine, carefree ground cover.

HOW TO GROW. Leadwort grows in Zones 6-10 in full sun or light shade. It needs well-drained soil supplemented with peat moss or leaf mold; good drainage is essential during the winter months because the dormant plants cannot tolerate soggy soil. Set plants 18 to 24 inches apart. For winter protection in Zone 6 apply a light mulch of salt hay or straw. Propagate by dividing the clumps in early spring just as new growth becomes evident. Leadwort spreads rather fast by underground roots, and may have to be divided every two to four years.

CHALK PLANT See *Gypsophila*
CHARITY See *Polemonium*

CHEIRANTHUS
C. allionii, also called *Erysimum asperum* (Siberian wallflower); *C. cheiri* (English wallflower)

Siberian wallflowers, which are true biennials, and English wallflowers, perennials that do best when grown as biennials, grow 9 to 18 inches high and are notable for their late-spring and early-summer displays of sweetly fragrant 1-inch flowers. Both wallflowers come in shades of yellow and orange, but English wallflowers also provide shades of pink, red, maroon, brown, mahogany and purple. They are excellent for cutting.

HOW TO GROW. Wallflowers do well in Zones 5-9, in full sun or light shade. They do best in well-drained soil with a pH of 6.0 to 8.0. As biennials, wallflowers are generally started each year from seeds sown in a nursery bed in early summer. When they are 1 to 2 inches tall, dig them up, pinch off the tip of the taproot of each plant to encourage a fibrous root system and replant 6 inches apart. When the plants are 3 to 4 inches tall, pinch off the stem tips to encourage multiple branching. In Zones 7-9 transplant to the garden in the fall. For winter protection in Zones 5 and 6, dig up the plants with as much soil as possible clinging to the roots and set them snugly together in a cold frame; transplant to the garden in early spring, setting them 6 to 12 inches apart. To ensure reproduction of the characteristics of especially choice plants, propagate them from stem

JUPITER'S-BEARD
Centranthus ruber

LEADWORT
Ceratostigma plumbaginoides

ENGLISH WALLFLOWER
Cheiranthus cheiri

For climate zones and months of flowering, see page 151.

PINK TURTLEHEAD
Chelone lyonii

cuttings taken in early summer and grown in the same manner as the seedlings.

CHELONE
C. lyonii (pink turtlehead)

Pink turtlehead grows 2 to 3 feet tall and in late summer and early fall bears short spikes of 1-inch flowers and dense, shiny dark green leaves. Turtleheads are easy to grow, pest resistant and especially suitable for planting in areas that get little sun.

HOW TO GROW. Turtleheads grow well in Zones 4-9, but must have moist or wet soil and light shade. Mulch the plants with 2 to 3 inches of compost, peat moss or ground corncobs in summer to help hold moisture in the soil during the blooming season. Set new plants about 18 inches apart. The most practical method of propagation is to divide the clumps in early spring every two or three years.

CHRYSANTHEMUM
C. coccineum, also called *C. roseum, Pyrethrum hybridum* (painted daisy, pyrethrum); *C. frutescens* (marguerite, Paris daisy); *C. maximum* (Shasta daisy); *C. morifolium,* also called *C. hortorum* (hardy chrysanthemum, florists' chrysanthemum); *C. parthenium,* also called *Matricaria capensis, Pyrethrum parthenium* (feverfew)

The wide variety of plants in the *Chrysanthemum* genus share one quality: all are long lasting when cut. In addition, most have a pleasing fragrance. But from there on, dissimilarities abound.

Varieties of the painted daisy range from 9 inches to 3 feet in height and bear red, pink or white flowers on slender stems. The flowers appear from early to midsummer, although a few scattered blossoms open now and then until frost; they may be single, with one ring of petals, or double, with overlapping rings of petals, or they may have raised pincushionlike centers similar to those of anemones. The dark green fernlike foliage forms a soft mound a few inches high.

The marguerite is a perennial in Zones 9 and 10, where it flowers throughout the year; elsewhere it is popular as a house plant or as a summer-flowering annual. The foliage forms a mound 2 to 3 feet tall with an equal spread.

The Shasta daisy stands as a living monument to the great plant breeder Luther Burbank, who for 15 years interbred wild species of chrysanthemums from various parts of the world to produce this modern mainstay of perennial gardens. Varieties range from 1 to over 3 feet tall; some begin to bloom in early summer and others continue well into the fall, even until frost. The flowers, as large as 6 inches across, come in single, double and anemone forms, and are nearly always snow white with occasional tinges of yellow. Superior varieties include Esther Read and Cobham's Gold, both 3-inch double types; Snow Cloud, a 3- to 4-inch anemone-centered double; and the spectacular Thomas Killin, a 6-inch anemone-centered semidouble.

The late-blooming hardy or florists' chrysanthemums are among the most varied, dependable and useful of all perennials. Older types bloomed so late in the fall that frost often came before some of the buds opened; today this defect has been eliminated. New handsome varieties come into flower as early as August. Colors include white and many shades of yellow, pink, lavender, red and bronze; many blossoms combine more than one color, and on some the second color appears on the backs of the petals. These varieties offer a number of different flower types and two plant shapes. Upright plants have stiff stalks rising 1 to 3 feet tall from clumps of foliage. Cushion types grow only 9 to 15 inches tall but may spread to 30 inches across; they

PAINTED DAISY
Chrysanthemum coccineum

bear so many small, short-stemmed flowers that the foliage is usually hidden.

The various blossom types of hardy chrysanthemums are classified by the National Chrysanthemum Society as follows (the plant heights given apply only to the upright chrysanthemum types, not to the cushion types):

Pompon chrysanthemums. The blossoms, about 1½ to 2 inches across, bloom in clusters on long stems throughout the fall and may be yellow-centered single types, with one loosely arranged ring of petals, or heavily petaled doubles. The plants grow about 2 feet tall.

Button chrysanthemums. The blossoms, less than an inch across, have petals that hug the center of the flower so tightly that they look as if they have been trimmed. Like the pompons, button chrysanthemums bloom in long-stemmed clusters in fall on 2-foot plants.

Decorative chrysanthemums. The 2- to 4-inch double flowers blossom from late summer to late fall. Plants usually grow 1½ to 3 feet tall.

Single-flowered chrysanthemums. The daisy-petaled single flowers have flat or slightly rounded central disks; an early-flowering strain known as Korean Hybrids has semi-double blossoms as well as singles.

Six other types of hardy chrysanthemums are generally not recommended for perennial gardens because they blossom late and require special protection from rain and frost in a greenhouse or temporary plastic-covered shelter, but they are included here for those chrysanthemum lovers willing to take the trouble to grow them:

Spoon-flowered chrysanthemums. The 3- to 5-inch flowers have tubular petals; the end of each petal flares into the shape of a spoon and is often lighter in color than the rest of the petal. The plants grow 2 to 2½ feet tall and bloom in late fall.

Quill-flowered chrysanthemums. These are similar to spoon-flowered chrysanthemums except that the ends of the tubular petals are closed.

Anemone-flowered chrysanthemums. The blossoms are singles or semidoubles with pincushionlike centers. They bloom in late fall on 3-foot plants.

Spider chrysanthemums. Sometimes called Fuji chrysanthemums, these flowers have unique petals—long, arching and curved upward at the tips. To channel the plant's energies into those top flowers, all blossoms except the top one on each stem are usually disbudded (page 49); the result is large blooms 3 to 5 inches across. The plants grow 3 to 4 feet tall.

Exhibition chrysanthemums. Sometimes called commercial, standard or football chrysanthemums, these are the giants of the genus, but they too must be disbudded to achieve the spectacular 6- to 8-inch blossoms seen in flower shops in late fall. The plants grow 3 to 6 feet tall.

Cascade chrysanthemums. Mostly single-flowered, these plants have extremely flexible stems up to 4 to 6 feet long.

Unlike these challenging hardy chrysanthemums, feverfews are easy to grow. Varieties rise 1 to 3 feet tall from clumps of pungent foliage and bear 1-inch yellow or white flowers in mid- to late summer. Some of the flowers are doubles; others have no petals at all, only a central disk.

Pot-grown chrysanthemums obtained from florists can be planted in the garden and are most likely to grow successfully if they are small-flowered types; most large-flowered varieties bloom late and their buds may be killed by frost. These florists' plants, which have been manipulated to cause them to blossom out of their normal season, will revert to their natural flowering season if later planted in the garden. Potted chrysanthemums are often treated by florists with a chemical that shortens their height with-

SHASTA DAISY
Chrysanthemum maximum 'Snow Cloud'

HARDY CHRYSANTHEMUM
Chrysanthemum morifolium

For climate zones and months of flowering, see page 151.

KAMCHATKA BUGBANE
Cimicifuga simplex 'White Pearl'

FRAGRANT TUBE CLEMATIS
Clematis heracleaefolia davidiana

out reducing their blossom size, but the dwarfing lasts only one season and the plants then revert to their normal size.

HOW TO GROW. Painted daisies, Shasta daisies and the hardy chrysanthemums recommended for gardens do well in Zones 4-10, but marguerites thrive only in Zones 9 and 10 and feverfews in Zones 6-10. Marguerites are treated as annuals in Zones 3-8, as are feverfews in Zones 3-5. All chrysanthemums do best in full sun, and all—especially hardy chrysanthemums—need soil that has been thoroughly cultivated and enriched with organic material such as compost, leaf mold or cow manure. The plants require ample watering during the growing season and good drainage while they are dormant in winter. Space plants 12 to 24 inches apart, depending on the size of the variety.

Painted daisies, Shasta daisies, except for named varieties, and feverfews can be grown from seeds sown in spring. Painted daisies and Shasta daisies will bloom the second year; feverfews will blossom in midsummer the first year. To multiply named varieties of painted and Shasta daisies, divide and reset clumps in spring. Marguerites may be propagated from stem cuttings at any time; they will usually blossom within a few weeks. To prolong the bloom of Shasta daisies, pick off flowers as soon as they fade. To prevent overcrowding, divide painted daisies and Shasta daisies after three or four years of flowering, feverfews after one or two years.

Hardy chrysanthemums require more care than most perennials because best results are secured when plants are reset each year. Start by buying growing plants for your garden. When they become 6 to 8 inches tall, feed them with 5-10-5 fertilizer at the rate of ½ pound per 100 square feet; repeat the feeding every week to 10 days until the buds show color, then discontinue. To make hardy chrysanthemums of the upright type bushier and sturdy enough to eliminate the need for staking, pinch off the tops of the stems; cushion chrysanthemums, which form many stems by themselves, do not need to be pinched off, nor, of course, do plants that are to be disbudded. Start pinching off when the plants are about 6 inches tall (*page 49*) and repeat the process until early summer every time the stems make 6 to 8 inches of growth. Dig up one or more plants of each variety of hardy chrysanthemum in fall, each with its own clump of soil and set them in a cold frame; place each variety in a separate flat or shallow box and label it. Put a light mulch of salt hay or straw over the plants after the soil freezes. To propagate new plants from those saved in the cold frame, cut off as many stolons, or underground stems, as you desire. The stolons, lighter in color than the rest of the roots, spread out at the base of the plants and are tipped with small new leaves. Only one stolon is needed to make a full-sized plant by fall. If more plants are needed, take cuttings in late spring from the new plants started from the freshly planted stolons; the stem cuttings root readily. Hardy chrysanthemums lose their vigor after one year of flowering, producing smaller and fewer blooms, so discard the clumps after removing the stolons and stem cuttings for new plants.

CIMICIFUGA
C. racemosa (cohosh bugbane, black snakeroot);
C. simplex, also called *C. foetida intermedia*
(Kamchatka bugbane)

Bugbanes are notable not only for their ability to grow in shade but for their 2-foot spires of tiny flowers, and their impressive leaves, some as long as 2 feet. The cohosh bugbane grows 5 to 8 feet tall and blooms in mid- and late summer. The Kamchatka bugbane grows about 3 feet tall and blooms in .fall; a particularly fine compact variety, is

White Pearl, pure white in color. All bugbanes are excellent for cutting.

HOW TO GROW. Bugbanes can be grown in Zones 3-9 in moist soil that has been well supplemented with peat moss or leaf mold; the soil should be watered deeply in dry weather. Light shade is ideal, but the plants will tolerate both full sun and deep shade. Set new plants about 12 inches apart. Mulch in fall with 2 inches of compost or rotted cow manure. New plants can be started by division of clumps in early spring; otherwise, clumps can remain undisturbed indefinitely.

CLEMATIS
C. heracleaefolia davidiana (fragrant tube clematis),
C. integrifolia caerulea (solitary blue clematis),
C. recta mandshurica (Manchurian ground clematis)

Although clematises are usually thought of as vines, these three varieties grow no more than 4 feet tall. The fragrant tube clematis grows 3 to 4 feet tall and in late summer and early fall bears clusters of fragrant 1-inch pale blue blossoms. The solitary blue clematis grows 1½ to 2 feet tall and from early summer to midsummer bears a single 1½-inch pale blue flower on each stem. The Manchurian ground clematis grows 3 to 4 feet tall and in early summer to midsummer is crowned with great clusters of fragrant ¾-inch white flowers; its 6-inch leaves are feather-shaped with five to nine leaflets. The flowers of all clematises are followed by fluffy seed pods.

HOW TO GROW. Clematises grow in Zones 4-9 in full sun or light shade. They must have well-drained, slightly acid to neutral soil (pH 6.0 to 7.0) that has been well supplemented with peat moss or leaf mold. Space plants 18 to 24 inches apart. Keep the soil cool and moist during the growing season by covering it with a 2- to 3-inch organic mulch of compost or peat moss. Do not cultivate around the plants; clematis' shallow roots are easily damaged. Because clematis stems are weak, a short, twiggy branch should be set in the ground next to each plant in the spring for support. New plants can be started from stem cuttings taken in summer to bloom the following year. Clematises can remain undisturbed indefinitely.

COLUMBINE See *Aquilegia*
CONEFLOWER See *Rudbeckia*
CONEFLOWER, PURPLE See *Echinacea*

CONVOLVULUS
C mauritanicus (ground morning-glory)

The ground morning-glory is a handsome trailing evergreen plant that is especially suited to the hot, sunny, dry gardens of the West Coast and Southwest; from late spring to late fall it bears 1-inch flowers above gray-green foliage.

HOW TO GROW. Ground morning-glories grow in Zones 8-10 in full sun. They need very well-drained, even gravelly, soil. Space plants about 3 feet apart and avoid overwatering, especially in winter. When plants get straggly, shear them back to the ground in spring. New plants can be started from clumps divided in spring, from seeds sown in fall to blossom the following summer or from stem cuttings made in late fall for flowers the next spring. Divide clumps after two or three years of flowering.

CORAL-BELLS See *Heuchera*

COREOPSIS
C. auriculata (eared coreopsis), *C. grandiflora* (big-flowered coreopsis), *C. verticillata* (thread-leaved coreopsis)

The yellow flowers of coreopsis are borne on slender

GROUND MORNING-GLORY
Convolvulus mauritanicus

BIG-FLOWERED COREOPSIS
Coreopsis grandiflora 'Sunburst'

For climate zones and months of flowering, see page 151.

CROWN VETCH
Coronilla varia

PAMPAS GRASS
Cortaderia selloana

wiry stems and bloom abundantly throughout the summer. The eared coreopsis grows 1 to 3 feet tall and has 2-inch flowers; a 1½- to 2-foot variety, Golden Star, has flowers with chestnut-brown centers, and another variety, the dwarf eared coreopsis, *C. auriculata nana,* grows only 5 to 6 inches tall and bears orange-yellow blossoms. The big-flowered coreopsis, the most popular species, grows 2 to 3 feet tall and has 2- to 3-inch blossoms; two fine varieties are Sunburst, with several rows of petals, and Mayfield Giant, with blossoms 3 inches or more across. The thread-leaved coreopsis, a spreading plant with 2-inch starlike flowers, grows 1 to 2 feet tall. Coreopsis can remain untended in fields or on sunny banks, where the plants will thrive and multiply indefinitely. They provide superb cut flowers.

HOW TO GROW. Coreopsis grows in Zones 4-10 in full sun. Infertile soil is satisfactory, but it must be well drained, especially during the winter dormant period. Space plants about 12 inches apart. New plants may be started easily from seeds or clump divisions in spring. Seeds often produce flowering plants late in the summer. Divide clumps after two or three years of flowering.

CORONILLA
C. varia (crown vetch)

Crown vetch, which grows 1 to 2 feet tall, bears small clusters of ½-inch pink-and-white flowers from early summer to late fall; the variety Penngift produces mostly pink flowers. Crown vetch is a tough, aggressively spreading plant that will crowd out its neighbors in a show garden but is well suited to a sunny bank, where it will take care of itself indefinitely. Its deep tenacious roots and thick fernlike leaves provide excellent erosion control where it is used as a ground cover.

HOW TO GROW. Crown vetch grows in Zones 3-10 in almost any soil if the location is sunny. Space plants about 3 feet apart. To propagate named varieties, dig up and divide the clumps in spring or fall. New plants can also be grown from seeds sown in spring to flower the following year; for vigorous growth, dust the seeds with nitrifying bacteria (available from seedsmen) before planting.

CORTADERIA
C. selloana, also called *C. argentea, Gynerium argenteum* (pampas grass)

Pampas grass, native to Argentina, is widely grown in warm-climate gardens both for its huge mounds of tough sawtooth-edged leaves and for its spectacular 1- to 3-foot flower plumes, which appear in late summer and fall. Plants usually grow 8 to 10 feet tall, but may become twice that height. Pampas grass therefore serves well in the rear of a shrub border or alone as a fast-growing windbreak. Its feathery plumes, the best of which are borne on female plants, range from silvery white to pink and may be dried for winter bouquets if picked before they become saturated with autumn rains.

HOW TO GROW. Pampas grass flourishes in Zones 8-10 in any soil, wet or dry, provided the location is sunny. To be sure of the best flowers, ask the nurseryman for female plants. Set them at least 6 feet apart. Pampas grass seldom needs division but can be divided for propagation.

CORYDALIS
C. lutea (yellow corydalis)

Nurserymen will sometimes list the yellow corydalis as "yellow bleeding heart" because it resembles its distant relative, the bleeding heart of the *Dicentra* genus. Yellow corydalis grows 12 to 15 inches tall and its gray-green fernlike foliage is attractive from spring until fall. The ¾-inch flowers are borne above the leaves from spring until mid-summer and sometimes later. The species often grows wild in cracks in old walls where drainage is excellent.

HOW TO GROW. Yellow corydalis grows in Zones 5-10 except in Florida and along the Gulf Coast; it does best in light shade, but will tolerate both full sun and deep shade. Excellent drainage is vital and the soil should be liberally supplemented with peat moss or leaf mold. Set plants 8 to 10 inches apart. New plants can be started by dividing and resetting clumps in early spring after two or three years of flowering or from stem cuttings taken in summer for flowers the following year. To prevent overcrowding, divide clumps after two or three years of flowering.

CRANE'S-BILL See *Geranium*
CROWN VETCH See *Coronilla*
CUPFLOWER See *Nierembergia*
CUPIDONE, BLUE See *Catananche*
CUPID'S-DART See *Catananche*

D

DAISY, BARBERTON See *Gerbera*
DAISY, BLUE See *Felicia*
DAISY, ENGLISH See *Bellis*
DAISY, GLORIOSA See *Rudbeckia*
DAISY, MICHAELMAS See *Aster*
DAISY, PAINTED See *Chrysanthemum*
DAISY, PARIS See *Chrysanthemum*
DAISY, SHASTA See *Chrysanthemum*
DAISY, TRANSVAAL See *Gerbera*
DAISY, TRUE See *Bellis*
DAY LILY See *Hemerocallis*

DELPHINIUM

D. cheilanthum formosum (garland delphinium); *D.* 'Connecticut Yankee' (Connecticut Yankee delphinium); *D. elatum* (candle delphinium, bee delphinium); *D. grandiflorum,* also called *D. chinense* (Chinese delphinium, Siberian delphinium); *D. zalil* (Zalil delphinium). (All also called larkspur)

The spirelike flowers of delphiniums—usually blue, lavender, purple or white, but sometimes pink, red or yellow—make a spectacular sight in the garden and provide some of the best cut flowers. The plants vary in height from 1 to 6 feet; the tall-growing types are breathtaking but fragile; the medium-sized strains are more popular not only because they seldom require staking but also because their stalks are a better length for flower arrangements. Delphiniums bloom abundantly in late spring and summer and again in fall if the flowers are removed before the seed pods develop. To produce this second crop, cut the stems just below the flowers; when the new growth at the base of the plants is about 6 inches tall, remove the original stems to the ground *(drawings, page 54).* The new stalks will bear flowers smaller than the first crop but no less colorful in about two and a half months—usually in early fall.

The garland delphinium grows 2 to 4 feet tall and bears spikes of 1½- to 2-inch flowers. Excellent strains are Belladonna, pale blue; Bellamosum, dark blue; Casa Blanca, white; Cliveden Beauty, light blue; and Sapphire, bright blue. The hybrid Connecticut Yankee is an exceptionally free-flowering plant about 2½ feet tall that bears spikes of 2½-inch blossoms in shades of blue, purple or lavender as well as white. The candle delphinium is a giant hybrid whose stalks may become 5 to 6 feet or more in height. The massive spikes are composed of 2- to 3-inch flowers with a single or double ring of petals; many of the flowers have contrasting centers, called "bees." Most candle del-

YELLOW CORYDALIS
Corydalis lutea

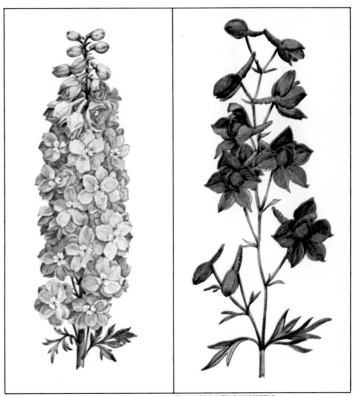

CANDLE DELPHINIUM
Delphinium elatum

CHINESE DELPHINIUM
Delphinium grandiflorum

For climate zones and months of flowering, see page 151.

ALLWOOD'S PINK
Dianthus allwoodii

SWEET WILLIAM
Dianthus barbatus

BORDER CARNATION
Dianthus caryophyllus

phinium blossoms are blue, purple or white, but there are also shades of pink, yellow and red; some excellent strains are Pacific Hybrids, Blackmore and Langdon Hybrids and Wrexham Hybrids.

The Chinese or Siberian delphinium is ideal for small gardens or for the front of borders because the plants become only 12 to 18 inches tall. This species has 1-inch flowers in shades of blue and white. Recommended strains are Azure Fairy, sky blue; Blue Butterfly, deep blue; and Cambridge Blue, medium blue. The Zalil delphinium is a lemon-yellow species from Persia, where its 1½-inch flowers are used to make a dye for silk. It grows only 12 to 18 inches tall, but its stems are weak and need staking.

HOW TO GROW. Delphiniums grow as perennials in Zones 3-7 and in a strip of Zone 9 on the West Coast where the nights are cool. They do best in full sun and a well-drained soil that has been enriched with compost, well-rotted cow manure or leaf mold. In Zones 8-10, where the summers are long and hot, delphiniums should be treated as hardy annuals; sow their seeds early in fall to flower the following year. In Zones 3-7 place plants 12 to 24 inches apart, depending on size, and set the crown, or top of the root structure, 1 to 2 inches beneath the surface of the soil. New plants can be grown from seeds sown in early summer to bloom the following year. Delphiniums lose their vigor after two or three years and should be replaced by young seedlings.

DIANTHUS

D. allwoodii (Allwood's pink), *D. barbatus* (sweet William), *D. caryophyllus* (border carnation), *D. plumarius* (border pink, cottage pink, grass pink, Scotch pink)

Pinks and carnations are perennials noted for their clove-like fragrance, whereas sweet Williams are biennials and lack fragrance. All are prized for their long blooming seasons and long-lasting cut flowers. Their foliage, which grows in dense grasslike tufts, is evergreen. Although *Dianthus* species vary from 2 inches to 3 feet in height, the best garden varieties are mostly 10 to 20 inches tall.

Allwood's pinks, which grow 12 to 18 inches high, are superb hybrids that combine the hardiness and free flowering of the border pink with the large blossoms of the carnation. The flowers, 1½ to 2 inches across, are red, pink, white or a combination of these colors; they provide a lavish display in spring and continue to bear some blooms into early fall. Sweet William is covered in mid- to late spring with massive flat-topped flower heads 3 to 5 inches across that are densely packed with tiny flowers in red, pink, white or combinations of those colors. The standard sweet William grows about 1½ to 2 feet tall; there are varieties that do not exceed 6 inches, but their blossoms are easily spattered by mud and their stems are too short for cutting. Some strains of sweet William will blossom the first year from seeds sown early in the spring, but they do not have the fine flowers of other types. The border carnation, 1½ to 2 feet tall, belongs to the same species as the greenhouse carnation, but is better suited to cold winters outdoors. Its 2-inch double flowers come in white, yellow, orange, pink, red and lavender, and open from early summer to fall. Grenadin and Teicher Hybrids are excellent strains. The border pink grows 12 to 15 inches tall and bears 1½-inch single, double or fringed blossoms in pink, rose, purple and white in mid- to late spring; Highland Hybrids is a recommended strain.

HOW TO GROW. Border carnations grow as perennials in Zones 6 and 7; Allwood's pinks and border pinks grow as perennials in Zones 4-7. All should be treated as biennials in Zones 8-10, where summers are hot. Sweet Williams grow as biennials in Zones 4-10. All need full sun and do best in a well-drained, light sandy soil. Plant *Dianthus* species 12 to 18 inches apart. The crown, or top of the root structure, must be level with the surface of the soil; never bury any part of the stems. The plants should not be mulched; their tender root tops and trailing stems require good air circulation at all times and must be kept as free from moisture as possible. New plants can be started from seeds sown in spring or early summer to flower the following year or from stem cuttings made in early summer; such plants are best moved to the garden in the fall. Pinks and carnations usually lose their vigor after their second flowering and should be replaced. Sweet Williams must be grown from seeds each year for new plants the following year; pull up and discard plants after they flower.

DICENTRA, also called DIELYTRA

D. eximia (fringed or plumed bleeding heart), *D. formosa* (western bleeding heart), *D. hybrids* (hybrid bleeding hearts), *D. spectabilis* (common bleeding heart)

No perennial is more familiar than the common bleeding heart, which grows 2½ to 3 feet tall and blossoms in mid- to late spring. Its arching stems, dripping with 1-inch heart-shaped deep pink flowers, are lined with graceful, deeply divided blue-green leaves. But by midsummer this Chinese species shrivels away and disappears until the following spring. Other, less well-known, species and hybrids outshine it, blooming longer and offering a variety of colors. All these plants have fernlike foliage and grow only about 12 to 15 inches high. One is the fringed or plumed bleeding heart, native to eastern North America. From midspring to late fall it bears ½-inch rose-pink flowers. The western bleeding heart, native to shady woodlands of the Pacific Coast, bears pale rosy lavender blooms in spring; an excellent white-flowered variety called Sweetheart blossoms from spring to fall. Hybrids bred by crossing fringed and western bleeding hearts are even more spectacular and produce a great abundance of ¾-inch flowers from late spring to midsummer and again in the fall, with a scattering of flowers in between. Recommended varieties include Adrian Bloom, crimson; Bountiful, deep pink; Debutante, pale pink; and Silversmith, creamy white.

HOW TO GROW. Bleeding hearts grow in Zones 4-10 except in Florida and along the Gulf Coast. They last for years in Zones 4-7, but are short lived in Zones 8-10 because of the long hot summers there. All grow best in light shade, but the common and hybrid bleeding hearts will also tolerate full sun if the soil is moist. Bleeding hearts do best in well-drained soil generously supplemented with peat moss or leaf mold. Plant the smaller kinds 15 to 18 inches apart, the larger ones about 2½ feet apart. New plants of common, fringed and western bleeding hearts can be grown from seeds sown in fall to flower the following year. Common bleeding hearts can also be propagated in spring from root cuttings and stem cuttings. Propagate the named varieties and hybrids by dividing clumps. To prevent overcrowding, divide the clumps in spring after three or four years of flowering; handle the roots carefully because they are extremely brittle.

DICTAMNUS

D. albus, also called *D. fraxinella*
(gas plant, fraxinella, dittany, burning bush)

The gas plant is named for the inflammable fumes released if its roots are cut; the gas given off when a plant is dug up may pop if ignited. The leaves also exude an inflammable oil. But fireworks are not the main attraction of the gas plant. Its shiny leathery dark green leaves, which

FRINGED BLEEDING HEART
Dicentra eximia

COMMON BLEEDING HEART
Dicentra spectabilis

For climate zones and months of flowering, see page 151.

GAS PLANT
Dictamnus albus purpureus

FOXGLOVE
Digitalis purpurea 'Shirley Hybrids'

smell like lemon peel when rubbed, form a handsome 2-foot mound. In early summer, spikes of 1½- to 2-inch pinkish purple or snow-white flowers rise 10 to 12 inches above the foliage. Mature gas plants—four to five years old —bloom most lavishly and will flourish indefinitely. The variety *D. albus giganteus,* also called *D. albus caucasicus,* has larger flowers and *D. albus purpureus,* also called *D. albus ruber,* has deep pinkish purple flowers. The seed pods are attractive in dried arrangements.

HOW TO GROW. Gas plants grow in Zones 3-8 in full sun or light shade in a well-drained soil enriched with compost. Set plants 3 to 4 feet apart. New plants can be started from seeds sown in spring to blossom in about three or four years. Gas plants grow best if left undisturbed.

DIELYTRA See *Dicentra*

DIGITALIS
D. ferruginea, also called *D. aurea* (rusty foxglove);
D. grandiflora, also called *D. ambigua* (yellow foxglove);
D. mertonensis (Merton foxglove);
D. purpurea (common foxglove)

The genus name *Digitalis* is familiar because the leaves of common foxglove provide the heart stimulant called by that name. The plant's spirelike stalks are lined with white, yellow, pink, rose, purple or rusty red flowers, each 1- to 3-inch speckle-throated flower shaped like the finger of a glove. Foxgloves bloom mainly in early summer but if the first stalks are cut off below the seed pods before the seeds mature, more flowers often appear in midsummer. Foxgloves are wild flowers in Europe, North Africa and the Near East and have become naturalized in this country, growing wild along partly shaded roadsides in western Washington, Oregon and Northern California. Most are biennials, but some species and hybrids are perennials.

The rusty foxglove is usually grown as a biennial or a short-lived perennial; 4 to 6 feet tall, it has rusty red flowers. The yellow foxglove, also a biennial or short-lived perennial, grows 2 to 3 feet tall and has honey-colored flowers blotched with brown. The Merton foxglove, a perennial that grows about 3 feet tall, has deep red flowers. The common foxglove, a biennial, grows 4 to 5 feet tall and has rosy purple or white flowers. It has been bred, however, to provide varieties of many distinctive characteristics. The Shirley Hybrids include many pastel shades, the Gloxiniaflora strain produces an abundance of wide-flaring flowers that all open simultaneously, and a 3-foot strain called Foxy comes into blossom so quickly—about five months after seeds are sown in the spring—that it can be grown as an annual. But the most striking strain is Excelsior Hybrids; its flowers are borne on all sides of the spike, rather than on one side as on other foxgloves, and face outward rather than downward.

HOW TO GROW. Foxgloves thrive in Zones 4-10 except in Florida and along the Gulf Coast in full sun or light shade, but in hot areas should be kept in partial to full shade. They do best in moist but well-drained soil. Plant foxgloves 15 to 18 inches apart. To prevent winter damage from excessive moisture around the thick crown of leaves where soil is not well drained, dig up the plants in the fall with dirt clinging to their roots, set them snugly together in a cold frame and, after the ground freezes, mulch with a 4-inch layer of salt hay or straw. Perennial foxgloves can be started by dividing and resetting clumps in early spring or fall, but are more commonly grown from seeds. Sow the seeds in mid- to late spring to get flowers the following summer. To prevent overcrowding, divide clumps after three or four years of flowering.

DITTANY See *Dictamnus*
DOLLAR PLANT See *Lunaria*

DORONICUM

D. caucasicum (Caucasian leopard's-bane); *D. pardalianch-es* (goldbunch leopard's-bane); *D. plantagineum excelsum,* also called *D.* 'Harpur Crewe' (showy leopard's-bane)

Most spring flowers are short, but leopard's-bane shoots up 1½ to 5 feet, flaunting bright yellow daisylike flowers 2 to 4 inches across. Usually borne singly on stalks, the flowers are excellent for cutting. Their height is accentuated by ground-hugging leaves that deteriorate by midsummer and may disappear entirely. To avoid an unkempt or bare appearance, set leopard's-bane beside plants whose leaves will provide a mask during summer and fall. The Caucasian leopard's-bane grows about 1½ feet tall; most varieties have flowers about 2 inches across. Recommended are Miss Mason (also sold as Madam Mason); Spring Beauty, a many-petaled type; and *D. caucasicum magnificum,* which bears blossoms slightly larger than usual. Goldbunch leopard's-bane bears its flowers in clusters on 2- to 3-foot stems. The showy leopard's-bane grows 3 to 5 feet tall and has flowers 3 to 4 inches across.

HOW TO GROW. Leopard's-banes grow in Zones 4-9 except in Florida and along the Gulf Coast. They do best in moist well-drained soil and light shade but will tolerate full sun in areas where summers are cool. Mulch plants with chunky peat moss or compost to conserve moisture around the roots, which are generally shallow, as well as to control weeds. Set plants about a foot apart. New plants can be grown from seeds sown in spring to flower the following year. Propagate named varieties by dividing clumps. Divide clumps when they become overcrowded—usually after two or three years of flowering.

DRACOCEPHALUM See *Physostegia*
DRAGONHEAD, FALSE See *Physostegia*
DROPWORT See *Filipendula*
DUSTY MILLER See *Centaurea*

E

ECHINACEA

E. purpurea, also called *Rudbeckia purpurea* (purple coneflower)

The garden varieties of the wild coneflower are drought-resistant 3-foot perennials that bear long-lasting bright-colored 3- to 4-inch blossoms shaped like sunflowers during late summer and early fall. A variety called The King has striking coral flowers with maroon centers; Bright Star has rosy red flowers with maroon centers; Robert Bloom has purple flowers with orange centers; and White Lustre, also called White King, has white blossoms with bronze centers. All have bold rough leaves 2 to 8 inches in length.

HOW TO GROW. Coneflowers grow in Zones 3-10 and do best in full sun but tolerate light shade. They require soil that is never soggy, especially during winter. Plant coneflowers 18 to 24 inches apart. New plants can be started from root cuttings or clump divisions in spring or fall to flower the following summer. To prevent overcrowding, divide clumps after three years of flowering.

ECHINOPS

E. 'Taplow Blue' (Taplow Blue globe thistle)

This eye-catching 3- to 4-foot plant bears striking 2- to 3-inch flower heads high above its distinctive foliage from midsummer to early fall. The deeply lobed leaves, up to a foot long, are shiny dark green above and woolly white beneath, and are tipped with spines. Globe thistles make

CAUCASIAN LEOPARD'S-BANE
Doronicum caucasicum
'Miss Mason'

PURPLE CONEFLOWER
Echinacea purpurea 'The King'

GLOBE THISTLE
Echinops 'Taplow Blue'

For climate zones and months of flowering, see page 151.

LONG-SPURRED EPIMEDIUM
Epimedium grandiflorum

FLEABANE
Erigeron hybrid

OLIVER SEA HOLLY
Eryngium oliverianum

excellent cut flowers, and hold their color when dried for winter arrangements if picked just as the flowers open.

HOW TO GROW. Globe thistles grow in Zones 3-10 in full sun; they must have well-drained soil and will tolerate very dry soil. Plant globe thistles 18 to 24 inches apart. New plants may be started from clump divisions or root cuttings taken in early spring to flower the same season. To prevent overcrowding, divide the clumps after three or four years of flowering.

EPIMEDIUM
E. grandiflorum, also called *E. macranthum* (long-spurred epimedium); *E. pinnatum*, also called *E. colchicum* (Persian epimedium); *E. rubrum*, also called *E. alpinum rubrum* (red epimedium); *E. versicolor sulphureum*, also called *E. sulphureum* (yellow epimedium); *E. youngianum*, also called *E. niveum* (snowy epimedium). (All also called bishop's-hat)

Most gardeners value epimediums for their delicate-looking but leathery-textured leaves, made up of 2- to 3-inch heart-shaped leaflets and borne on wiry stems about 9 to 12 inches tall. In early spring the foliage is light green interlaced with pink veins; by midsummer it is a glossy deep green; in fall it turns reddish bronze. The masses of ½-inch blossoms, often multicolored, appear above the foliage in late spring to early summer and are excellent for cutting. The flowers of long-spurred epimedium may be deep rose, yellow, violet or white; Persian epimedium, bright yellow with purplish brown markings; red epimedium, a mixture of red and yellow; yellow epimedium, pale yellow; and snowy epimedium, white.

HOW TO GROW. Epimediums grow in Zones 3-8 and do best in light shade and moist soil supplemented with compost, peat moss or leaf mold. Set plants 8 to 10 inches apart. Clumps may be divided for new plants in fall or early spring, or can remain undisturbed indefinitely.

ERIGERON
E. hybrids (fleabane)

These bushy 1½- to 2½-foot plants produce 2-inch yellow-centered blossoms, usually in shades of pink to purple, in summer. Typical varieties are Foerster's Liebling and Pink Jewel, both bright pink; and Wuppertal, rich violet. Fleabanes are excellent as cut flowers.,

HOW TO GROW. Fleabanes grow in Zones 4-10 and do best in full sun in relatively infertile but well-drained sandy soil. Set plants about a foot apart. Plants are best propagated by dividing clumps in spring. To prevent overcrowding, divide clumps after two or three years of flowering.

ERYNGIUM
E. amethystinum (amethyst sea holly),
E. oliverianum (Oliver sea holly)

The sea holly, a European wild flower that grows on beach dunes, has spiny leaves that look like holly foliage. Amethyst sea holly is a bushy plant 1½ to 2 feet tall, its many-branched stems tipped from midsummer to early fall with ½-inch blue flowers that have spiny ruffs. Even the upper parts of the stems are bluish. The hybrid Oliver sea holly grows 3 to 4 feet tall. Sea holly blossoms make excellent cut flowers and, if picked when fully open, will hold their color when dried.

HOW TO GROW. Sea holly grows in Zones 4-10 and does best in full sun and dry sandy soil. Set plants 12 to 18 inches apart. New plants can be started from seeds sown in spring or root cuttings taken in fall or early spring for flowers the following year. The clumps spread slowly and can remain undisturbed indefinitely.

EUPATORIUM

E. coelestinum, also called *Conoclinium coelestinum*
(mistflower, hardy ageratum)

Mistflowers grow wild in the eastern part of the United States and are easily cultivated in gardens in most parts of the country. In late summer they bear 3- to 4-inch flat-topped clusters of blue blossoms on 1½- to 3-foot stems. The heart-shaped leaves are hairy and have sawtoothed edges. Mistflowers are excellent for cutting.

HOW TO GROW. Mistflowers grow in Zones 3-10 in any well-drained garden soil; they do best in full sun, but will tolerate light shade. Plant them 1½ to 2 feet apart. Mistflower roots are shallow; mulch the plants with chunky peat moss or compost to conserve moisture around the roots as well as to control weeds. New plants can be started from clump divisions in spring, from seeds sown in spring or from stem cuttings taken in spring. All will flower the following year. Clumps spread rapidly and should be dug up and divided after a year or two of flowering.

EUPHORBIA

E. corollata (flowering spurge); *E. cyparissias* (cypress spurge); *E. epithymoides,* also called *E. polychroma*
(cushion spurge)

Like their relatives the poinsettias, spurges have petallike leaves called bracts that appear to be blossoms; the true flowers are set in the centers of the bracts. Flowering spurge grows 1½ to 3 feet tall; its delicate stems and minute white bracts open from early to midsummer. Its glossy leaves turn dark red in the fall. The stems of cypress spurge are set with 1- to 2-inch grayish green needlelike leaves; dense heads of ½-inch yellow bracts appear on the tops of the 1-foot stems in late spring and early summer. Cushion spurge grows a foot tall and spreads to 2 feet wide. In late spring and early summer, the tops of the plants are covered with clusters of bright yellow 1-inch bracts; their leaves also turn red in the fall.

HOW TO GROW. Cypress and cushion spurges grow in Zones 3-9; flowering spurge can also survive the summers in Zone 10. All do best in full sun and well-drained soil. Plant spurges 18 to 24 inches apart. New plants of flowering and cushion spurges are best grown from seeds sown in spring for flowers the following year. Cypress spurge can be propagated by clump division in the spring; otherwise, plants can remain undisturbed indefinitely.

F

FELICIA

F. amelloides, also called *F. capensis, Agathaea coelestis, Aster rotundifolius* (blue daisy, blue marguerite)

A perennial in warm regions, the blue daisy forms a thick 6-inch mound of 1-inch leaves, from which rise 1- to 2-foot stalks bearing 1½-inch blossoms; the variety Santa Anita has flowers as large as 3 inches across. Plants will bloom all year long if flowers are removed as they fade.

HOW TO GROW. Blue daisies grow as perennials in Zones 9 and 10 in full sun and well-drained soil. In Zones 4-8 blue daisies grow as annuals when started from seeds sown indoors in early spring for summer bloom. Set plants 6 to 12 inches apart. If plants become straggly, cut them back to a height of 3 to 6 inches to force healthy new growth. New plants can be started from clump divisions in spring or from seeds sown in early spring to flower continuously from midsummer on, or from stem cuttings taken at any time to flower within a few months. To prevent overcrowding, divide plants after two or three years of flowering.

FEVERFEW See *Chrysanthemum*

For climate zones and months of flowering, see page 151.

MISTFLOWER
Eupatorium coelestinum

CUSHION SPURGE
Euphorbia epithymoides

BLUE DAISY
Felicia amelloides

DROPWORT
Filipendula hexapetala flore pleno

BLANKETFLOWER
Gaillardia aristata

GAZANIA
Gazania longiscapa

FILIPENDULA

F. camtschatica (Kamchatka meadowsweet), *F. hexapetala* (dropwort, meadowsweet), *F. rubra* (prairie meadowsweet, queen of the prairie), *F. ulmaria* (European meadowsweet, queen of the meadow)

Meadowsweets are topped by tiny flowers in clusters up to a foot across. The dropwort and its heavily petaled double form, *F. hexapetala flore pleno,* grow 15 to 18 inches tall and have long fernlike leaves from which slender flower stalks arise in late spring. The other, taller species have large coarse palm-shaped or deeply lobed leaves. The 4- to 10-foot Kamchatka meadowsweet has white flowers in early summer; the 6-foot prairie meadowsweet, fragrant pale pink flowers in late spring and early summer; and the 4-foot European meadowsweet, fragrant white flowers in late spring and early summer.

HOW TO GROW. Meadowsweets grow in Zones 4-8 in full sun or light shade. All do best in very wet soil, but dropworts also tolerate dry soil. Plant dropworts about 12 inches apart, other species 2 to 3 feet apart. Propagate named varieties by dividing clumps in spring; start other types from seeds sown in fall for flowers in two years. All types can remain undisturbed indefinitely.

FLAX See *Linum*
FLAX, NEW ZEALAND See *Phormium*
FLEABANE See *Erigeron*
FLEECEFLOWER, REYNOUTRIA See *Polygonum*
FORGET-ME-NOT See *Myosotis*
FOUR-O'CLOCK See *Mirabilis*
FOXGLOVE See *Digitalis*
FRAXINELLA See *Dictamnus*
FUNKIA See *Hosta*

G

GAILLARDIA

G. aristata, also called *G. grandiflora*
(blanketflower, gaillardia)

Blanketflowers bear bright 2½- to 4-inch blossoms continuously from early summer until frost. The flowers, which are excellent for cutting, are held on slender stems above mounds of hairy foliage. Among the many fine varieties are Sun Dance and Baby Cole, both about 8 inches tall with red yellow-tipped petals; Burgundy, 2 feet tall with red flowers; and Sun God, 2 feet tall with yellow flowers.

HOW TO GROW. Blanketflowers can be grown throughout Zones 3-10 and do best in full sun and well-drained garden soil. In heavy clay soil the leaves grow at the expense of the flowers, and the plants are also likely to die in winter. Plant blanketflowers 10 to 12 inches apart. New plants can be started from seeds sown early in spring to blossom the same year; propagate named varieties from clumps divided and reset in spring or from root cuttings taken in spring to bloom the same year. The clumps should be dug up and divided in spring when they become overcrowded, usually after two or three years of flowering.

GAS PLANT See *Dictamnus*
GAY-FEATHER See *Liatris*

GAZANIA

G. longiscapa (gazania, treasure flower); *G. uniflora*, also called *G. leucolaena* (trailing gazania)

In the mild climates of Zones 8-10, particularly in the Southwest and Southern California, gazanias often blossom all year, although the greatest display appears from early spring through early summer. Treasure flowers grow 6 to 12 inches tall and have daisylike blossoms up to 4 inches across; the colors, ranging from creamy white through yellow to blazing orange, and from lavender and pink to deep bronzy red, usually appear in sharply contrasting concentric rings. Trailing gazanias creep along the ground, forming a mat of foliage 4 to 8 inches tall. Their slender 2- to 6-inch leaves are silvery gray, and their 2½-inch flowers are white, yellow, orange or bronzy red.

HOW TO GROW. Gazanias grow as perennials in Zones 8-10 and as annuals in Zones 3-7 in full sun and well-drained soil. Set plants about a foot apart. New plants can be started from clump divisions or from seeds sown in early spring to flower the same year. To prevent overcrowding, divide clumps after three or four years of flowering.

GENTIAN See *Gentiana*

GENTIANA
G. asclepiadea (willow gentian), *G. septemfida.*
(Both called gentian)

Blue is the usual color of gentian flowers, but some varieties have white or yellow blossoms. The willow gentian grows 2 to 3 feet tall and has slender stems lined with prominently veined 2- to 3-inch leaves. During mid- to late summer, the upper 6 to 8 inches of each stem are studded with 1½-inch flowers. *G. septemfida,* which blossoms at the same time as willow gentian, grows only 8 to 12 inches tall. It has 1-inch white-throated deep blue flowers.

HOW TO GROW. Gentians grow in Zones 4-8 and do best in light shade. They need a moist acid soil (pH of 5.0 to 6.5) liberally supplemented with peat moss or leaf mold. Plant gentians 12 to 18 inches apart. New plants are best started from seeds sown in fall for flowers the following year. The clumps seldom require division.

GERANIUM
G. endressii (Pyrenean crane's-bill), *G. grandiflorum* (lilac crane's-bill), *G. ibericum* (Iberian crane's-bill), *G. sanguineum* (blood-red crane's-bill)

Crane's-bills are related to the common geranium *(Pelargonium)* but belong to a different genus. They bear 1- to 2-inch flowers almost all summer and form attractive mounds of dark usually deeply lobed foliage. Two fine 18-inch varieties of Pyrenean crane's-bill are Johnson's Blue, light blue, and Wargrave Pink, deep pink; both bloom from early summer to fall. Lilac crane's-bill, 15 to 18 inches tall, produces red-veined blue flowers from late spring until frost. Iberian crane's-bill, 12 to 18 inches tall, has purple flowers in early to midsummer. Most types of blood-red crane's-bill have purplish red flowers and grow about 12 inches tall, but spread to about twice that in diameter; a pink-flowered variety, *G. sanguineum prostratum (G. lancastriense),* grows 4 to 6 inches tall with a spread of 18 inches. All the blood-red crane's-bills blossom from early summer to early fall, when their leaves turn bright red.

HOW TO GROW. Pyrenean and Iberian crane's-bills grow in Zones 4-8, the lilac and blood-red crane's-bills grow in Zones 4-10. All do best in full sun and grow in almost any garden soil. Plant crane's-bills about a foot apart. New plants of named varieties are best started from stem cuttings taken in summer; the species types not given variety names can be grown from seeds sown in spring or fall. All will flower the following year. Clumps do best undisturbed.

GERBERA (GERBERIA)
G. jamesonii (gerbera daisy, Barberton daisy, Transvaal daisy)

In the gardens of mild-climate areas gerbera daisies offer a continuous display of blossoms from spring to late

GENTIAN
Gentiana septemfida

LILAC CRANE'S-BILL
Geranium grandiflorum

BARBERTON DAISY
Gerbera jamesonii

For climate zones and months of flowering, see page 151.

fall. Their long-lasting 4- to 5-inch blossoms are borne on leafless 12- to 18-inch stems, and their colors range from white through cream, yellow, orange, pink, salmon and rose to red. The flowers may be singles, with one ring of petals, or heavily petaled doubles. The 8- to 12-inch leaves are shallowly lobed, dark green above and woolly white beneath, and rise directly from the ground.

HOW TO GROW. Gerbera daisies can be grown in Zones 8-10. They need full sun, except in very hot areas, and a moist well-drained soil liberally supplemented with peat moss or compost. Plant gerbera daisies 12 to 15 inches apart, setting the crown, or top of the root structure, level with the surface of the soil. Feed the plants every other month from early spring to late fall by scattering a handful of 5-10-10 fertilizer around each plant and scratching it into the soil. Seeds sown in midwinter will flower the following summer. Sow them barely beneath the surface of the soil; keep moist until the seedlings emerge. New plants may be started from divisions of clumps in spring. Clumps should be divided when they become overcrowded, usually after three or four years of flowering.

GERBERIA See *Gerbera*

GEUM
G. borisii (Boris avens), *G. chiloense* (Chilean avens). (Both called geum)

The handsome 2- to 3-inch flowers of geums, which are available as semidoubles (more than one row of petals) and doubles (heavily overlapping petals), resemble roses, and the genus is in fact a member of the rose family. Geums bloom from midspring to midsummer with occasional flowers until frost if faded blossoms are removed before they produce seeds. Colors include many shades of yellow, orange and red. Most flower stalks grow 1½ to 2 feet tall from clumps of dark green finely divided foliage. Boris avens bears bright orange flowers. There are many excellent varieties of Chilean avens, including Princess Juliana, semidouble, bronzy orange; Fire Opal, semidouble, scarlet; Lady Stratheden, semidouble, golden yellow; and Mrs. Bradshaw, double, scarlet.

HOW TO GROW. Geums grow well in Zones 5-10 in rich moist soil, but need good drainage, especially in winter. They do best in full sun but tolerate light shade. Plant geums 10 to 12 inches apart. New plants are best started from clump divisions in spring. To prevent overcrowding, divide clumps after two or three years of flowering.

GLOBEFLOWER See *Trollius*
GOATSBEARD See *Aruncus*
GOLDENROD See *Solidago*

GYPSOPHILA
G. bodgeri (Bodger babies'-breath), *G. paniculata* (babies'-breath), *G. repens* (creeping babies'-breath). (All also called chalk plant)

The lacy stems and myriad blossoms of babies'-breath add airy grace to a summertime border or bouquet. The popular forms of the hybrid *G. bodgeri* grow 15 to 18 inches tall and blossom mostly in mid- to late spring but bear scattered flowers later in the summer; two excellent varieties with pink flowers are Rosy Veil (Rosenschieler) and Pink Star. *G. paniculata* provides the most widely grown types of babies'-breath. The plants grow in mounds 3 to 4 feet tall and an equal distance across. Bristol Fairy and Perfecta, both white, and Flamingo, pink, bear masses of tiny ¼-inch flowers mostly in early summer, but produce occasional flowers until frost, provided the first stalks

CHILEAN AVENS
Geum chiloense 'Fire Opal'

BABIES'-BREATH
Gypsophila paniculata 'Bristol Fairy'

are removed when they fade. If the flowers are picked when fully open and dried upside down in a shaded, airy place, they make excellent winter bouquets. The creeping babies'-breath most often grown is G. *repens rosea*, a 6-inch type that bears pink flowers in mid- to late spring; its trailing stems may spread to a diameter of 1½ to 2 feet.

HOW TO GROW. Babies'-breath flourishes in Zones 4-8 and in Zone 9 on the West Coast. It does best in full sun and well-drained, neutral or even slightly alkaline soil (pH 6.5 to 7.5). The common name chalk plant reflects its need for lime, which must be added if the soil is acid. Plant babies'-breath 18 to 24 inches apart in early spring. In Zones 4 and 5 protect babies'-breath over winter with a mulch such as salt hay or straw. Most of the plants grown are varieties that are best propagated professionally by grafting. Grafted plants have a gnarled joint where the stem and root meet and this joint should be set about 1 inch below the soil level so that the graft can develop its own root system. Babies'-breath does not spread underground and clumps can remain undisturbed indefinitely.

H

HAREBELL, CARPATHIAN See *Campanula*
HELEN FLOWER See *Helenium*

HELENIUM

H. autumnale (sneezeweed, Helen flower)

Despite its common name, this delightful plant does not provoke sneezing. Modern varieties of the North American wild flower bloom in late summer and early fall, decorating the garden with great clusters of 2-inch daisy-like flowers in shades that range from yellow to mahogany. Recommended varieties are Bruno, 3 to 3½ feet tall, deep reddish brown; Butterpat, 3 to 3½ feet tall, golden yellow; Chippersfield Orange, 3½ to 4 feet tall, gold; Copper Spray, 3 to 3½ feet tall, orange; and Pumilum Magnificum, about 2 feet tall, soft yellow. The flowers of all varieties are excellent for cutting.

HOW TO GROW. Sneezeweeds grow throughout Zones 3-10 in almost any soil in full sun, but they do best if the site is moist. Set plants 12 to 18 inches apart. Pinch out the tips of the stalks in early summer to force additional branches and flowers. New plants can be started by dividing clumps. To prevent overcrowding, clumps should be divided every other year.

HELIANTHUS

H. decapetalus flore pleno, also called *H. multiflorus* (double thin-leaved sunflower)

In its single-flowered form—with one ring of petals —this sunflower grows wild along the East Coast from Quebec to Georgia, and its double-flowered garden varieties —those that have many overlapping petals—can be grown almost anywhere. In mid- to late summer they produce golden 4-inch dahlialike blossoms. Because these plants are about 4 feet tall and have coarse leaves, they should be set at the back of a border.

HOW TO GROW. Double sunflowers can be grown throughout Zones 3-10 in almost any soil as long as the site is sunny. Plant them 18 to 24 inches apart. Double sunflowers spread rapidly; to prevent them from crowding other plants in a border, dig them up and divide them every other year in either spring or fall.

HELIOPSIS

H. scabra (rough heliopsis)

The garden varieties of heliopsis grow about 3 feet tall and bear double (heavily petaled) or semidouble yellow

SNEEZEWEED
Helenium autumnale

DOUBLE THIN-LEAVED SUNFLOWER   ROUGH HELIOPSIS
Helianthus decapetalus flore pleno   *Heliopsis scabra* 'Gold Greenheart'

For climate zones and months of flowering, see page 151.

CHRISTMAS ROSE
Helleborus niger

DAY LILY
Hemerocallis hybrid

or orange flowers 3 to 4 inches across from midsummer to fall. Recommended varieties are Gold Greenheart, green-centered golden-yellow flowers; Gold Plume and Incomparabilis, both with orange-yellow flowers; and Light of Loddon, bright yellow flowers. Heliopsises are valuable in the back of a border for their bright colors and extended blooming season; their flowers, borne on long stems, are excellent for cutting.

HOW TO GROW. Heliopsises grow in Zones 3-9 and do best in full sun, especially when the soil is enriched with compost or leaf mold and there is ample moisture. Set plants about 2 feet apart. Heliopsises spread by underground roots, and the clumps should be dug up and divided in either spring or fall when they become overcrowded, usually after every three or four years of flowering.

HELIOTROPE, GARDEN See *Valeriana*

HELLEBORUS

H. niger (Christmas rose), *H. orientalis* (Lenten rose)

Both Christmas and Lenten roses are 12- to 15-inch plants that, despite their names, are more closely related to buttercups than to roses. The Christmas rose produces 2- to 4-inch white blossoms with prominent yellow pollen-bearing stamens. It blooms any time from late fall to early spring, depending upon the climate, and individual flowers last a month or more. The variety *H. niger altifolius* has flowers up to 5 inches across. The flowers will last longer if protected by a temporary plastic-covered frame to keep off snow and ice. The blossoms of the Lenten rose, usually about 2 inches across, vary in color from white to chocolate brown and purple and even green; they open between early and midspring. The flowers of both species are suitable for cutting, but before placing in water, the stem ends should be seared with a match or candle flame. Both species have leathery evergreen leaves; the roots of both are poisonous if eaten.

HOW TO GROW. Christmas roses grow in Zones 4-8 and Lenten roses grow in Zones 4-9. Both do best in partial shade and a moist, neutral or slightly alkaline (pH 7.0 to 8.0) soil that has been liberally supplemented with peat moss, leaf mold or compost. In spring place the plants 12 to 15 inches apart, setting the crowns, or tops of the root structures, about 1 inch below the top of the soil. Each spring apply a 1-inch mulch of compost or well-rotted cow manure around the plants. New plants are best grown from seeds sown in early autumn, but require three or four years to reach flowering size. Do not divide clumps.

HEMEROCALLIS

H. hybrids (hybrid day lilies)

Day lilies used to be either yellow or orange, but today's hybrids cover a spectrum from palest yellow through orange to pink, red and dark mahogany. Day lilies known as polychromes are a blend of related shades; bi-color and eyed day lilies combine different hues. There are now so many varieties, each blossoming at a different time, that they can be planted to bloom successively from early spring until frost. A wide range of heights is also available, from miniatures that grow 15 to 18 inches tall to giants that reach 4 feet or more. Blossoms may be less than 3 or more than 8 inches across and may have a single ring of petals or a double row of overlapping petals. Although individual blossoms are short lived, day lilies are excellent for bouquets; cut whole stalks and remove the faded flowers as new buds open indoors.

HOW TO GROW. Day lilies of one variety or another flourish in every part of the United States and southern Canada, and you will find that local nurserymen stock a wide choice of types for your area. Types whose foliage remains green all year usually need a winter mulch such as salt hay or straw from Zone 5 north. Day lilies grow in almost any soil, but do best in well-drained soil liberally enriched with compost or leaf mold. They flower more freely in full sun, but will tolerate light shade; in hot areas, afternoon shade is desirable. Plant day lilies 1½ to 2 feet apart. Clumps should be divided for propagation in spring or fall or when they become overcrowded, usually after every four to six years of flowering.

HESPERIS
H. matronalis (dame's rocket, sweet rocket, dame's violet)

Dame's rocket, native to Europe, grows so readily that it has become a wild flower in this country. The plants reach a height of 2 to 3 feet and from midspring to midsummer bear large, loose clusters of fragrant ¾-inch purple, lilac or white flowers. If faded flowers are removed before they form seeds, the plants may continue to blossom until early fall.

HOW TO GROW. Dame's rockets grow in Zones 4-8 and in Zone 9 on the West Coast in almost any moist well-drained soil in full sun or light shade. Plant them 15 to 18 inches apart. New plants can be started from seeds sown in spring for flowers the following year. Since dame's rocket usually is a short-lived perennial, sow seeds each year to be sure of having flowering plants the following season.

HEUCHERA
H. sanguinea (coral-bells, alumroot)

The name coral-bells once described the color as well as the shape of the blossoms of this graceful perennial, but today the flowers' colors range from pure white to fiery red. The foliage, bronze-colored 1- to 2-inch heart-shaped leaves that remain on the plants the year round, provides a handsome background for the hundreds of ¼-inch flowers that are borne on wiry 1- to 2-foot stems from late spring until early fall. Recommended varieties of coral-bells are Fire Sprite, rose red; Freedom, rose pink; June Bride, white; Pluie de Feu, bright red; and Rosamundi, coral. Coral-bells can be placed in the front of a border or used to line a path or accent a rock garden. They also make excellent cut flowers.

HOW TO GROW. Coral-bells thrive in Zones 4-10 except in Florida and along the Gulf Coast. They flower most profusely in full sun, but will tolerate light shade, especially in hot areas. Because they have shallow roots, coral-bells require moist well-drained soil that has been liberally enriched with organic materials such as compost, peat moss or leaf mold. Coral-bells hybrids may be grown successfully from commercial seeds and will blossom when two years old. Set plants about a foot apart. New plants can be started from divisions of clumps or from leaf cuttings taken in spring. The clumps should be divided in spring or fall whenever they become overcrowded, usually after every four or five years of flowering.

HIBISCUS
H. moscheutos, also called *H. palustris* (rose mallow)

Rose mallows, colorful relatives of the hollyhock, bear enormous red, white or pink flowers 6 to 12 inches in diameter from midsummer until frost. The wild rose mallow is native to swampy land from Massachusetts to Florida, and west to Missouri. Garden varieties may grow up to 8 feet, but unless the soil is extremely moist in summer, mature plants seldom exceed 5 feet. Southern Belle and Avalon Hybrids are recommended strains that can be

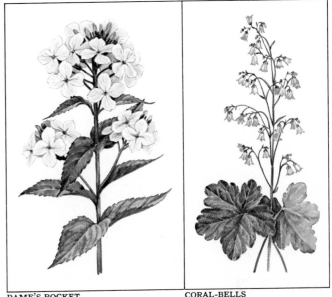

DAME'S ROCKET
Hesperis matronalis

CORAL-BELLS
Heuchera sanguinea 'Freedom'

ROSE MALLOW
Hibiscus moscheutos

For climate zones and months of flowering, see page 151.

grown from seeds. More colorful than the seed strains are named varieties that must be purchased as plants (and are therefore more expensive). Among the best of these are Cotton Candy, soft pink; Ruby Dot, pure white with red center; and Satan, deep velvety crimson. Because of the rose mallow's height, all types should be placed at the back of the garden or in a group by themselves.

HOW TO GROW. Rose mallows grow in Zones 4-9. They do best in full sun but will tolerate light shade. Although they can grow in almost any soil, they prefer moist ground liberally supplemented with compost, leaf mold or other organic material. Rose mallows should be spaced about 3 feet apart. If you are setting out growing plants, place the crowns, or tops of the root structures, 3 to 4 inches beneath the soil. To start plants from seeds, sow early in spring; the new plants will produce only a few flowers the first year, but will come into full bloom in subsequent years. Home-grown seeds produce good results if the parent plants are types that are sold in seed form (such as Southern Belle and Avalon Hybrids); propagation of named varieties that are not sold in seed form (such as Cotton Candy) requires professional skills. Because rose mallow clumps do not spread underground, the plants can be allowed to remain undisturbed indefinitely.

HOLLY, SEA See *Eryngium*
HOLLYHOCK See *Althaea*
HONESTY See *Lunaria*

HOSTA (FUNKIA)

H. crispula, also called *H. fortunei albo-marginata, H. caerulea albo-marginata* (white-edged plantain lily); *H. decorata,* also called *H.* 'Thomas Hogg' (blunt-leaved plantain lily); *H.* 'Honeybells' (Honeybells plantain lily); *H. lancifolia* (narrow-leaved plantain lily); *H. plantaginea,* also called *H. subcordata grandiflora* (fragrant plantain lily); *H. sieboldiana,* also called *H. glauca* (Siebold's plantain lily); *H. undulata* (wavy-leaved plantain lily); *H. ventricosa* (blue plantain lily). (All also called hosta)

Although plantain lilies, or hostas, produce attractive 1- to 1½-inch lilylike flowers atop slender leafless stalks, they are valued more for the mounds of highly decorative foliage that they present from spring until frost. The white-edged plantain lily, 1½ to 2 feet tall, has dark green leaves with broad white edges; individual leaves are almost a foot long and half that wide; the pale purple flowers open in midsummer. The blunt-leaved plantain lily, 12 inches tall, has white-margined leaves about 6 inches long and 4 inches wide; its violet-colored flowers bloom in late summer. Honeybells, a 2-foot hybrid, has light green leaves almost a foot long and half that wide; its fragrant violet-striped white flowers bloom in late summer. The variety of the narrow-leaved plantain lily called *H. lancifolia albo-marginata* grows about 15 inches tall and has white-edged leaves 5 inches long and 3 inches wide; it bears violet flowers lined with white that open in late summer and early fall. The variety *H. lancifolia minor alba,* also called *H. minor alba,* grows 10 inches tall and has glossy green leaves topped by white flowers in late summer. The fragrant plantain lily grows 1½ feet tall and has bright greenish yellow leaves a foot long and 6 inches wide; its white flowers open in late summer and early fall and are noted for their fragrance. Siebold's plantain lily grows 2 feet tall and has distinctive blue-green striped leaves about 15 inches long and 10 inches wide; its creamy lavender flowers, which appear in midsummer, are borne on stalks that barely extend above the foliage. Wavy-leaved plantain lily, 10 inches tall, has green leaves marked with central bands of white; its

FRAGRANT PLANTAIN LILY
Hosta plantaginea

GOLDFLOWER ST.-JOHN'S-WORT
Hypericum moserianum

light purple flowers open in midsummer. The blue plantain lily, 2½ feet tall, has leaves about 10 inches long and 6 inches wide; its violet flowers open in midsummer.

HOW TO GROW. Plantain lilies grow throughout Zones 3-9 and thrive in moist soil liberally enriched with compost or leaf mold. They do best in light shade but will tolerate full sun or deep shade. Space plants 12 to 24 inches apart, depending on the size of the species. New plants can be started by dividing clumps in early spring. Clumps may otherwise remain undisturbed indefinitely.

HYPERICUM
H. moserianum (goldflower St.-John's-wort)

The blossoms of this hybrid bring a lively note of color to gardens from midsummer to early fall. The five-petaled cup-shaped blossoms, clustered at the ends of 2- to 3-foot stems, are about 2 inches across and have centers crowded with golden pollen-bearing stamens with red tips. The leaves retain their color throughout the year in mild climates but die down to the ground in cold winters.

HOW TO GROW. Goldflower St.-John's-wort can be grown in Zones 7-10 in full sun or light shade. It grows in almost any soil, but does best in a moist soil that has been well supplemented with peat moss or leaf mold. Set plants 16 to 24 inches apart. The stems should be cut to ground level each year to force healthy new growth. New plants can be propagated from stem cuttings taken in summer for flowers the following year.

I

IBERIS
I. sempervirens (evergreen candytuft)

The low-growing evergreen candytuft is almost completely covered with 2-inch clusters of tiny dazzling white flowers from early spring to early summer. Plants grow 6 to 9 inches tall and spread as much as 2 feet across. The narrow leaves, 1 to 2 inches long, are attractive throughout the year. Superior hybrids include Purity, which flowers abundantly in spring, and Autumn Snow, which blossoms in fall as well as in spring.

HOW TO GROW. The evergreen candytuft can be grown throughout Zones 3-10 in full sun or light shade and well-drained garden soil. Set plants 12 to 15 inches apart. Shear off the old flower stems as soon as they stop blossoming to encourage the growth of fresh new stems. New plants can be started from seeds sown in early spring for flowers the following year, but named varieties must be propagated from stem cuttings taken in midsummer.

INCARVILLEA
I. delavayi (Delavay incarvillea)

The Delavay incarvillea, sometimes called hardy gloxinia, is a handsome but seldom-grown perennial. From midspring to midsummer it sends up 1½- to 2-foot leafless stems topped by clusters of flowers, each of which may be as much as 3 inches across.

HOW TO GROW. Delavay incarvillea can be grown in Zones 6-10 in full sun or light shade. It does best in soil that has been liberally enriched with compost or leaf mold; good drainage is essential during the dormant winter season. Set plants 12 to 15 inches apart. Remove flowers as they fade to extend the blooming season. New plants can be grown from seeds sown in spring, but may not blossom until the third year. It is possible to divide and reset clumps, but the plants flourish most vigorously if allowed to remain undisturbed.

INDIGO, FALSE See *Baptisia*

For climate zones and months of flowering, see page 151.

EVERGREEN CANDYTUFT
Iberis sempervirens

DELAVAY INCARVILLEA
Incarvillea delavayi

TALL BEARDED IRIS
Iris, bearded hybrid

IRIS

I. hybrids (bearded iris, beardless iris, aril iris),
I. pseudacorus (yellow flag iris)

There are more than 200 species of irises that grow wild (or did once) and thousands of hybrids, but all have two characteristics in common: sword-shaped leaves and a distinctive flower structure consisting of three usually erect petals, called standards, and three outer petals, or sepals, called falls, that hang down from the base of the blossom. Between each pair of standards and falls rise the flower's reproductive organs, often crowned with colorful crests. Irises come in a stunning range of colors—hence the name iris, after the Greek goddess of the rainbow.

There are two broad categories of hybrid irises—bearded and beardless. On bearded irises each of the falls is ornamented with a fuzzy, often brightly colored strip, or beard. Bearded irises include the familiar standard bearded hybrids as well as the group of hybrids called aril irises, which are distinguished by their rounded flowers, veined petals and subdued colors. The colors of standard bearded irises range from snowy white through every conceivable shade, including yellow, orange, pink, red, blue, lavender, purple, brown and near black; more often than not the standards and falls are of different colors. The height of standard bearded irises ranges from 3 inches to 40 inches or more, with flowers 1½ to 8 inches across.

Plant height, flower size and blooming season are the key factors in the American Iris Society classification of standard bearded irises: MINIATURE DWARF BEARDED IRISES, less than 10 inches tall, bear 1½- to 2-inch flowers in midspring. STANDARD DWARF BEARDED IRISES (sometimes called Lilliputs), 10 to 15 inches tall, have 2- to 2½-inch flowers. INTERMEDIATE BEARDED IRISES, 15 to 28 inches tall, have 2- to 4-inch flowers, but both bloom slightly later in spring than miniature dwarf irises. MINIATURE TALL BEARDED IRISES (sometimes called table irises), 18 to 26 inches tall, have flowers up to 2½ inches across; BORDER BEARDED IRISES, up to 28 inches tall, have 3- to 4-inch flowers; and TALL BEARDED IRISES, more than 28 inches tall, have 4- to 8-inch flowers; all three types blossom from late spring to early summer. REBLOOMING BEARDED IRISES, of varying heights and sizes, blossom in spring and again any time from midsummer through fall. ARIL IRIS HYBRIDS grow 2 to 3 feet tall and from late spring to early summer bear 4- to 6-inch bearded flowers, mostly in tan and smoky shades. Many have prominently veined petals.

Beardless iris hybrids are classified into four groups: LOUISIANA HYBRIDS grow 2 to 3 feet tall and bear 3- to 4-inch flowers ranging in color from white through cream and yellow to bronze, pink, red, blue, purple and near black; the flowers blossom in mid- to late spring in Zones 8-10 and in early summer farther north. JAPANESE IRISES grow up to 3½ feet tall; their flat-topped blossoms—often 6 to 8 inches across, but sometimes as large as 10 inches—come in many shades and mottlings of rose, purple and blue as well as in white, and bloom in early to midsummer. SIBERIAN IRIS HYBRIDS grow up to 3 feet tall and have 3-inch flowers in many colors from pure white to deep reddish purple with most blossoms in shades of deep blue, purple and violet; they bloom profusely in early summer and are long lasting, some flowers remaining in bloom for a week. SPURIA IRIS HYBRIDS grow to a height of more than 3 feet. Their 4-inch flowers, which bloom in spring and early summer and are excellent for cutting, come in white, cream, yellow, brown, blue and purple; some blossoms blend several colors and others have distinct veins in a second color.

A direct descendant from wild species, the nearly indestructible yellow flag iris bears bright yellow brown-veined

JAPANESE IRIS
Iris, beardless hybrid

YELLOW FLAG IRIS
Iris pseudacorus

flowers, 1½ to 2 inches across, in early to midsummer. It is at its best in wet places, such as beside ponds, and may be planted to grow untended indefinitely, as if wild.

HOW TO GROW. All irises bloom best in full sun, but soil, moisture and climatic requirements vary with the types. Standard bearded irises do well throughout Zones 3-10 except in Florida and along the Gulf Coast, and will grow in any well-drained soil. Aril bearded hybrids grow best in the arid west and southwest areas of Zones 8-10; they need well-drained neutral soil. Both standard bearded irises and aril bearded irises grow from thick underground stems, called rhizomes, that creep along just beneath the surface of the soil; plant both types from midsummer to early fall, setting them 10 to 15 inches apart, with the tops of the rhizomes even with the surface of the soil. Both can be propagated by dividing the rhizomes. In arid areas of Zones 8-10, to which they are best suited, aril bearded irises should be dug up and reset after flowering each year; in areas with more rainfall than they prefer, they should be dug up early each summer after they have flowered and stored in dry sand until fall. Standard bearded irises multiply rapidly and reach their peak of loveliness in the third and fourth flowering seasons; after flowering, the rhizomes should be dug up, divided and replanted.

Among the beardless irises, Louisiana irises grow best in Zones 7-10, Japanese irises in Zones 5-8 and Siberian irises in Zones 3-8. Spuria irises grow in Zones 4-10, although most varieties do not blossom as freely in northern gardens as they do in southern ones. Spuria irises prefer neutral soil, but Louisiana, Japanese and Siberian irises require acid soil with a pH of 5.5 to 6.5; add sulfur if necessary to acidify the soil. Both Louisiana and Japanese irises do best in very moist soil liberally supplemented with peat moss, leaf mold or compost; Siberian and spuria irises thrive in moist but well-drained soil. Plant all of them in fall 15 to 18 inches apart. Spuria irises usually require two or three years to become fully established and should remain undisturbed indefinitely. All of the other beardless hybrids can be propagated by dividing clumps in early fall. Otherwise they can be left alone for as long as 8 or 10 years, when they may become overcrowded.

Yellow flag irises, which grow in Zones 5-10, thrive on neglect as long as they have moist soil. Space plants 18 to 24 inches apart. Clumps can be left undisturbed indefinitely, or dug up for division to start new plants.

J

JACOB'S-LADDER See *Polemonium*
JERUSALEM CROSS See *Lychnis*
JUPITER'S-BEARD See *Centranthus*

K

KNIPHOFIA

K. uvaria, also called *K. aloides, K. pfitzerii, Tritoma uvaria* (red-hot poker, poker plant, torch lily, kniphofia, tritoma)

The blossoms of red-hot pokers are unusual 12-inch lance-shaped spikes made up of 1½- to 2-inch tubular flowers. In the original species the flowers were yellow at the bottom, shading upward to the fiery red tips from which the plant derives its name. Modern hybrids, however, are available in many colors from pure white through delicate shades of yellow to rosy red. Some bloom from early summer into fall. Most varieties grow 2 to 2½ feet tall, although some may reach 6 feet. Their long narrow leaves resemble coarse grass, and their flowers, beloved by hummingbirds, are long lasting, both in gardens and in bouquets.

HOW TO GROW. Red-hot pokers can be grown in Zones 6-

SIBERIAN IRIS
Iris sibirica

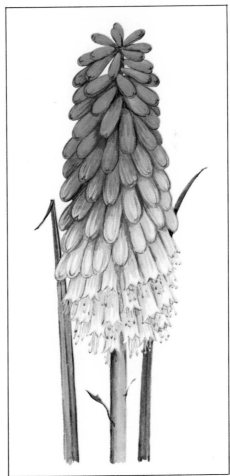

RED-HOT POKER
Kniphofia uvaria 'Springtime'

For climate zones and months of flowering, see page 151.

PERENNIAL PEA
Lathyrus latifolius

10 in full sun and well-drained garden soil. Plant them 1½ to 2 feet apart. In Zones 6 and 7 tie the leaves together over each clump in the fall, and protect the plants with a winter mulch of salt hay, straw or pine needles. New plants can be started from seeds sown in early spring or from clump divisions in spring, but require two or three years to reach flowering size. Except for propagation purposes, red-hot pokers are best if undisturbed indefinitely.

L

LAMB'S EARS See *Stachys*
LANTERN PLANT, CHINESE See *Physalis*
LARKSPUR See *Delphinium*

LATHYRUS
L. latifolius (perennial pea)

This hardy 4- to 8-foot-long vine bears clusters of five to nine 1½-inch blossoms from early summer to early fall at the ends of 12-inch stems. The original species is a washed-out magenta, but varieties come in pink, reddish purple and pure white. Perennial peas can be planted to climb on fences, trellises, brush or rocks.

HOW TO GROW. Perennial peas grow in Zones 3-10 in full sun and almost any well-drained soil. Space plants 18 to 24 inches apart. Remove faded flowers to extend the blooming season. Start new plants by sowing seeds in late fall or early spring; they will bloom the following year.

LAVANDULA
L. officinalis, also called *L. spica, L. vera* (true lavender)

The fragrance of true lavender is one of the joys of a perennial garden; it rises primarily from the clusters of ½-inch lavender or purple blossoms that circle the plant's wiry stems in mid- to late summer. The silvery gray leaves, shaped like blunt 1-inch needles, produce the same scent when rubbed; both flowers and foliage have long been used, after drying, for sweet-smelling sachets and potpourris. True lavender is an excellent choice for rock gardens and the edges of paths and borders; it also provides delightful cut flowers. Fine varieties include Gray Lady, 2 feet tall and deep lavender; Twickel Purple, 3 feet tall and also deep lavender; and Hidcote, 1 foot tall and deep purple. These varieties are sold only as growing plants, but a good type available in seed form is Munstead, which grows about 15 inches tall and produces mauve flowers.

HOW TO GROW. True lavender grows in Zones 5-10 in full sun and well-drained soil. Space plants 15 to 18 inches apart. New plants of the varieties sold only as growing plants should be started from stem cuttings taken at any time to bloom the following summer. Types ordinarily sold as seeds, such as Munstead, can be started from home-grown seeds sown in spring to bloom that summer. Cut off the heads of the plants after the flowers fade to encourage fresh growth. Let the plants grow undisturbed indefinitely.

LAVENDER, SEA See *Limonium*
LAVENDER, TRUE See *Lavandula*
LAVENDER COTTON See *Santolina*
LEADWORT See *Ceratostigma*
LEOPARD'S-BANE See *Doronicum*

LIATRIS
L. pycnostachya (Kansas or cattail gay-feather), *L. scariosa* (tall gay-feather), *L. spicata* (spike gay-feather). (All also called liatris)

The tiny fuzzy blossoms of most gay-feathers usually begin to open at the top of the plants' 1½-foot flower spikes rather than in the normal bottom-to-top sequence

TRUE LAVENDER
Lavandula officinalis 'Hidcote'

SPIKE GAY-FEATHER
Liatris spicata 'Silver Tips'

of other plants. The Kansas gay-feather grows 4 to 6 feet tall and bears rosy lavender or white flowers in late summer and early fall. Two notable varieties of the tall gay-feather blossom in early fall: September Glory, with deep purple flowers, and White Spire, with pure white blossoms; both grow 5 to 6 feet tall. The spike gay-feather also boasts two fine varieties: the 18-inch Kobold, with deep rosy purple flowers, and the 3-foot Silver Tips, with lavender blossoms; both bloom in mid- to late summer.

HOW TO GROW. Gay-feathers grow in Zones 3-10 in full sun or light shade. Soil must be well drained in winter in northern zones. Space plants 12 to 15 inches apart. Start new plants of named varieties by clump division in spring; others can be grown from seeds sown in spring to bloom the second year. To prevent overcrowding, divide clumps after three or four years of flowering.

LILY, PLANTAIN See *Hosta*
LILY, TORCH See *Kniphofia*
LILY-TURF See *Liriope* and *Ophiopogon*

LIMONIUM
L. latifolium (wide-leaved sea lavender, hardy statice)

The slender many-branched 1½- to 2-foot-tall flower stalks of sea lavender appear from mid- to late summer and are soon hidden beneath broad billows of tiny pink-to-lavender blossoms. Two lovely varieties are the violet Violetta and the pink-flowered Collier's Pink. Sea lavenders are excellent for borders, and since they are very resistant to salt spray, they are unexcelled for seaside planting. They also make superb cut flowers and dried bouquets; to dry them, cut sea lavenders when they are fully open and hang them upside down in a shady, airy place.

HOW TO GROW. Sea lavenders grow well in Zones 3-10 in full sun in well-drained soil. Space plants 18 to 24 inches apart. New plants can be started from seeds sown in early spring, but usually require three or four years to reach flowering size. Clumps should remain undisturbed indefinitely.

LINUM
L. flaven (golden flax), *L. narbonnense* (Narbonne flax), *L. perenne* (perennial flax)

Flaxes are noted for their never-failing supply of dainty 1-inch flowers from early summer to early fall if the blossoms, which last only a single day, are removed after they fade. Most types of golden flax grow a foot or more in height but there is a 6-inch variety, *L. flaxum compactum;* all bear bright yellow flowers and blossom in midsummer. Narbonne flax, generally about 2 feet tall, bears blue flowers with white centers from late spring to midsummer; an abundantly flowering variety, Heavenly Blue, grows a little more than a foot tall. The 10-inch perennial flax produces flowers from early to midsummer; most are pale blue but *L. perenne album* is a fine white-flowered variety. All types have 2-inch needlelike blue-green leaves that make the plants attractive even when not flowering. Flaxes have a spread equal to their height and are especially useful at the front of a border or in rock gardens.

HOW TO GROW. Golden and Narbonne flaxes grow in Zones 5-10 and perennial flax grows in Zones 4-10. None grow in Florida and along the Gulf Coast. They do best in full sun and well-drained soil. Space plants 12 to 18 inches apart. New plants can be started from cuttings taken from nonflowering stems in summer to bloom the following year or from seeds sown in spring or summer to blossom the next summer. Do not divide flax plants.

LION'S-HEART, VIRGINIA See *Physostegia*

For climate zones and months of flowering, see page 151.

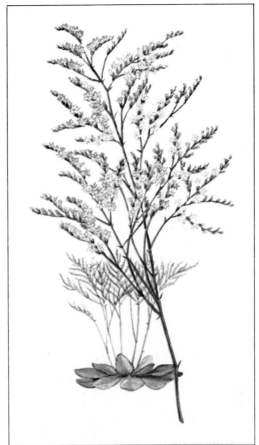

WIDE-LEAVED SEA LAVENDER
Limonium latifolium

PERENNIAL FLAX
Linum perenne

BIG BLUE LILY-TURF
Liriope muscari

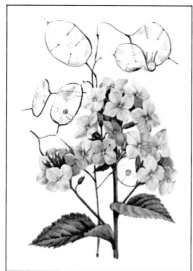

HONESTY
Lunaria annua

LUPINE
Lupinus 'Russell Hybrid'

LIRIOPE
L. muscari, also called *L. platyphylla* (big blue lily-turf),
L. spicata (creeping lily-turf)

Lily-turfs are of special interest to gardeners in the South and Southwest, where their foliage remains green in most seasons. The big blue lily-turf, 12 to 18 inches tall, forms clumps of grasslike leaves up to 2 feet long from which rise 6- to 12-inch spikes of ¼-inch flowers. The flowers bloom from midsummer to fall and are followed by tiny black berries. Most types have purple flowers and dark green leaves, but several varieties are available with white or lavender flowers and white- or yellow-striped leaves. Creeping lily-turf, often used as a ground cover, spreads by underground runners and grows up to a foot tall. It has long grasslike leaves, slender 6- to 8-inch spikes of ¼-inch pale lilac or white flowers that bloom from midsummer to fall, and blue-black berries. The flowers of both species, though short-stemmed, are good for cutting.

HOW TO GROW. Big blue lily-turf grows in Zones 6-10, creeping lily-turf in Zones 4-10. They will grow in almost any soil; they do best in light shade but will tolerate a wide range of light conditions, growing very slowly in deep shade and withstanding sun (except in the hottest areas) if the soil is sufficiently moist. Space plants about 12 inches apart. Cut off old leaves in the spring to encourage the growth of new foliage. New plants can be started from clumps divided and reset in early spring, but the clumps can remain undisturbed indefinitely.

LIVE-FOREVER See *Sedum*
LOOSESTRIFE See *Lythrum*

LUNARIA
L. annua, also called *L. biennis* (honesty, dollar plant, money plant, moneywort, moonwort)

Honesty—a biennial sometimes grown as an annual—is best known for the flat translucent centers of its seed pods, which are widely used in dried arrangements; however, its many clusters of sweet-scented purple, pink or white blossoms make it splendid in the garden too. The flowers bloom in late spring and early summer, followed by the round or oval 1-inch pods in early fall. Honesty grows up to 3 feet tall and has large coarsely toothed leaves. To dry the seed pods for winter bouquets, gather them as soon as they start to turn brown (they often rot during wet weather if allowed to ripen on the plants). Rub off the outer parts of the pods to expose the central disks.

HOW TO GROW. Honesty grows well in Zones 5-10 in full sun or light shade in almost any well-drained soil. Space plants 12 to 15 inches apart. Honesty generally multiplies in the garden by sowing its own seeds, often coming up year after year without further care. It can be grown from seeds sown in midsummer to bloom the following spring; if treated as an annual and sown in early spring, the plants flower later in the spring but never become as large and colorful as those grown as biennials.

LUNGWORT See *Pulmonaria*
LUPINE See *Lupinus*

LUPINUS
L. 'Russell Hybrid' (Russell Hybrid lupine)

Russell Hybrid lupines provide some of the grandest flowers of the gardening year. Their blue, white, yellow, red or pink blossoms, up to an inch across, are tightly set along 2 feet or more of their 3- to 5-foot stems; they bloom from midspring to midsummer. The handsome foliage is deeply divided into many palmlike segments.

HOW TO GROW. Russell Hybrid lupines can be grown in Zones 4-7 and the West Coast sections of Zones 8 and 9; ideal locations are New England, the Maritime Provinces, the Pacific Northwest and regions just north of the Great Lakes. Lupines do best in full sun or partial shade and a well-drained, neutral or slightly acid soil. Space plants 18 inches apart. In spring and fall dust bone meal lightly around the plants to encourage the development of blossoms in midsummer. Propagate from seeds sown in spring or summer to flower the next year. Before sowing, dust the seeds with a nitrifying powder, available from seedsmen. Plants can also be grown from 4- to 6-inch stem cuttings taken in early spring with a tiny piece of the top of the root structure, or crown, attached; they will flower the following year. Clumps can remain undisturbed until they lose vigor, usually after three or four years, when they should be replaced.

LYCHNIS

L. chalcedonica (Maltese cross, Jerusalem cross, scarlet lightning); *L. coronaria*, also called *Agrostemma coronaria* (rose campion, mullein pink); *L. viscaria*, also called *Viscaria viscosa* (German catchfly)

These *Lychnis* species differ greatly from one another, The Maltese cross bears 1½-inch clusters of scarlet blossoms shaped like small Maltese crosses atop 2- to 3-foot stems in summer. The 2-foot rose campion, mainly a biennial, has woolly whitish leaves; its angular stems bear 1-inch bright rose-purple or white flowers in summer. The German catchfly bears abundant clusters of ¾-inch deep rose blossoms from early summer to midsummer; a many-petaled double variety, Flore Pleno, is excellent for cutting.

HOW TO GROW. All three species grow in Zones 3-10 except in Florida and along the Gulf Coast. They do best in full sun but grow in any well-drained soil; good drainage is essential in cold areas. Set plants 12 to 15 inches apart. Maltese cross and rose campion are best grown from seeds sown in spring or fall to bloom in one or two years. Clumps may remain undisturbed indefinitely. German catchfly should be propagated by dividing clumps in early spring. Divide clumps after three or four years of flowering.

LYTHRUM

L. salicaria (purple loosestrife, lythrum)

The wild form of purple loosestrife is 5 to 6 feet tall, but a number of fine varieties are short enough to be suitable for gardens. Their 1-inch blossoms are borne on slender spikes more than a foot tall, rising high above dark green willowlike leaves. Among the best are Happy, dark pink and up to 18 inches tall; Morden Gleam, carmine and up to 4 feet tall, with foliage that turns red purple in the fall; Morden Pink, rose pink and about 3 feet tall; Morden Rose, rose and about 3 feet tall; and Robert, rose red and up to 2 feet tall, with scarlet foliage in the fall. All are effective in a border and in moist sunny semiwild settings.

HOW TO GROW. Purple loosestrifes grow in Zones 3-10 except in Florida and along the Gulf Coast. They do best in full sun but tolerate light shade and grow in almost any soil. Space plants 15 to 18 inches apart. New plants may be propagated by dividing and resetting clumps in spring or fall after three years of flowering.

M

MACLEAYA

M. cordata, also called *Bocconia cordata*
(pink plume poppy)

The imposing 6- to 8-foot plume poppy has pink 12-inch flower clusters, opening from bronze buds in mid- to late

MALTESE CROSS
Lychnis chalcedonica

GERMAN CATCHFLY
Lychnis viscaria 'Flore Pleno'

PURPLE LOOSESTRIFE
Lythrum salicaria 'Morden Pink'

For climate zones and months of flowering, see page 151.

PINK PLUME POPPY
Macleaya cordata

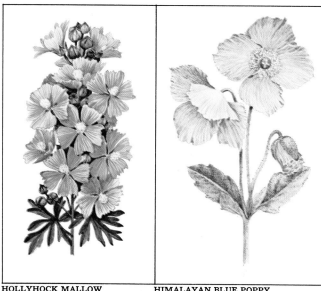

HOLLYHOCK MALLOW
Malva alcea fastigiata

HIMALAYAN BLUE POPPY
Meconopsis betonicifolia

summer. The flowers have no petals, but numerous pollen-bearing stamens rise over the upper 2 to 3 feet of the stems to produce an airy effect; seed pods are similar in appearance to the blossoms and continue the plumelike appearance into the fall. Heart-shaped deeply lobed leaves are gray-green above and nearly white underneath; they range in size from a foot across at ground level to 1 to 3 inches at the base of the flower stalks. Plume poppies are best set off by themselves where their lower foliage is not hidden and where their quickly spreading roots cannot encroach on other plants. The flowers are good for cutting and can be dried for winter use if cut when three quarters open and hung in a dry room.

HOW TO GROW. Plume poppies grow in Zones 3-10 except in Florida and along the Gulf Coast. They grow in sun or light shade and almost any soil, but do best in moist soil that has been well supplemented with peat moss or leaf mold. Space plants 3 to 4 feet apart. Plants can be started from clump divisions, root cuttings or seeds sown in spring; all will bloom the next year. To prevent overcrowding, clumps should be divided after three or four years.

MALLOW See *Malva*
MALLOW, POPPY See *Callirhoë*
MALLOW, PRAIRIE See *Sidalcea*
MALLOW, ROSE See *Hibiscus*
MALTESE CROSS See *Lychnis*

MALVA

M. alcea (hollyhock mallow)

Hollyhock mallows bear masses of bright pink blossoms from midsummer to late fall. The popular variety *M. alcea fastigiata* crowds its 2-inch flowers at the top of 3- to 4-foot stems, above downy palm-shaped leaves.

HOW TO GROW. Hollyhock mallows grow in Zones 4-10 except in Florida and along the Gulf Coast. They do well in full sun or light shade and almost any soil, and can tolerate hot sunny locations. Space plants 12 inches apart. New plants can be started from clump divisions, from cuttings taken in spring or summer or from seeds sown in summer to bloom the following year. The clumps can remain undisturbed indefinitely.

MARGUERITE See *Chrysanthemum*
MARGUERITE, BLUE See *Felicia*
MARGUERITE, GOLDEN See *Anthemis*
MARVEL-OF-PERU See *Mirabilis*
MEADOW RUE See *Thalictrum*
MEADOWSWEET See *Filipendula*

MECONOPSIS

M. betonicifolia, also called *M. baileyi* (Himalayan blue poppy); *M. cambrica* (Welsh poppy)

Meconopsis species are related to true poppies *(page 136).* The Himalayan blue poppy, native to western China and Tibet, grows 2 to 5 feet tall and in early and midsummer bears clusters of glistening sky-blue gold-centered flowers about 2 inches across. The Welsh poppy, from Western Europe, grows 12 to 18 inches tall and in summer produces slightly smaller yellow or orange flowers; some varieties bear heavily petaled double blossoms.

HOW TO GROW. Himalayan blue and Welsh poppies grow in the cool moist sections of Zones 6-8, particularly the Pacific Northwest. They do best in light shade and need an acid soil (pH 5.5 to 6.5) that has been well supplemented with leaf mold or peat moss. Good drainage, important the year round, is vital in winter. Space plants 12 to 15 inches apart. Himalayan blue poppies must be grown from seeds sown in spring or summer. They should not be allowed to blossom until their third year, and any flower buds that develop before that time should be picked off; if young plants are allowed to blossom they soon die. Most Welsh poppies can be grown from seeds sown in spring or summer to blossom the next year or from clumps divided in early spring to bloom the same year; the heavily petaled double types can be grown only from clump divisions.

MILFOIL See *Achillea*

MIRABILIS

M. jalapa (four-o'clock, marvel-of-Peru)

Four-o'clocks are appropriately named; their blossoms open in late afternoon, scenting the air with a delightful fragrance before closing the next morning. The plants grow up to 3 feet tall and blossom continuously from midspring to late fall. The 1-inch trumpet-shaped flowers come in white, pink, red, yellow and violet, and more than one color may appear on the same plant. The dense leaves are shiny green, sometimes sticky and 2 to 6 inches long.

HOW TO GROW. Four-o'clocks may be grown as perennials in Zones 9 and 10 in full sun and well-drained soil that has been well supplemented with organic material such as compost or leaf mold. Set plants 18 to 24 inches apart. New plants may be started from seeds sown in spring to blossom by midsummer. In Zones 4-8 four-o'clocks are widely grown as annuals, but the plants can survive the winters if they are dug up in the fall and stored in a frost-free place, such as a cellar. In Zones 9 and 10 perennial four-o'clocks should remain undisturbed indefinitely.

MISTFLOWER See *Eupatorium*

MONARDA

M. didyma (bee balm, Oswego tea, sweet bergamot)

Bee balms, which exude a delightful mint fragrance, bear slender tubular flowers in 2- to 3-inch circular whorls from early to midsummer and sometimes later. The plants, up to 3 feet tall, have rough hairy leaves. The easy-to-grow varieties include Adam, bright red; Cambridge Scarlet, crimson; Croftway Pink and Granite Pink, rose pink; and Mahogany, dark red. Bee balms are favorites of bees and attract hummingbirds; they make fine cut flowers.

HOW TO GROW. Bee balms grow in Zones 4-10 except in Florida and along the Gulf Coast, in full sun or light shade; they do best in moist soil that has been well supplemented with organic material such as peat moss or leaf mold. Space plants 12 to 15 inches apart. To prolong flowering, remove faded flowers before they produce seeds. New plants can be started from clump divisions. To prevent overcrowding, divide clumps after every three or four years of flowering.

MONDO GRASS See *Ophiopogon*
MONEYWORT See *Lunaria*
MONKSHOOD See *Aconitum*
MOONWORT See *Lunaria*
MORNING-GLORY, GROUND See *Convolvulus*
MOUNTAIN BLUET See *Centaurea*
MUGWORT See *Artemisia*
MULLEIN See *Verbascum*

MYOSOTIS

M. alpestris, also called *M. rupicola* (alpine forget-me-not); *M. scorpioides semperflorens*, also called *M. palustris semperflorens* (dwarf perpetual forget-me-not); *M. sylvatica*, also called *M. oblongata* (woodland forget-me-not)

These tiny sky-blue yellow-centered flowers are among

FOUR-O'CLOCK
Mirabilis jalapa

BEE BALM
Monarda didyma 'Adam'

FORGET-ME-NOT
Myosotis scorpioides semperflorens

For climate zones and months of flowering, see page 151.

MAUVE CATMINT
Nepeta faassinii

BLUE CUPFLOWER
Nierembergia caerulea

the first cheery signs of spring. Pink and white varieties are also available. The alpine forget-me-not grows about 6 inches tall, the woodland type about a foot; both bloom until early summer. The dwarf perpetual forget-me-not, despite its name, grows up to a foot tall and blossoms from late spring until frost.

HOW TO GROW. Forget-me-nots thrive in Zones 3-10 in light shade and moist soil supplemented with peat moss or other organic material. Set plants 9 to 12 inches apart. Alpine and woodland types are generally treated as biennials and are started from seeds sown outdoors in summer to bloom in spring. To grow them as annuals, sow seeds indoors very early in spring to bloom in late spring or early summer. New plants of dwarf perpetual forget-me-nots should be started from clumps divided in late summer or from stem cuttings taken in summer to bloom the next year. Divide clumps after three or four years of flowering.

N

NEPETA

N. faassinii, also called *N. mussinii* (mauve catmint)

Mauve catmint grows 12 to 18 inches tall, forming soft mounds of mint-scented, crinkled gray-green leaves about an inch long. From early summer through fall it is covered with clusters of tiny lavender flowers that have a pungent fragrance. The plants are excellent for edging a path.

HOW TO GROW. Mauve catmint grows in Zones 4-10 except in Florida and along the Gulf Coast, in full sun in almost any well-drained soil. Space plants 12 to 18 inches apart. To encourage occasional bloom until frost, cut the flower stalks back to the foliage mound after the first flowers have faded. In fall cover the plants with a winter mulch such as salt hay or evergreen boughs; leave old stalks on the plants as added protection. Start new plants from stem cuttings taken in summer to blossom the following year. Plants may remain undisturbed indefinitely.

NIEREMBERGIA

N. caerulea, also called *N. hippomanica* (blue cupflower); *N. frutescens* (tall cupflower); *N. repens,* also called *N. rivularis* (white cupflower)

Cupflowers, grown as annuals in most of North America, are treated in mild climates as true perennials. All bear 1-inch flowers. A popular variety of blue cupflower called Purple Robe grows 6 to 12 inches tall and bears violet blossoms from early spring to late fall. The tall cupflower has blue- or purple-tinged white blossoms from midsummer to early fall on plants that become 2 to 3 feet tall. The white cupflower, a creeping species only 4 to 6 inches tall, bears creamy white flowers from midsummer to early fall.

HOW TO GROW. Cupflowers grow as perennials in Zones 8-10 in moist but well-drained soil; they do best in light shade but can stand full sun in places that remain relatively cool. Set plants 6 to 12 inches apart. To encourage continuous bloom and force new growth for the following year, pick off old flowers in the fall and cut foliage and stems almost to the ground. Blue and tall cupflowers can be treated as annuals and grown from seeds sown indoors in early spring; they should be transplanted to the garden in early summer for blooming the same year. New plants of white cupflower can be grown from clump divisions or from 3- to 4-inch pieces of stems. To prevent overcrowding, divide clumps in spring after three or four years of flowering. Blue and tall cupflowers can remain undisturbed until they lose vigor, usually after three years of flowering.

O

OBEDIENT PLANT See *Physostegia*

OENOTHERA

O. missouriensis (Ozark sundrops); *O. tetragona*, also called *O. fruticosa youngii* (Young's sundrops)

Sundrops are related to evening primroses and are sometimes mistakenly called by that name; however, evening primroses open at night and sundrops blossom during the day. Ozark sundrops are sprawling plants that eventually become 9 to 12 inches high; they bear 4- to 5-inch cup-shaped golden-yellow flowers throughout the summer and have slender willowlike leaves 1 to 3 inches long. Young's sundrops grow about 2 feet tall and produce 1½-inch flowers throughout the summer; their leaves are 3 to 6 inches long. Two fine varieties are Yellow River, about 2 feet tall, with 2-inch lemon-yellow flowers, and Fyrverkerii, which grows only about a foot tall but bears many 2-inch golden-yellow flowers. Fyrverkerii's young stems and flower buds are a shiny reddish brown.

HOW TO GROW. Sundrops grow in Zones 4-10 in full sun and well-drained soil; excellent drainage is especially important during winter to prevent winterkill. Space plants 12 to 15 inches apart. Divide clumps for propagation or when they become overcrowded, usually after every third year of flowering.

OPHIOPOGON

O. jaburan (white lily-turf),
O. japonicus (dwarf lily-turf, mondo grass)

The lily-turfs of the genus *Ophiopogon* look very much like the lily-turfs called *Liriope (page 130)*. They have evergreen foliage and small spikes of ¼-inch flowers. White lily-turf forms large clumps of narrow leaves up to 3 feet long that lie nearly flat on the ground; from these clumps rise white flowers that bloom in early summer and are followed by ¼-inch violet-blue berries. Dwarf lily-turf spreads underground, sending up grasslike leaves 8 to 12 inches long; it bears pale lilac flowers in midsummer followed by ¼-inch blue berries. Both species are excellent for edging walks or as ground covers.

HOW TO GROW. Lily-turfs can be grown in Zones 8-10 in full sun to deep shade; they do best in light shade in soil that is kept moist and has been well supplemented with organic material such as peat moss or leaf mold. Space plants 6 to 12 inches apart. Plants can be allowed to remain undisturbed indefinitely, but may be dug up and divided for propagation in spring.

OSWEGO TEA See *Monarda*

P

PAEONIA

P. lactiflora, also called *P. albiflora* (Chinese peony);
P. officinalis (common peony);
P. tenuifolia (fern-leaved peony)

The red shoots of peonies emerging from the ground have signaled spring for generations of gardeners. All have unforgettable fragrance, are unexcelled for cutting and may live 20 to 30 years or longer.

To most gardeners the term peony means plants from the Chinese species, native to parts of China, Siberia and Japan. Mature Chinese peony plants reach 2 to 4 feet in height and breadth and in late spring and early summer send forth flowers that may be as much as 10 inches across. The blossoms are classified as single, Japanese (or anemone) and double. Single flowers have one row of five or more petals with a central mass of golden pollen-bearing stamens; Japanese or anemone-flowered varieties have two or more rows of petals and centers made up of feathery petallike structures called staminodes. Both of these flow-

SUNDROPS
Oenothera tetragona 'Yellow River'

DWARF LILY-TURF
Ophiopogon japonicus

For climate zones and months of flowering, see page 151.

135

CHINESE PEONY
Paeonia lactiflora 'Philippe Rivoire'

ICELAND POPPY
Papaver nudicaule

er types are light enough on their stems to survive wind and rain. Double flowers, with so many petals that the centers are nearly or wholly concealed, are the most popular, but require staking. All range from snowy white through pale yellow to many shades of pink to deepest red.

Although there are superb new varieties of Chinese peonies, many of the best are inexpensive longtime classics. One of the greatest white varieties in the world, Festiva Maxima, made its debut in 1851; Walter Faxon, a handsome pink, came out in 1904; and the deep red Philippe Rivoire was named in 1911.

The common peony, *P. officinalis*, a wild flower from France to Albania, has been grown in gardens since ancient times. Although the wild form normally has single dark crimson flowers about 5 inches across, there are double types with white, pink or red blossoms. They grow 2 to 3 feet tall and blossom in spring, a week or two ahead of Chinese peonies.

The fern-leaved peony has dark crimson single or double flowers about 3 inches across and blooms in spring, a month before Chinese peonies blossom. Native to Eastern Europe, it grows about 1½ feet tall and its fernlike foliage is ornamental throughout the summer. For indoor arrangements cut the flowers as soon as the buds open, leaving at least three leaves on each stem so that the plant can rebuild its strength for another year.

HOW TO GROW. Peonies do best in cold climates, even surviving temperatures of 40° or more below zero. They can be grown in Zones 3-8 and in the West Coast area of Zone 9 where nights are cool. They flourish in well-drained soil; although they prefer full sun, they will do well in light shade, provided the area is not invaded by tree roots. The planting hole should be about 2 feet in diameter and 1½ feet deep, and the soil liberally supplemented with peat moss or leaf mold. (Do not use manure; it may make the roots rot and foster disease.) For each plant, mix a double handful of bone meal with the soil. Plant peonies in early fall. Nurseries sell three- to five-bud divisions of named varieties, which should be set so that the tops of the buds are no more than 2 inches below the surface of the soil. In heavy clay soil plant them 1 inch deep. Shallow planting will not hurt the plants; it encourages flower production. Twice a year, in early spring and fall, sprinkle a handful of bone meal around each plant and scratch it into the soil. Peonies usually take three to five years to attain mature size; there may be no blossoms the first year and only a few the second season. Once planted, peonies can be left to grow undisturbed indefinitely. Propagation of new plants by any method is difficult for the home gardener; new divisions of named varieties should be purchased.

PAMPAS GRASS See *Cortaderia*
PANSY See *Viola*

PAPAVER
P. nudicaule (Iceland poppy),
P. orientale (Oriental poppy)

The flowers of both these species are eye catching—Iceland poppies because of their abundance and Oriental poppies because of their size and brilliance. At close hand, the blossoms of both species seem to be made of silky tissue; most come in single-flowered form, with four or six petals, and in semidouble form, with up to a dozen petals. Gardeners are usually satisfied to enjoy the blossoms of Iceland and Oriental poppies outdoors, but they also make delightful bouquets if the flowers are cut just as the buds begin to burst open. Sear the stem ends immediately with a match or candle flame, then place the flowers in warm water (about 100° F.). Their seed pods are attractive and can be used in dried bouquets.

The Iceland poppy (best treated as a biennial or annual in the United States and Canada) has soft gray-green foliage growing in low clumps from which sprout wiry stems up to 2 feet tall. The sweet-scented 2- to 4-inch flowers come in many shades of red, pink, orange and yellow as well as white. Champagne Bubbles, with flowers of the same colors, is an especially fine strain. In most areas the blossoms appear from late spring until frost, but in hot climates they bloom in early spring. The flowers are dramatic when grown in the front of a border, especially if massed in large groups.

The common types of Oriental poppies are a flamboyant orange red, but newer varieties are available in a range of colors from white through delicate shades of pink to deep red. Many varieties have a black blotch at the base of each petal; all are studded in the center with a mound of black pollen-bearing stamens. The blossoms are 6 to 12 inches across and are borne on hairy-leaved plants 2½ to 4 feet tall. Especially recommended varieties are Barr's White, white with black spots; Helen Elizabeth, clear blood red; and the lushly petaled double-flowered Crimson Pompon, which is orange scarlet. Oriental poppies blossom in early summer, and their foliage dies down and disappears in mid- to late summer; for this reason they are best set among other plants, such as babies'-breath *(page 120),* whose developing foliage will cover the yellowing leaves of the poppies. In fall Oriental poppies send up fresh leaves that last through winter.

HOW TO GROW. Both species do best in full sun and very well-drained soil. Iceland poppies grow in Zones 2-10 and must be started from seeds. In Zones 2-7 seeds sown in early spring may blossom during the summer of the first year and make a striking display the second year; then the plants generally weaken and die. In Zones 8-10 Iceland poppies are generally treated as annuals; seeds sown in late summer provide flowers the following spring. Space Iceland poppies 8 to 10 inches apart.

Oriental poppies are perennials in Zones 3-8 and in the parts of Zone 9 on the West Coast where the nights are cool. Space the plants 15 to 18 inches apart. New plants can be started from 4- to 6-inch root cuttings of dormant plants taken in mid- to late summer and planted as shown in the drawings on page 87; they usually flower when two years old. Set the tops of the root cuttings 3 inches below the surface of the soil.

PEA, PERENNIAL See *Lathyrus*
PEARLY EVERLASTING See *Anaphalis*

PENSTEMON
P. gloxinioides (penstemon, beardtongue)

Penstemons grow from low clumps of dark green foliage and send up thin spikes of 2-inch white or white-throated pink, red or lavender flowers. Prairie Fire is a durable scarlet-crimson variety that grows up to 3 feet tall and blossoms most of the summer if faded flowers are removed; Firebird, crimson, grows 1½ to 2 feet tall and also blossoms most of the summer; Newberry, purplish blue, grows 12 inches tall and blossoms in early summer and occasionally again later in the season; Indian Jewels, 1½ to 2 feet tall, comes in all the penstemon colors and blossoms mostly in early summer, although it may flower again in fall if faded flowers are removed before producing seeds.

HOW TO GROW. Penstemons grow in Zones 6-10, but are extremely sensitive to winter moisture and do best in raised beds. In gardens where the drainage is not excellent, the

ORIENTAL POPPY
Papaver orientale

PENSTEMON
Penstemon gloxinioides 'Firebird'

For climate zones and months of flowering, see page 151.

137

plants should be dug up in the fall and stored until spring in protected cold frames. Penstemons will grow in full sun or light shade, and need acid soil (pH 5.5 to 6.5) that has been liberally enriched with compost or leaf mold. Set plants 12 to 18 inches apart. In Zones 6 and 7 penstemons may be treated like other perennials, but should be protected with a 4- to 6-inch-thick winter mulch of salt hay or straw. Seed-grown types can also be grown there as annuals if started indoors in midwinter for flowers 12 to 14 weeks later. In Zones 8-10 new plants of seed-grown types should be started in summer to flower the following spring. For home propagation of named varieties, which are sold as living plants, take stem cuttings in spring to produce new flowering plants the following year, or divide clumps in early spring. Clumps of mature plants should be dug up and divided every other year of flowering.

PEONY See *Paeonia*

PHLOX
P. carolina, also called *P. suffruticosa* (Carolina phlox); *P. divaricata,* also called *P. canadensis* (Canada phlox, wild blue phlox); *P. paniculata,* also called *P. decussata* (garden phlox, summer phlox); *P. subulata* (moss phlox, moss pink, ground pink)

Phloxes are the most widely grown perennials, for good reasons. They bear spectacular flowers, many of which are fragrant, and they are easy to grow. The original species and many early varieties of Carolina, garden and moss phloxes are still cultivated, although long surpassed by new ones with clearer colors and larger blossoms.

Carolina phlox grows 2½ to 3 feet tall and has 8- to 10-inch conical clusters of hundreds of ¾-inch pink or white fragrant flowers. It blooms for about six weeks from early to midsummer, starting a full month before garden phlox. If the first blossoms are cut, plants often bloom again in late summer or early fall. Two outstanding varieties are Miss Lingard, pure white, and Rosalinde, pink.

The 1-foot-tall Canada phlox and its variety Lapham's phlox, *P. divaricata laphamii,* are lovely in late spring. The soft blue or white flowers, less than an inch across, are borne in loose clusters that cover the plants completely. Canada phlox is most often used in the front of a border, but also grows untended in lightly shaded wooded areas. If faded flowers are sheared off, the plant produces fresh foliage that is attractive all season.

The 2- to 4-foot garden phlox is the backbone of most summer gardens, since varieties are available to bloom almost any time from early summer to late summer. They bear huge clusters of sweetly scented disk-shaped flowers an inch or more across, in colors ranging from snowy white through every shade of pink to red and from pale blue to deep purple. Many varieties' flowers have conspicuous central eyes of contrasting colors. Individual clusters on a single stem are often of bouquet size, 12 to 14 inches tall and 6 to 10 inches or more across, but the flowers fade quickly when cut. Removing faded flower heads, however, encourages a second flowering and, more important, prevents the ripening and dispersal of seeds, which generally produce undesirable plants that crowd out the superior named varieties.

A favorite for rock gardens, moss phlox begins the gardener's year in early spring with sheets of vivid color made up of thousands of flowers clothing the tops of 4- to 5-inch plants. The flowers on newer varieties may be an inch across and are available in white as well as many shades of pink, red, blue and lavender. Moss phlox has evergreen foliage of closely set, tiny needlelike leaves. After the flow-

CANADA PHLOX
Phlox divaricata laphamii

GARDEN PHLOX
Phlox paniculata 'Starfire'

ers fade, the tops of the plants should be sheared back about halfway; the plants then produce fresh foliage and may blossom again, sparsely, in the fall.

HOW TO GROW. All the phloxes described can be grown in Zones 3-9, but do best in Zones 4-7. Carolina and garden phloxes grow in full sun or light shade, in a moist soil rich in compost or leaf mold. Space these plants about 18 inches apart. In spring when young shoots are 4 to 6 inches tall, thin each clump to four or five shoots spaced 4 to 6 inches apart to get the largest possible flower clusters (drawings, page 49). New plants of Carolina phlox can be started from stem cuttings taken in summer to flower the following year; garden phlox can be grown from 2-inch root cuttings taken in fall to flower in two years. To propagate both, divide clumps in spring or fall after four or five years of flowering.

Canada phlox does best in light shade in moist soil rich in organic matter, but will grow in full sun if there is sufficient moisture. Set plants 8 to 12 inches apart. New plants may be grown from stem cuttings taken in summer to flower the following year or by dividing clumps after the plants have had two years of flowering.

Moss phlox needs full sun and well-drained soil. Set plants 8 to 12 inches apart. New plants can be started easily from stem cuttings taken in summer to flower the next year or from clump divisions taken in spring after the flowers fade. Before planting the divisions, cut foliage halfway to the ground to lessen the load on the sparse root system.

PHORMIUM
P. tenax (New Zealand flax)

The sword-shaped leaves of New Zealand flax, which grow in massive clumps 4 to 8 feet high, dominate many West Coast gardens, especially in Southern California. The leaves of several varieties are dramatically colored. Most are shades of purplish red, although one type, the variegated New Zealand flax, has prominent ivory-white stripes. In early summer and midsummer the plants extend zigzag stalks with 1- to 2-inch mahogany or yellow flowers about 2 feet above the tops of the leaves. New Zealand flax is tough enough to withstand heat, wind and seaside conditions. Because of its bold lines New Zealand flax is most often used in gardens as an accent plant.

HOW TO GROW. New Zealand flax thrives along the West Coast in Zones 9 and 10, but it is often grown in Zone 8 even though its foliage may be damaged during the winter. (Injured leaves should be cut away; new ones will replace them in the spring.) The plant grows in full sun and almost any soil, wet or dry. Set plants 6 feet apart. Start new plants from divisions of clumps in early spring before new growth starts. Clumps usually need dividing after four or five years to prevent overcrowding.

PHYSALIS
P. alkekengi, also called P. alkekengi franchetii
(Chinese lantern plant, bladder cherry)

The Chinese lantern plant is valued for its inflated orange-red seed coverings which resemble miniature Chinese lanterns. The plants should be set apart, for they tend to spread and overwhelm other garden plants. They grow 1 to 2 feet tall, bearing 2- to 3-inch leaves that obscure tiny white flowers in summer. Inside each 2-inch-long lantern is an edible but insipid-tasting scarlet berry. For winter bouquets, pick the stems in fall just as the lanterns turn color, remove the leaves and hang the stems upside down to dry in a shady, airy place.

HOW TO GROW. Chinese lantern plants grow throughout Zones 3-10 in almost any soil in full sun or light shade. Set

NEW ZEALAND FLAX
Phormium tenax rubrum

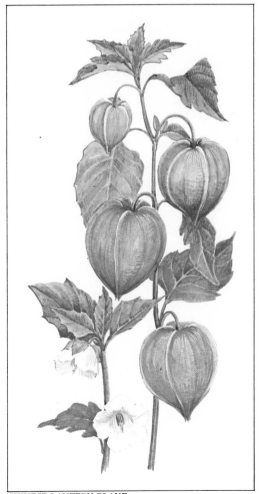

CHINESE LANTERN PLANT
Physalis alkekengi

For climate zones and months of flowering, see page 151.

FALSE DRAGONHEAD
Physostegia virginiana 'Vivid'

BALLOONFLOWER
Platycodon grandiflorus mariesii

the plants about 2 feet apart. New plants can be grown from seeds sown in spring, from root cuttings taken in fall or spring or from clump divisions in fall or spring; all will produce lanterns during the first growing season. Chinese lantern plants can remain undisturbed indefinitely.

PHYSOSTEGIA
P. virginiana, also called *Dracocephalum virginianum*
(false dragonhead, obedient plant, Virginia lion's-heart)

The flowers of false dragonheads, which resemble those of snapdragons, open during late summer and early fall. The plants grow 2 to 4 feet tall and have dark green willowlike leaves 3 to 5 inches long. The flower spikes, 8 to 10 inches long, are made up of four widely spaced vertical rows of small flowers. Among recommended varieties of false dragonhead, Vivid grows 2 feet tall and has deep pink flowers, Summer Glow grows 3 to 4 feet tall and has pale pink flowers, and Summer Snow grows about 2 feet tall and has translucent white flowers.

HOW TO GROW. False dragonheads can be grown throughout Zones 3-10 in sun or shade and in almost any soil, wet or dry. Set plants 15 to 18 inches apart. New plants can be started from divisions of clumps. To prevent overcrowding, dig up and divide clumps every second year of flowering.

PINCUSHION FLOWER See *Scabiosa*
PINK See *Dianthus*
PINK, GROUND See *Phlox*
PINK, MOSS See *Phlox*
PINK, MULLEIN See *Lychnis*

PLATYCODON
P. grandiflorus (balloonflower, Chinese bellflower)

Balloonflowers get their name from the way each flower bud swells before its starry petals unfold. The plants bear 2- to 3-inch cuplike blossoms on stems 2 to 3 feet tall. The flowers bloom throughout the summer and come in blue, pale pink or white. *P. grandiflorus mariesii,* a variety called Maries' balloonflower, grows 18 inches tall and comes only in blue and white. The flowers are excellent for cutting, but their stems should be seared with a match or candle flame before being placed in water.

HOW TO GROW. Balloonflowers grow in Zones 3-10 except in Florida and along the Gulf Coast. They thrive in full sun or light shade in well-drained garden soil. Set plants 12 to 18 inches apart. Be careful in spring when cultivating in the area where you have planted balloonflowers; they do not sprout until other plants have begun to grow, and it is easy to dig them up inadvertently. New plants can be started from seeds sown in spring or summer, but do not flower for two or three years. The clumps do not spread and should remain undisturbed.

PLEURISY ROOT See *Asclepias*
PLUMBAGO See *Ceratostigma*
POKER PLANT See *Kniphofia*

POLEMONIUM
P. caeruleum (Jacob's-ladder, Greek valerian, charity),
P. reptans (creeping Jacob's-ladder),
P. richardsonii (Richardson's Jacob's-ladder)

Jacob's-ladders are among the first perennials to produce new growth in spring, sending up mounds of feathery apple-green leaves that are topped from late spring to midsummer with soft clusters of dainty cup-shaped blossoms an inch or less across. Jacob's-ladder, with sky-blue flowers, and its pure white variety, *P. caeruleum album,* grow 2 to 2½ feet tall. Creeping Jacob's-ladder, a sprawling plant, reaches a height of only 6 to 8 inches and has blue or white flowers. Richardson's Jacob's-ladder bears blue-to-purple flowers on 9-inch stems in early summer.

HOW TO GROW. Jacob's-ladders grow in Zones 2-8 and do best in light shade and moist but well-drained soil that has been supplemented with compost, peat moss or leaf mold. They may also be grown in full sun if additional moisture is provided. Space plants about 18 inches apart. New plants can be grown from clump divisions or stem cuttings taken in spring or summer to bloom the next year. To prevent overcrowding, divide clumps after three or four years of flowering.

POLYGONUM
P. reynoutria (Reynoutria fleeceflower, dwarf polygonum)

The Reynoutria fleeceflower grows 12 to 18 inches tall and bears great numbers of tiny pink flowers that open from red buds in late summer and fall; its 1-inch heart-shaped leaves turn brilliant red in fall. The plant is easy to grow, and because its roots spread rapidly underground, it makes a good ground cover, but it should not be used where the roots may encroach upon other plants.

HOW TO GROW. Reynoutria fleeceflowers grow in Zones 4-8 and the West Coast strip of Zone 9, and thrive in full sun and almost any soil. Space plants 18 to 24 inches apart. Shear the plants to the ground early each spring to encourage fresh, vigorous growth. Propagate by division of clumps; if new plants are not desired, old plants can remain undisturbed indefinitely.

POPPY See *Papaver*
POPPY, CALIFORNIA TREE See *Romneya*
POPPY, HIMALAYAN BLUE See *Meconopsis*
POPPY, MATILIJA See *Romneya*
POPPY, PLUME See *Macleaya*
POPPY, WELSH See *Meconopsis*
PRIMROSE See *Primula*

PRIMULA
P. auricula (auricula primrose); *P. beesiana* (Bee's primrose); *P. bullesiana* (Bulle's primrose); *P. bulleyana* (Bulley's primrose); *P. cockburniana* (Cockburn's primrose); *P. cortusoides* (Cortusa primrose); *P. denticulata* (Himalayan primrose); *P. elatior* (oxlip primrose); *P. japonica* (Japanese primrose); *P. juliae* (Julia primrose); *P. polyantha* (polyanthus primrose); *P. rosea* (rose primrose); *P. sieboldii* (Siebold's primrose); *P. veris,* also called *P. officinalis* (cowslip); *P. vulgaris,* also called *P. acaulis* (English or true primrose)

Of the more than 500 kinds of primroses, the 15 species and hybrids recommended here are among the easiest to grow and among the most beautiful to behold. They present a procession of handsome blossoms, ½ to 2 inches across, that usually appear in 2- to 6-inch clusters. The flowers bloom from early to late spring.

The sweet-scented auriculas bear their clusters of 1-inch single (one ring of petals) or heavily petaled double blossoms atop 6- to 8-inch stems in midspring; the flowers range in color from creamy white through gray, rose, copper, chestnut red and reddish purple to deep blue, and appear above thick, leathery evergreen leaves. Four types that bear their flowers in candelabralike tiers from midspring to early summer are Bee's primrose, 1½ to 2 feet tall, with rosy lilac yellow-eyed flowers; Bulley's primrose, about 2½ feet tall, with golden-yellow flowers; Bulle's primrose, a cross between Bee's primrose and Bulley's primrose that grows about 2 feet tall and comes in shades of cream, rose, mauve, rust red, wine red and purple; and

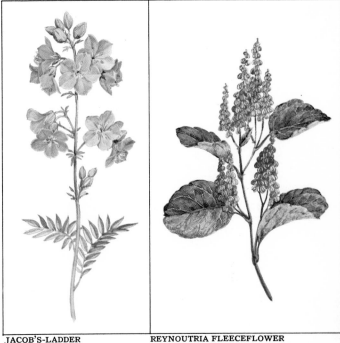

JACOB'S-LADDER
Polemonium caeruleum

REYNOUTRIA FLEECEFLOWER
Polygonum reynoutria

HIMALAYAN PRIMROSE
Primula denticulata

For climate zones and months of flowering, see page 151.

JAPANESE PRIMROSE
Primula japonica

POLYANTHUS PRIMROSE
Primula polyantha

Cockburn's primrose, about 1½ feet tall, with coppery scarlet flowers.

The Cortusa primrose bears clusters of bright rosy pink flowers on 8- to 10-inch stems in midspring, sometimes with two tiers of flowers on a stem. The Himalayan primrose bears ½-inch soft lilac flowers in 2-inch ball-like clusters atop 8- to 12-inch stems in early spring and has foliage that is covered with a whitish yellow powder; the flowers of the variety *P. denticulata cachemiriana*, the Kashmir primrose, are purple with yellow centers. The oxlip primrose has evergreen leaves and produces large clusters of pale yellow blossoms on 8-inch stems in midspring. The Japanese primrose, one of the most popular of the candelabra types, grows about 2 feet tall and bears white, pink, rose, deep crimson or terra-cotta blossoms from late spring to early summer. The Julia primrose produces wine-red flowers, but its hybrid, called Juliana, is available in white, cream, yellow, pink, red and deep purple; the plants grow about 3 inches tall and blossom so profusely in midspring that their evergreen foliage becomes hidden.

The polyanthus primrose, the most familiar primrose, grows 8 to 12 inches tall and in midspring bears immense clusters of single or double flowers, some as large as silver dollars. A hybrid with evergreen foliage, it comes in an amazing color range, with seedlings often showing up in striped or blended combinations of white, gray, ivory, yellow, pink, lavender, salmon, burnt orange, copper, bronze, chestnut, brown, blue and purple.

The rose primrose sends up its flowering stems before its leaves appear in midspring; the plants grow 8 to 10 inches tall and have clusters of rose-pink flowers. Varieties of Siebold's primrose come in white, pink, rose, crimson and purple; the flowers are borne in clusters on 8- to 10-inch stems in midspring above crinkled scallop-edged leaves that die away in late summer and reappear the following spring. The cowslip is an evergreen species about 8 inches tall; its flowers bloom in midspring and are normally cream to yellow in color, but selections are also available in copper red and purple, as well as in a double yellow form known as hose-in-hose, in which one cuplike flower is set within another. The delightfully fragrant English primrose, so often mentioned by Elizabethan poets, blooms singly on 6-inch stems in midspring and has evergreen leaves. One of the parents of the polyanthus primrose, it is normally a soft "primrose" yellow in color, but also comes in pink, red, apricot, amber, blue and purple, and in heavily petaled double as well as single forms.

HOW TO GROW. When William Wordsworth wrote, "A primrose by a river's brim," he was noting a situation that all primroses find congenial. None should be allowed to become dry at any time, and some—notably Bee's, Bulle's, Bulley's, Japanese, rose and Siebold's primroses—need more than ordinary amounts of moisture and thrive in boggy situations, such as beside a pond or brook. All grow best in partial shade and an acid soil well supplemented with organic matter such as leaf mold or compost. Auricula, Cortusa and polyanthus primroses grow well in Zones 3-8; Himalayan, Julia, Siebold's and English primroses in Zones 4-8; oxlip primroses, Japanese primroses and cowslips in Zones 5-8; and Bee's, Bulle's, Bulley's, Cockburn's and rose primroses in Zones 6-8. Primroses like cool moist weather, especially during summer, and do best in southern Canada, the Great Lakes region, New England, the Pacific Northwest and a narrow strip along the coast of Northern California.

Space plants 6 to 12 inches apart. New plants of named varieties and most heavily petaled double forms (but not strains of polyanthus primroses) can be propagated only by dividing clumps immediately after the plants have flowered. All other primroses are most easily grown from seeds. If seeds are sown in a bed protected by a cold frame in late fall, the plants will sprout in the spring and probably blossom a second season. Since some types, such as the Japanese primrose, often act as biennials, especially in mild climates, and die after flowering, sow a few seeds each year to ensure a steady supply of flowering plants. Many species drop seeds yearly, and the seedlings are worth keeping. Primrose clumps should be dug up and divided immediately after the plants flower when they become overcrowded, usually every year or two.

PULMONARIA
P. angustifolia (blue or cowslip lungwort),
P. saccharata (Bethlehem sage)

Blue lungwort and Bethlehem sage are excellent for shady gardens and provide a display of colors in spring when their drooping clusters of trumpet-shaped ½-inch pink flowers soon change to sky blue; the blue lungwort is also available in pink- and white-flowering varieties. The blue lungwort grows 8 to 12 inches tall and has 4- to 6-inch leaves. Bethlehem sage blooms from late spring to early summer; it grows about a foot tall and has white-spotted 3- to 6-inch leaves.

HOW TO GROW. Blue lungworts and Bethlehem sage grow well in Zones 3-9 except in Florida and along the Gulf Coast. They need shade and moist soil well supplemented with organic material such as peat moss, compost or leaf mold. Space plants about 10 inches apart. New plants can be grown from seeds sown in early spring or from clumps divided in early fall; water clump divisions well to enable them to develop a root system before cold weather. Propagated either way, new plants will bloom the following year. Divide clumps after three or four years of flowering.

PYRETHRUM See *Chrysanthemum*

Q

QUEEN OF THE MEADOW See *Filipendula*
QUEEN OF THE PRAIRIE See *Filipendula*

R

RED-HOT POKER See *Kniphofia*
ROCKET See *Hesperis*

ROMNEYA
R. coulteri (matilija poppy, California tree poppy)

The fragrant flowers of the matilija poppy are distinctive: they are 3 to 6 inches across and have golden centers surrounded by six snow-white petals that resemble crumpled silk. They bloom from early summer to early fall, one on each of the short branches that cover the 4- to 8-foot plants. Although they are rather short lived, lasting only two to four days, they make handsome bouquets; pick them just before the buds open and sear the ends with a match or candle flame before putting them in water.

HOW TO GROW. Matilija poppies do best in the southwestern parts of Zones 8-10 where rainfall is scant in the summer, but can also be grown in Zones 6 and 7 if given excellent drainage and if covered with a thick winter mulch such as salt-marsh hay. They require full sun and flower most freely in dry infertile soil. They are best planted by themselves because their underground roots spread rapidly and can encroach on other plants. Space plants 3 to 4 feet apart. Cut plants back to about 6 inches from the ground in early fall to encourage fresh growth the following year. New plants should be grown from seeds sown in

BLUE LUNGWORT
Pulmonaria angustifolia

MATILIJA POPPY
Romneya coulteri

For climate zones and months of flowering, see page 151.

143

spring, but require two or three years to reach flowering size. Plants are best left to grow undisturbed indefinitely.

ROSE, CHRISTMAS See *Helleborus*
ROSE, LENTEN See *Helleborus*
ROSE CAMPION See *Lychnis*

RUDBECKIA

R. fulgida (orange coneflower); *R. hirta gloriosa,* also called *R. gloriosa* (gloriosa daisy); *R. laciniata* (cut-leaved coneflower)

Rudbeckia coneflowers are often confused with coneflowers in the genus *Echinacea (page 115).* The distinguishing characteristic of *Rudbeckia* coneflowers is their color, always a shade of yellow with a dark center; *Echinacea* coneflowers come in other colors. Outstanding, easy-to-grow varieties of the orange coneflower are Goldquelle, a 2½-foot plant that bears lemon-yellow heavily petaled double flowers 3 inches or more across in late summer and early fall, and Goldsturm, which grows 2 feet tall and bears 3- to 4-inch golden-yellow flowers from midsummer to mid-fall. The gloriosa daisy, a handsome 2½-foot hybrid that bears 5- to 7-inch daisylike flowers all summer long in many shades of yellow, orange and mahogany, all with dark brown centers; the flowers come in single form with one ring of petals, or heavily petaled doubles. An excellent descendant of the old-fashioned cut-leaved coneflower is the 4- to 5-foot variety Golden Globe, whose heavily petaled 3-inch bright yellow blossoms appear in late summer and early fall; it spreads rapidly and should be planted where it will not encroach upon neighboring plants.

HOW TO GROW. Coneflowers thrive in Zones 3-10 in well-drained soil and full sun, but tolerate light shade. Space plants 12 to 15 inches apart. Gloriosa daisies should be grown only from seeds sown in early spring; plants will blossom the first year and live for many years, multiplying in the garden by dropping their own seeds. Propagate all other types by clump divisions. To prevent overcrowding, divide clumps every other year of flowering.

S

SAGE See *Salvia*
SAGE, BETHLEHEM See *Pulmonaria*
ST.-JOHN'S-WORT See *Hypericum*

SALVIA

S. azurea (blue sage); *S. haematodes* (bloodvein sage); *S. pitcherii* (Pitcher's sage); *S. superba,* also called *S. virgata nemerosa* (violet sage). (All also called salvia)

Most perennial sages have blue or violet flowers, distinguishing them from the popular annual, scarlet sage. The blue sage grows 3 to 4 feet tall and sends out slender spikes of ½-inch sky-blue flowers in late summer and early fall. Pitcher's sage closely resembles the blue sage, but its flowers are a darker blue. Bloodvein sage grows about 3 feet tall and from early to midsummer bears great masses of ½-inch lavender-blue flowers on many stems. It often acts as a biennial and dies after flowering. It has 4- to 9-inch red-veined gray-green leaves, most of which lie flat on the ground. The violet sage, a hybrid, grows 2 to 3 feet tall and bears short spikes of ½-inch violet flowers from early to midsummer. Its variety East Friesland has dark violet flowers and grows 1½ feet tall. All sages make excellent cut flowers.

HOW TO GROW. Sages will grow in Zones 5-10, and blue sage will also grow in Zone 4. They do best in full sun and very well-drained soil. Space plants 15 to 18 inches apart. Blue sage, bloodvein sage and Pitcher's sage can be grown

ORANGE CONEFLOWER
Rudbeckia fulgida 'Goldsturm'

BLOODVEIN SAGE
Salvia haematodes

PITCHER'S SAGE
Salvia pitcherii

from seeds sown in summer to flower the next year; blue sage, Pitcher's sage and violet sage can be propagated from stem cuttings taken in early summer to flower the following year, but the cuttings are difficult to root. Clumps should remain undisturbed indefinitely.

SANTOLINA
S. chamaecyparissus, also called *S. incana* (lavender cotton); *S. virens* (green lavender cotton)

Lavender cotton is valued more for its foliage and shrub-like appearance than for its flowers. It has woody stems and fernlike, aromatic, silvery gray foliage. If left unpruned, lavender cotton may grow 2 feet tall and 3 feet across. Most gardeners never even see the 3/4-inch buttonlike yellow flowers that bloom from early to midsummer because they shear the plants back occasionally to stimulate growth of fresh new foliage. Lavender cotton is effective in mass plantings in a border or as an edging along a garden path. Green lavender cotton presents a bright green counterpart to lavender cotton, and the two species are often used together.

HOW TO GROW. Lavender cottons grow as perennials in Zones 7-10 and as annuals elsewhere. They need full sun but will thrive in almost any soil. Set plants 18 to 24 inches apart. Old plants should be cut to a height of 4 to 6 inches in the spring to encourage fresh new growth. New plants can be started from stem cuttings taken in spring or summer. Clumps can remain undisturbed indefinitely.

SCABIOSA
S. caucasica (pincushion flower)

Prominent dark gray pollen-bearing stamens that stand out like pins from the center of the pincushion flower give the plant its name. The 2- to 2½-foot stalks bear 3-inch blossoms from summer to early fall, and even later if faded flowers are removed. In addition to the light blue of the basic species, mauve, lavender, violet, blue and white varieties are available.

HOW TO GROW. Pincushion flowers will grow in Zones 3-10 except in Florida and along the Gulf Coast. They do best in full sun and need soil that is moist during the growing season and extremely well drained in winter. Plant pincushion flowers 12 to 15 inches apart. New plants can be grown from clump divisions or from seeds sown in summer for blooming the following year. To prevent overcrowding, divide clumps every two to four years.

SCARLET LIGHTNING See *Lychnis*
SEA PINK See *Armeria*

SEDUM
S. spectabile
(showy stonecrop, also called live-forever, sedum)

The showy stonecrop grows about 18 inches tall and from late summer to late fall bears 3- to 4-inch clusters of tiny ivory, pink or red flowers at the ends of its stems. Its thick leaves die to the ground each year, but the plant is noted for its strength; it is tolerant of drought and is pest free. Several excellent varieties are available, including Brilliant, raspberry red; Carmine, rose red; Meteor, deep carmine red; and Star Dust, ivory. The showy stonecrop is suitable for borders as well as rock gardens.

HOW TO GROW. The showy stonecrop grows well throughout Zones 3-10 in full sun or light shade in almost any soil, preferably well drained. Set plants 18 to 24 inches apart. New plants can be started from stem cuttings taken in summer to bloom the next year or by clump divisions. Except for propagation purposes, leave clumps undisturbed.

LAVENDER COTTON
Santolina chamaecyparissus

PINCUSHION FLOWER
Scabiosa caucasica

SHOWY STONECROP
Sedum spectabile 'Meteor'

For climate zones and months of flowering, see page 151.

HYBRID PRAIRIE MALLOW
Sidalcea hybrid

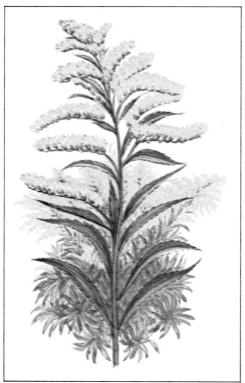

HYBRID GOLDENROD
Solidago 'Goldenmosa'

SENNA, WILD See *Cassia*

SIDALCEA

S. hybrids (hybrid prairie mallow; often sold under the name miniature hollyhock)

Prairie mallows grow 1½ to 4 feet tall and have a great many branching spikes, covered in mid- to late summer with 1- to 1½-inch cup-shaped flowers ranging in color from blush pink to crimson. If faded flowers are removed, the plants will blossom through midfall. The leaves of the prairie mallows are an attractive palm shape that is scalloped or deeply lobed. One excellent strain is Rosy Gem, whose color reflects its name. Prairie mallows are excellent for cutting.

HOW TO GROW. Prairie mallows grow well in Zones 5-10 except in Florida and along the Gulf Coast. They need full sun and well-drained soil. Strains of hybrid prairie mallows such as Rosy Gem must be started from seeds sown in summer to bloom the next year. Once established, plants can be multiplied by dividing clumps, which develop quite rapidly and usually need to be dug up and divided every three or four years.

SNAKEROOT See *Cimicifuga*
SNEEZEWEED See *Helenium*
SNEEZEWORT See *Achillea*

SOLIDAGO

S. hybrids (hybrid goldenrod)

Although goldenrods may be more familiar as wild flowers than as garden flowers, several delightful goldenrod perennials have recently been developed; their 10- to 12-inch yellow flower heads, composed of many tiny blossoms, combine especially well in borders with lavender and purple hardy asters. Some begin to blossom in midsummer, others later, and last through fall. Among the best varieties of hybrid goldenrods are Goldenmosa, which has dark yellow flowers in late summer and grows up to 3 feet tall; Leraft, which has bright golden-yellow flowers in late summer and is also 3 feet tall; Peter Pan, also known as Goldstrahl, which has bright canary-yellow flowers in early fall and grows up to 2½ feet tall.

HOW TO GROW. Goldenrods grow in full sun or very light shade in Zones 3-10, and thrive in almost any soil. Set plants 18 inches apart. New plants of named varieties should be started by clump divisions; clumps should be divided when they become overcrowded, usually after every three or four years of flowering.

SOLIDASTER

S. luteus, also called *S. hybridus, Aster hybridus luteus, Asterago lutea* (solidaster)

In 1909 a nurseryman in Lyons, France, achieved the unusual feat of crossing an aster and a goldenrod, plants from two separate genera. The resulting hybrid, named solidaster—from *Solidago* (goldenrod) and *Aster*—inherited its golden-yellow color from its goldenrod parent and its masses of ½-inch starlike flowers from the aster side of the family. Its flowers, good for cutting, blossom from midsummer to early fall; the plant grows 1½ to 2 feet high and may billow to spread twice that wide.

HOW TO GROW. Solidasters can be grown in Zones 5-10 except in Florida and along the Gulf Coast. They do best in well-drained soil and full sun, but will tolerate light shade. Set plants 15 to 18 inches apart. New plants can be started by dividing and resetting clumps in spring or fall. To prevent overcrowding, clumps should be divided after every three years of flowering.

SPEEDWELL See *Veronica*
SPIDERWORT, VIRGINIA See *Tradescantia*
SPIREA, FALSE See *Astilbe*
SPURGE See *Euphorbia*

STACHYS

S. macrantha, also called *S. grandiflora, Betonica grandiflora* (big betony, woundwort); *S. olympica,* also called *S. lanata* (lamb's ears, woolly betony)

Big betony, which may grow as tall as 3 feet, bears spikes of 1-inch deep violet flowers in early and midsummer. The flowers, good for cutting, are arranged in closely set whorls along the spikes. The wrinkled hairy leaves of this species are heart-shaped and have scalloped edges. Lamb's ears, or woolly betony, is most notable for its silvery white tongue-shaped leaves, which are 4 to 6 inches long. This species grows 12 to 18 inches tall and begins to bear spikes of small pinkish purple flowers in early summer; they will bloom until frost if faded flowers are removed. The foliage is highly prized.

HOW TO GROW. Both species grow in Zones 3-10 except in Florida and along the Gulf Coast. They do best in full sun and very well-drained soil. Space plants 12 to 18 inches apart. New plants may be started by sowing seeds in early spring for flowering the following year or by dividing clumps in early spring or early fall. To prevent overcrowding, divide clumps after two or three years of flowering.

STATICE See *Limonium*

STOKESIA

S. laevis, also called *S. cyanea*
(Stokes's aster, cornflower aster)

The Stokes's aster, a wild flower particularly suited to cultivation in the southeastern United States, grows 12 to 18 inches tall and bears a continuous crop of 3- to 4-inch asterlike flowers from midsummer until fall; its shiny leaves are 2 to 8 inches long. In addition to the popular blue variety, there are types with white, pink, purple and pale yellow blossoms. All are excellent for cutting.

HOW TO GROW. Stokes's asters can be grown in Zones 5-10. They do best in full sun and need very well-drained soil, particularly in Zones 5 and 6. Set plants 12 to 15 inches apart. New plants can be started from divisions of clumps or root cuttings made in spring, or from seeds sown in spring to flower the next year. To prevent overcrowding, clumps should be divided every three or four years.

STONECROP See *Sedum*
SUCCORY, BLUE See *Catananche*
SUNDROPS See *Oenothera*
SWEET WILLIAM See *Dianthus*
SWEET WOODRUFF See *Asperula*

T

THALICTRUM

T. aquilegifolium (columbine meadow rue); *T. dipterocarpum* (Yunnan meadow rue); *T. rochebrunianum* (lavender mist meadow rue); *T. speciosissimum,* also called *T. glaucum, T. rugosum* (dusty meadow rue)

The lacy fernlike foliage of meadow rues enhances the cloudlike clusters of tiny blossoms that engulf the plants' tops. Most species grow 3 to 4 feet tall and are effective at the back of a border or in a shady nook. The blossoms are excellent for cutting.

Columbine meadow rue, 2½ to 3 feet tall, sends up huge clusters of lavender, white or rose-pink flowers from late spring to early summer. An excellent strain is Purple

SOLIDASTER
Solidaster luteus

BIG BETONY
Stachys macrantha

LAMB'S EARS
Stachys olympica

STOKES'S ASTER
Stokesia laevis

For climate zones and months of flowering, see page 151.

LAVENDER MIST MEADOW RUE
Thalictrum rochebrunianum

CAROLINA THERMOPSIS
Thermopsis caroliniana

VIRGINIA SPIDERWORT
Tradescantia virginiana

Mist, whose flowers are a rich rosy purple. Yunnan meadow rue grows up to 5 feet tall and in late summer and early fall bears enormous clusters of lavender flowers. Lavender mist meadow rue, probably the finest species of meadow rue available, bears masses of rosy lavender flowers with yellow pollen-bearing stamens. It blossoms from midsummer to early fall. The dusty meadow rue has fragrant fuzzy yellow flowers that blossom in great clusters in midsummer. Its handsome bluish green leaves help make it a favorite for cut-flower arrangements.

HOW TO GROW. Lavender mist meadow rue will grow in Zones 4-10, the other species in Zones 5-10, but none will grow in Florida and the Gulf Coast area. They do best in moist soil enriched with compost or leaf mold. Meadow rues thrive in very light shade, but tolerate full sun if the soil is moist. Excellent drainage in winter is vital in Zones 4 and 5. A light winter mulch such as salt hay or straw is advisable from Zone 6 north. Plant meadow rues 15 to 18 inches apart. They can be started from the current season's seeds, sown in summer or fall to bloom two years later. Clumps may be divided in spring for propagation or left undisturbed indefinitely.

THERMOPSIS
T. caroliniana (Carolina thermopsis)

The Carolina thermopsis bears pea-shaped blossoms in 10- to 12-inch spikes from early to midsummer atop broadly spreading plants that grow 3 to 4 feet tall. The flowers, which are good for cutting, combine well with blue delphiniums, which flower at the same time.

HOW TO GROW. Carolina thermopsis grows throughout Zones 3-10. It does best in fertile well-drained soil and full sun, although it can tolerate light shade. Set plants 3 to 4 feet apart. Propagate new plants from newly produced seeds, sown in summer to bloom two years later; dust the seeds before planting with a nitrifying bacteria sold by seedsmen. Clumps can remain undisturbed indefinitely.

THISTLE, GLOBE See *Echinops*
THRIFT See *Armeria*

TRADESCANTIA
T. virginiana (Virginia spiderwort)

Modern varieties of the Virginia spiderwort grow about 18 inches tall and bear 1½- to 3-inch flowers in shades of violet blue, pink and red, as well as white. Although individual flowers live only one day, new ones continue to open from spring through early summer. By late spring the foot-long grasslike leaves and stems become weak and floppy; if cut to the ground at that time they will blossom again in the fall. Good named varieties are Blue Stone, deep blue; Pauline, orchid pink; Purple Dome, brilliant purple; Red Cloud, rosy red; and Snowcap, white.

HOW TO GROW. Virginia spiderworts grow in Zones 4-10 in almost any soil but do best in moist soil and light shade. Set plants 12 to 15 inches apart. Clumps of named varieties can be divided for propagation in spring after three or four years of flowering. New plants can also be grown from seeds sown in spring or summer to flower the following year; their color, however, is unpredictable.

TRITOMA See *Kniphofia*

TROLLIUS
T. cultorum (hybrid globeflower), *T. europaeus* (common globeflower), *T. ledebourii* (Ledebour globeflower)

Globeflowers, relatives of the buttercup, bear yellow-to-orange flowers 2 to 4 inches across and bloom from late spring to late summer if flowers are removed as they fade. They grow 1 to 2 feet tall and have palmlike leaves; the flower stalks of some varieties reach 3 feet in moist rich soil. Hybrid globeflowers, widely grown in Europe, are not generally available in the U.S. in the form of living plants, but seeds of these excellent large-flowered hybrids can be purchased. The common globeflower has 2-inch yellow flowers with dark yellow centers, and the Ledebour globeflower has 2- to 2½-inch orange flowers. All globeflowers are long lasting when cut.

HOW TO GROW. Globeflowers grow in Zones 3-10 except in Florida and along the Gulf Coast. They thrive in full sun or light shade. They are suited to moist soil—even the wet ground beside a pool or brook—but the soil must be liberally supplemented with peat moss, leaf mold, compost or cow manure. Plant globeflowers 10 to 12 inches apart. New plants can be started by clump divisions or by sowing seeds in the fall to bloom the following spring. Divide clumps after four or five years of flowering.

TURTLEHEAD See *Chelone*

V

VALERIAN See *Valeriana*
VALERIAN, GREEK See *Polemonium*
VALERIAN, RED See *Centranthus*

VALERIANA
V. officinalis (common valerian, garden heliotrope)

The common valerian bears tiny pinkish white flowers in airy 4-inch clusters in mid- to late summer; their fragrance resembles that of heliotrope, accounting for the plant's other common name. Plants grow 3 to 4 feet tall and have attractive fernlike foliage; the flowers are excellent for cutting.

HOW TO GROW. Common valerian grows in Zones 3-10 in sun or shade in almost any soil, and even tolerates very moist conditions. Space plants 15 to 18 inches apart. New plants can be started from clump divisions or from seeds sown in summer to flower the following year. Divide clumps after every three years of flowering.

VERBASCUM
V. hybrids (hybrid mullein)

Hybrid mulleins are stately many-branched plants with large fuzzy gray leaves that grow in low clumps. The 3- to 4-foot stems are laden with 1-inch pink, white, yellow, amber or lavender flowers from midsummer to early fall. Fine varieties are Pink Domino, with rosy pink flowers, and Cotswold Gem, with purple-centered yellow flowers.

HOW TO GROW. Mulleins will grow in Zones 4-10 in full sun and almost any well-drained soil; excellent drainage is vital in northern areas. Plant mulleins 12 to 15 inches apart. Since plants sometimes die after blossoming, start new plants each year as replacements. Propagate named varieties from root cuttings taken in early spring to blossom the same year. New plants can also be grown from seeds sown in spring or early summer to blossom the next year; their color, however, cannot be foretold.

VERONICA
V. incana (woolly speedwell); *V. longifolia*, also called *V. maritima* (clump speedwell); *V. spicata* (spike speedwell); *V. teucrium*, also called *V. latifolia* (Hungarian speedwell)

Speedwells are highly valued as long-blooming plants that grow 12 to 18 inches tall and bear colorful 6- to 8-inch spikes of tiny flowers. The woolly speedwell has silvery

LEDEBOUR GLOBEFLOWER
Trollius ledebourii

COMMON VALERIAN
Valeriana officinalis

HYBRID MULLEIN
Verbascum hybrids

For climate zones and months of flowering, see page 151.

SPIKE SPEEDWELL
Veronica spicata 'Minuet'

VIOLA
Viola williamsii

PANSY
Viola wittrockiana

leaves and bears light blue flowers in early and midsummer; the variety Saraband has deep violet flowers all summer. The most famous variety of clump speedwell, *V. longifolia subsessilis,* bears royal-blue flowers on slender 2-foot spikes from midsummer until fall; another variety called Icicle has white flowers. Three excellent 18-inch varieties of the spike speedwell blossom all summer: Barcarolle, deep pink; Minuet, medium pink; and Pavane, rose pink. Crater Lake Blue, a superb variety of the Hungarian speedwell, bears deep blue flowers all summer.

HOW TO GROW. Speedwells grow in Zones 3-10 except in Florida and along the Gulf Coast. They need full sun and well-drained soil. Set plants 12 to 15 inches apart. Start named varieties from stem cuttings in spring and summer for flowering the next year. Divide clumps in spring or fall after every three or four years of flowering.

VIOLA
V. odorata (sweet violet); *V. williamsii* (viola, tufted pansy); *V. wittrockiana,* also called *V. tricolor hortensis, V. tricolor maxima; V. tricolor* (both called pansy)

Sweet violets grow about 8 inches tall and from mid- to late spring produce ¾-inch pink, white or purple flowers, some single, with one ring of petals, some heavily petaled doubles. The familiar pansy grows about 8 inches tall and has 2- to 3-inch flowers in many shades and combinations of yellow, pink, dark red, brown, blue, purple and white. Although a true perennial, the pansy weakens with the arrival of hot weather and is treated as a biennial. Plants blossom profusely from early spring to midsummer. Viola flowers are similar to pansies but are smaller and generally come in solid shades of blue, purple, yellow and red, as well as white. Violas blossom from early spring until frost in Zones 3-8, from winter until midsummer in Zones 9 and 10. All three species make lovely, fragrant cut flowers.

HOW TO GROW. Sweet violets grow in Zones 6-10, violas and pansies in Zones 3-10. All do best in light shade and moist soil liberally enriched with compost or leaf mold. Set plants 8 inches apart. Propagate sweet violets by clump division; single-flowered varieties can also be grown from seeds sown in summer to blossom the following year. Pansies are easily grown from seeds in Zones 3-8; sow the seeds outdoors in midsummer in light shade, then transplant them to a sunny reserve garden until the following spring. To protect the evergreen leaves over winter in Zones 3-6, apply a 4- to 6-inch mulch of salt hay or straw. If early flowering is desired, grow the plants over winter in a cold frame. In Zones 9 and 10 sow pansy seeds in late summer; the plants will grow through the fall and blossom during winter and spring. Many types of violas can be started from seeds in the same manner as pansies, but named varieties must be propagated from stem cuttings or clump divisions in early spring for flowers the same season, or in early fall for flowers the following year.

VIOLET See *Viola*
VIOLET, DAME'S See *Hesperis*
VISCARIA See *Lychnis*

W
WALLFLOWER See *Cheiranthus*
WINE-CUP See *Callirhoë*
WOLFSBANE See *Aconitum*
WORMWOOD See *Artemisia*
WOUNDWORT See *Stachys*

Y
YARROW See *Achillea*

150

Appendix

Where and when perennials bloom

To indicate which species and varieties of plants will flourish in the region where you live, the encyclopedia entries in the preceding chapter include recommended growing areas keyed to the numbered zones on this map, which divides North America into 10 zones according to the depth of winter cold. The encyclopedia also indicates when each species usually blooms—spring, summer or fall. Calendar dates for the seasons—and for blooming—vary, of course, depending on the climate zone where the plant is being grown; within each zone, moreover, blooming time will vary according to local terrain, rainfall, nearness to bodies of water and the severity of a given winter. The table below lists the approximate months corresponding to the seasons in each zone (except for Zone 1, which embraces unpopulated subarctic regions). The fall season is considered to extend to the first frost, which generally takes place at approximately the time noted in the final column.

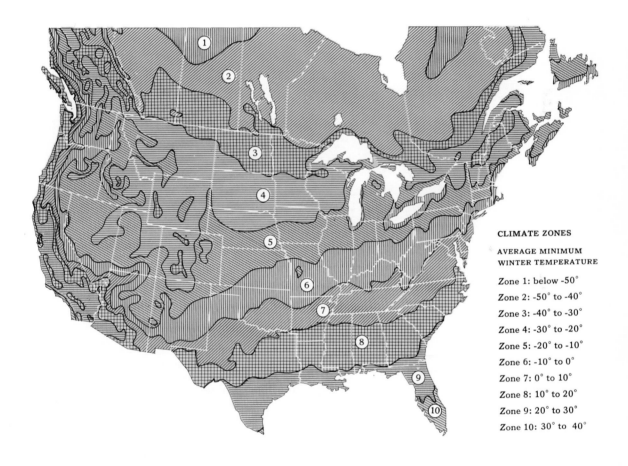

CLIMATE ZONES

AVERAGE MINIMUM
WINTER TEMPERATURE

Zone 1: below -50°

Zone 2: -50° to -40°

Zone 3: -40° to -30°

Zone 4: -30° to -20°

Zone 5: -20° to -10°

Zone 6: -10° to 0°

Zone 7: 0° to 10°

Zone 8: 10° to 20°

Zone 9: 20° to 30°

Zone 10: 30° to 40°

FLOWERING SEASONS IN YOUR ZONE

ZONE	SPRING	SUMMER	FALL	ZONE
1	(perennials not grown)			1
2	Mid-April to mid-June	Mid-June through July	August to early September	2
3	Early April to mid-June	Mid-June through July	August to mid-September	3
4	Late March to mid-June	Mid-June to mid-August	Mid-August to late September	4
5	Mid-March through May	June through August	September	5
6	Mid-March through May	June through August	September to early October	6
7	Early March through May	June through August	September to mid-October	7
8	Mid-February to mid-May	Mid-May to mid-September	Mid-September to late October	8
9	Mid-January to mid-April	Mid-April through September	October through November	9
10	January through March	April through September	October through December	10

Characteristics of 147 perennials and biennials

	FLOWER COLOR					FLOWER SIZE			FLOWER TYPES			BLOOMING SEASONS				PLANT HEIGHT			NOTED FOR		LIGHT		SOIL	
	White	Yellow to orange	Pink to red	Blue to purple	Multicolor	Under 1 inch	1 to 3 inches	Over 3 inches	One per stem	Spikes	Clusters	Spring	Summer	Fall	Winter	Under 2 feet	2 to 3 feet	Over 3 feet	Fragrance	Distinctive foliage	Sun	Partial shade	Well drained	Moist to wet
ACANTHUS MOLLIS (bear's-breech)	●		●				●		●				●					●		●	●	●		
ACHILLEA FILIPENDULINA (fern-leaved yarrow)		●			●				●			●	●					●		●	●			
ACHILLEA MILLEFOLIUM 'FIRE KING' (common yarrow)			●		●				●			●	●	●			●		●	●	●			
ACONITUM CAMMARUM SPARKIANUM (Spark's Variety monkshood)				●			●			●			●					●				●		●
ADONIS VERNALIS (spring adonis)	●	●					●	●			●	●				●					●	●		
ALTHAEA ROSEA (hollyhock)			●					●		●			●					●			●		●	●
ANAPHALIS YEDOENSIS (Japanese pearly everlasting)	●						●				●		●			●				●	●	●	●	
ANCHUSA AZUREA (Italian bugloss)				●			●				●		●				●				●			
ANEMONE HYBRIDA (Japanese anemone)	●		●				●				●		●	●			●				●	●		
ANTHEMIS TINCTORIA (golden marguerite)		●					●		●				●	●			●			●	●			
AQUILEGIA HYBRIDA (columbine)	●	●	●	●	●		●	●			●	●	●				●				●	●		
ARMERIA PLANTAGINEA (sea pink)			●				●				●	●	●			●					●		●	
ARTEMISIA ALBULA 'SILVER KING' (wormwood)	●			●							●		●					●		●	●		●	
ARUNCUS SYLVESTER (goatsbeard)	●					●					●		●					●				●		●
ASCLEPIAS TUBEROSA (butterfly weed)		●					●				●		●				●				●		●	
ASPERULA ODORATA (sweet woodruff)	●				●		●				●	●				●			●			●		●
ASTER FRIKARTII (aster)			●			●	●				●	●	●	●		●					●			
ASTER NOVI-BELGII (Michaelmas daisy)	●		●	●			●				●		●	●				●			●			
ASTILBE ARENDSII (astilbe)	●		●			●				●			●				●			●	●	●		●
BAPTISIA AUSTRALIS (blue false indigo)				●			●			●			●					●			●			
BELLIS PERENNIS (English daisy)	●		●			●			●			●	●	●	●	●							●	
BERGENIA CORDIFOLIA (heart-leaved bergenia)	●		●					●		●	●	●				●				●	●	●		
BOLTONIA LATISQUAMA (pink boltonia)			●				●	●					●	●				●			●			
BRUNNERA MACROPHYLLA (Siberian bugloss)				●	●					●	●	●				●						●		●
CALLIRHOE INVOLUCRATA (low poppy mallow)			●				●		●				●								●		●	
CAMPANULA MEDIUM (Canterbury bell)	●		●	●			●		●				●				●				●	●	●	
CAMPANULA PERSICIFOLIA (peach-leaved bellflower)	●		●				●		●				●			●					●	●	●	
CASSIA MARILANDICA (wild senna)		●						●			●		●					●			●			
CATANANCHE CAERULEA (Cupid's-dart)				●			●		●				●	●						●	●		●	
CENTAUREA MONTANA (mountain bluet)			●				●		●				●	●		●					●			
CENTAUREA RUTIFOLIA (dusty miller)		●	●	●			●						●				●			●	●			
CENTRANTHUS RUBER (Jupiter's-beard)	●	●					●				●		●				●	●			●		●	
CERATOSTIGMA PLUMBAGINOIDES (leadwort)			●				●				●		●	●		●				●	●	●		
CHEIRANTHUS CHEIRI (English wallflower)		●	●	●			●				●	●				●			●		●	●		
CHELONE LYONII (pink turtlehead)			●				●			●			●	●			●					●		●
CHRYSANTHEMUM COCCINEUM (painted daisy)	●							●	●				●			●					●	●	●	
CHRYSANTHEMUM MAXIMUM (Shasta daisy)	●						●	●					●	●		●	●				●		●	
CHRYSANTHEMUM MORIFOLIUM (hardy chrysanthemum)	●	●	●		●	●	●	●	●					●		●	●				●		●	
CIMICIFUGA SIMPLEX (Kamchatka bugbane)	●						●			●				●				●				●		●
CLEMATIS HERACLEAEFOLIA DAVIDIANA (fragrant tube clematis)			●				●				●		●	●		●			●		●			
CONVOLVULUS MAURITANICUS (ground morning-glory)				●			●	●	●				●	●		●					●		●	
COREOPSIS GRANDIFLORA (big-flowered coreopsis)		●					●		●				●				●				●		●	
CORONILLA VARIA (crown vetch)	●		●			●					●		●			●					●		●	
CORTADERIA SELLOANA (pampas grass)	●		●					●		●			●					●		●	●		●	
CORYDALIS LUTEA (yellow corydalis)		●				●					●	●	●			●					●	●	●	
DELPHINIUM ELATUM (candle delphinium)	●	●	●	●				●		●			●					●			●		●	
DELPHINIUM GRANDIFLORUM (Chinese delphinium)			●	●			●			●			●			●					●		●	
DIANTHUS ALLWOODII (Allwood's pink)	●		●				●		●				●			●			●		●		●	
DIANTHUS BARBATUS (sweet William)	●		●		●		●				●		●	●		●			●		●		●	

Unless variety names are given, the information above includes the colors and sizes of all recommended varieties of the species listed.

Species	FLOWER COLOR					FLOWER SIZE			FLOWER TYPES			BLOOMING SEASONS				PLANT HEIGHT			NOTED FOR		LIGHT		SOIL	
	White	Yellow to orange	Pink to red	Blue to purple	Multicolor	Under 1 inch	1 to 3 inches	Over 3 inches	One per stem	Spikes	Clusters	Spring	Summer	Fall	Winter	Under 2 feet	2 to 3 feet	Over 3 feet	Fragrance	Distinctive foliage	Sun	Partial shade	Well drained	Moist to wet
DIANTHUS CARYOPHYLLUS (border carnation)	●	●	●				●						●	●		●			●		●		●	
DICENTRA EXIMIA (fringed bleeding heart)			●		●				●			●	●	●		●				●	●	●	●	●
DICENTRA SPECTABILIS (common bleeding heart)			●			●					●	●					●			●	●	●	●	●
DICTAMNUS ALBUS PURPUREUS (gas plant)	●					●		●		●			●				●		●	●	●		●	
DIGITALIS PURPUREA (foxglove)	●	●	●	●			●			●			●					●			●	●	●	
DORONICUM CAUCASICUM (Caucasian leopard's-bane)		●				●	●		●			●				●					●	●	●	
ECHINACEA PURPUREA (purple coneflower)	●		●				●						●	●			●				●	●	●	
ECHINOPS 'TAPLOW BLUE' (globe thistle)				●		●	●						●	●				●		●	●	●	●	
EPIMEDIUM GRANDIFLORUM (long-spurred epimedium)	●	●	●	●	●	●				●	●	●				●				●		●	●	●
ERIGERON HYBRIDS (fleabane)			●	●		●							●				●				●		●	
ERYNGIUM OLIVERIANUM (Oliver sea holly)			●	●	●		●						●	●			●			●	●		●	
EUPATORIUM COELESTINUM (mistflower)				●				●			●			●			●				●	●	●	
EUPHORBIA EPITHYMOIDES (cushion spurge)		●				●						●				●				●	●	●	●	
FELICIA AMELLOIDES (blue daisy)				●		●			●			●	●	●	●	●					●		●	
FILIPENDULA HEXAPETALA FLORE PLENO (dropwort)	●					●				●	●		●			●			●	●	●			●
GAILLARDIA ARISTATA (blanketflower)		●	●		●	●	●	●					●	●		●					●		●	
GAZANIA LONGISCAPA (gazania)	●	●	●			●	●		●	●	●	●	●			●					●		●	
GENTIANA SEPTEMFIDA (gentian)			●			●							●			●						●		●
GERANIUM GRANDIFLORUM (lilac crane's-bill)			●			●	●				●	●	●			●			●					
GERBERA JAMESONII (Barberton daisy)	●	●	●					●				●	●	●		●					●		●	●
GEUM CHILOENSE (Chilean avens)		●	●			●					●	●	●			●				●	●		●	●
GYPSOPHILA PANICULATA (babies'-breath)	●		●			●					●		●	●			●				●		●	
HELENIUM AUTUMNALE (sneezeweed)		●	●			●		●					●	●		●	●				●			●
HELIANTHUS DECAPETALUS FLORE PLENO (double thin-leaved sunflower)		●					●	●					●					●			●			●
HELIOPSIS SCABRA (rough heliopsis)		●			●		●	●					●	●			●				●			●
HELLEBORUS NIGER (Christmas rose)	●						●	●	●			●		●	●	●						●	●	
HEMEROCALLIS HYBRIDS (day lily)		●	●		●			●	●			●	●	●		●	●	●			●	●	●	●
HESPERIS MATRONALIS (dame's rocket)	●		●			●				●	●	●	●				●		●		●	●	●	●
HEUCHERA SANGUINEA (coral-bells)	●		●			●			●	●	●	●	●			●				●	●	●	●	●
HIBISCUS MOSCHEUTOS (rose mallow)	●		●				●	●					●	●				●			●	●	●	●
HOSTA PLANTAGINEA (fragrant plantain lily)	●					●		●		●			●	●		●			●	●	●	●	●	●
HYPERICUM MOSERIANUM (goldflower St.-John's-wort)		●				●			●				●	●		●				●	●	●	●	
IBERIS SEMPERVIRENS (evergreen candytuft)	●					●					●	●	●			●				●	●	●	●	●
INCARVILLEA DELAVAYI (Delavay incarvillea)			●			●					●		●			●				●	●	●		
IRIS, BEARDED HYBRID (tall bearded iris)	●	●	●	●	●		●	●	●			●	●				●		●		●	●	●	
IRIS, BEARDLESS HYBRID (Japanese iris)	●	●	●	●	●			●	●				●				●	●			●		●	●
IRIS PSEUDACORUS (yellow flag iris)		●				●			●				●				●				●			●
IRIS SIBIRICA (Siberian iris)	●		●	●		●			●				●				●			●	●		●	●
KNIPHOFIA UVARIA (red-hot poker)	●	●	●		●		●	●		●			●	●			●	●			●		●	
LATHYRUS LATIFOLIUS (perennial pea)	●		●				●				●		●	●				●			●		●	
LAVANDULA OFFICINALIS (true lavender)				●		●	●			●			●			●	●		●	●	●		●	
LIATRIS SPICATA (spike gay-feather)				●		●	●			●			●				●	●			●		●	●
LIMONIUM LATIFOLIUM (wide-leaved sea lavender)			●	●		●					●		●			●					●		●	
LINUM PERENNE (perennial flax)	●		●			●	●					●	●			●				●	●		●	
LIRIOPE MUSCARI (big blue lily-turf)	●			●		●				●			●	●		●				●	●	●	●	●
LUNARIA ANNUA (honesty)	●		●	●		●				●	●	●	●				●			●	●	●	●	
LUPINUS 'RUSSELL HYBRID' (lupine)	●	●	●	●		●				●	●	●	●				●				●	●	●	
LYCHNIS CHALCEDONICA (Maltese cross)			●			●					●		●				●				●			●
LYCHNIS VISCARIA 'FLORE PLENO' (German catchfly)			●			●					●	●	●			●				●	●		●	

Unless variety names are given, the information above includes the colors and sizes of all recommended varieties of the species listed.

CHARACTERISTICS OF PERENNIALS AND BIENNIALS: CONTINUED

	FLOWER COLOR					FLOWER SIZE			FLOWER TYPES			BLOOMING SEASONS				PLANT HEIGHT			NOTED FOR		LIGHT		SOIL	
	White	Yellow to orange	Pink to red	Blue to purple	Multicolor	Under 1 inch	1 to 3 inches	Over 3 inches	One per stem	Spikes	Clusters	Spring	Summer	Fall	Winter	Under 2 feet	2 to 3 feet	Over 3 feet	Fragrance	Distinctive foliage	Sun	Partial shade	Well drained	Moist to wet
LYTHRUM SALICARIA (purple loosestrife)			●				●			●			●	●				●			●	●	●	●
MACLEAYA CORDATA (pink plume poppy)	●						●				●		●					●			●	●		●
MALVA ALCEA FASTIGIATA (hollyhock mallow)			●				●		●				●	●				●			●	●		
MECONOPSIS BETONICIFOLIA (Himalayan blue poppy)				●			●		●				●			●	●					●	●	
MIRABILIS JALAPA (four-o'clock)	●	●	●	●	●		●				●		●	●			●		●		●			
MONARDA DIDYMA (bee balm)			●				●				●		●				●		●		●	●		●
MYOSOTIS SCORPIOIDES SEMPERFLORENS (dwarf perpetual forget-me-not)	●		●	●		●				●	●	●	●			●						●		●
NEPETA FAASSINII (mauve catmint)			●		●		●			●			●			●			●	●	●	●		
NIEREMBERGIA CAERULEA (blue cupflower)			●				●				●		●			●					●	●	●	●
OENOTHERA TETRAGONA (sundrops)		●					●		●				●	●		●					●		●	
OPHIOPOGON JAPONICUS (dwarf lily-turf)			●				●			●			●			●				●	●	●	●	
PAEONIA LACTIFLORA (Chinese peony)	●	●	●				●	●	●			●				●	●		●	●	●			
PAPAVER NUDICAULE (Iceland poppy)	●	●	●			●	●		●			●	●			●					●		●	
PAPAVER ORIENTALE (Oriental poppy)	●		●				●	●	●			●	●			●	●				●		●	
PENSTEMON GLOXINIOIDES (penstemon)	●		●	●			●			●			●	●		●					●		●	
PHLOX DIVARICATA (Canada phlox)	●		●				●			●	●	●				●			●		●	●		
PHLOX PANICULATA (garden phlox)	●		●	●	●		●				●		●			●	●		●		●	●		
PHORMIUM TENAX (New Zealand flax)		●	●					●	●		●		●					●		●	●	●		
PHYSALIS ALKEKENGI (Chinese lantern plant)		●			●						●		●			●					●	●		
PHYSOSTEGIA VIRGINIANA (false dragonhead)	●		●				●	●		●			●	●		●	●				●	●		
PLATYCODON GRANDIFLORUS (balloonflower)	●		●	●			●						●			●					●	●	●	
POLEMONIUM CAERULEUM (Jacob's-ladder)	●		●				●		●	●	●		●			●					●	●	●	
POLYGONUM REYNOUTRIA (Reynoutria fleeceflower)			●			●					●		●	●		●				●	●	●		
PRIMULA DENTICULATA (Himalayan primrose)			●				●		●		●	●				●				●		●	●	
PRIMULA JAPONICA (Japanese primrose)	●		●				●		●	●		●				●				●		●		
PRIMULA POLYANTHA (polyanthus primrose)	●	●	●	●	●		●			●	●	●				●				●		●		
PULMONARIA ANGUSTIFOLIA (blue lungwort)	●		●	●	●		●			●	●	●				●						●		
ROMNEYA COULTERI (matilija poppy)	●						●	●	●				●	●				●	●	●	●		●	
RUDBECKIA FULGIDA (orange coneflower)		●					●	●	●				●	●			●				●	●	●	
SALVIA HAEMATODES (bloodvein sage)			●				●		●	●			●				●			●		●		
SALVIA PITCHERII (Pitcher's sage)			●				●			●			●					●			●		●	
SANTOLINA CHAMAECYPARISSUS (lavender cotton)		●			●			●					●				●		●	●	●	●	●	
SCABIOSA CAUCASICA (pincushion flower)	●		●	●			●		●				●	●		●				●				●
SEDUM SPECTABILE (showy stonecrop)	●		●			●					●		●	●		●				●	●	●	●	
SIDALCEA HYBRIDS (hybrid prairie mallow)			●				●		●	●			●				●	●	●		●	●		●
SOLIDAGO HYBRIDS (hybrid goldenrod)		●					●			●			●	●			●				●	●		
SOLIDASTER LUTEUS (solidaster)		●					●				●		●	●		●					●	●		
STACHYS MACRANTHA (big betony)			●				●	●		●			●			●					●		●	
STACHYS OLYMPICA (lamb's ears)			●				●			●			●			●				●	●		●	
STOKESIA LAEVIS (Stokes's aster)	●	●	●	●			●	●					●	●		●				●		●		
THALICTRUM ROCHEBRUNIANUM (lavender mist meadow rue)			●			●		●			●		●	●				●		●	●	●	●	●
THERMOPSIS CAROLINIANA (Carolina thermopsis)		●					●	●		●			●					●			●	●	●	
TRADESCANTIA VIRGINIANA (Virginia spiderwort)	●		●	●			●				●	●	●			●					●	●		
TROLLIUS LEDEBOURII (Ledebour globeflower)		●					●	●	●			●	●			●					●	●		●
VALERIANA OFFICINALIS (common valerian)			●			●					●		●					●	●	●	●	●		
VERBASCUM HYBRIDS (hybrid mullein)	●	●	●				●			●			●	●			●				●		●	
VERONICA SPICATA (speedwell)			●			●				●			●	●		●				●	●		●	
VIOLA WILLIAMSII (viola)	●	●	●	●		●			●			●	●	●	●	●						●		●
VIOLA WITTROCKIANA (pansy)	●	●	●	●	●		●		●			●	●			●						●		●

Unless variety names are given, the information above includes the colors and sizes of all recommended varieties of the species listed.

154

Picture credits

The sources for the illustrations that appear in this book are shown below. Credits for the pictures from left to right are separated by semicolons, from top to bottom by dashes. Cover —Evelyn Hofer. 4—Keith Martin courtesy James Underwood Crockett; Leonard Wolfe. 6—"Picking Chrysanthemums by Night" by Suzuki Harunobu, Nellie P. Carter Collection, Courtesy Museum of Fine Arts, Boston. 13—Drawings by Matt Greene. 17—Humphrey Sutton. 18,19—Evelyn Hofer. 20 —James Underwood Crockett. 21—Evelyn Hofer except top Peter Hunt. 22,23,24—Evelyn Hofer. 25—Evelyn Hofer except left Gottlieb Hampfler. 26,27—Jerome Eaton. 28,29 —Humphrey Sutton. 30,31,32—Evelyn Hofer. 34,38,40,42, 44,46,47,49—Drawings by Matt Greene. 50—Drawings by Davis Meltzer and Rebecca Merrilees. 51,52,53—Drawings by Davis Meltzer. 54—Drawings by Matt Greene. 59 through 65—Steinbicker-Houghton. 66,67—Costa Manos from Magnum. 68,69—Gene Daniels from Black Star. 70,71—Steven C. Wilson. 72,73—Steinbicker-Houghton. 74,75—Steinbicker-Houghton; Evelyn Hofer. 76,77—Steinbicker-Houghton. 78 —Humphrey Sutton. 81,82,84,86,87—Drawings by Matt Greene. 90 through 150—Illustrations by Allianora Rosse. 151—Map by Adolph E. Brotman.

Acknowledgments

For their help in the preparation of this book, the editors wish to thank the following: Fumie Adachi, Japan Society, New York City; Agricultural Extension Service, Texas A&M University, College Station, Texas; Agricultural Extension Service, University of Florida, Institute of Food and Agricultural Sciences, Gainesville, Fla.; Clifford W. Benson, Secretary, American Iris Society, St. Louis, Mo.; Mr. and Mrs. Robert B. Branstead, Bethesda, Md.; Marian T. Brodnax, Publicity Director, American Day Lily Society, Birmingham, Ala.; Brother Charles, Mission Gardens, Techny, Ill.; Miss Isabel M. Chappell, Bethesda, Md.; Ira B. Cross, Berkeley, Calif.; A. F. DeWerth, Floriculture Section, Texas A&M University, College Station, Texas; Mrs. William Dines, President, American Primrose Society, Redmond, Wash.; Jerome A. Eaton, Director, Old Westbury Gardens, Old Westbury, N.Y.; Professor Charles C. Fischer, Department of Floriculture and Ornamental Horticulture, Cornell University, Ithaca, N.Y.; Fred Galle, Director of Horticulture, Callaway Gardens, Pine Mountain, Ga.; Miss Gladys Guinn, Bethesda, Md.; Mr. and Mrs. Reuben Guzman, Danville, Calif.; Cyrus Happy, Tacoma, Wash.; Mrs. William W. Hoffman, Bar Harbor, Me.; Keiso Ishizu, Sunnyslope Gardens, San Gabriel, Calif.; Ted King, King's Chrysanthemums, Hayward, Calif.; Dr. Leslie Laking, Director, Royal Botanical Gardens, Hamilton, Ontario; Larry Leuthold, Extension Horticulturist, Cooperative Extension Service, Kansas State University, Manhattan, Kansas; Mildred D. McCormick, Bar Harbor, Me.; Mrs. Samuel Eliot Morison, Northeast Harbor, Me.; Dr. Neil G. Odenwald, Louisiana Cooperative Extension Service, Louisiana State University A&M College, University Station, La.; John C. Portelroy, President, National Chrysanthemum Society, Inc., U.S.A., Baldwin, N.Y.; Robert Schreiner, Schreiner's Gardens, Salem, Ore.; Dr. Thomas J. Sheehan, Department of Ornamental Horticulture, University of Florida, Gainesville, Fla.; Mr. and Mrs. Frank P. Sheppard, East Hampton, N.Y.; George H. Spalding, Botanical Information Consultant, Los Angeles State and County Arboretum, Los Angeles, Calif.; Mr. and Mrs. Walter H. Stryker, Forge Village, Mass.; Alex J. Summers, President, American Hosta Society, Roslyn, N.Y.; Theodore S. Swanson, Swanson's Land of Flowers, Seattle, Wash.; Mr. and Mrs. R. Amory Thorndike, Bar Harbor, Me.; Andre Viette, Martin Viette Nurseries, East Norwich, N.Y.; Mr. and Mrs. George Paul Watts, Armonk, N.Y.; Mrs. Troy R. Westmeyer, President, Society for Japanese Irises, Stamford, Conn.; Roy T. Whitesel, Silver Spring, Md.; Wayne C. Whitney, Department of Horticulture and Forestry, University of Nebraska, Lincoln, Neb.; Dr. Gwendolyn B. Wood, President, Potomac Chrysanthemum Society, Bethesda, Md.

Bibliography

Berrall, Julia S., *The Garden, An Illustrated History*. The Viking Press, 1966.

Brooklyn Botanic Garden, *Handbook on Propagation*. Brooklyn Botanic Garden, 1970.

Coats, Alice M., *Flowers and Their Histories*. McGraw-Hill Book Company, 1968.

Collingridge Books, *Pictorial Gardening*. The Hamlyn Publishing Group, Ltd., 1969.

Cumming, Roderick W., *The Chrysanthemum Book*. D. Van Nostrand Company, Inc., 1964.

Cumming, Roderick W. and Robert E. Lee, *Contemporary Perennials*. The Macmillan Company, 1960.

Free, Montague, *All About the Perennial Garden*. The American Garden Guild and Doubleday and Company, Inc., 1955.

Free, Montague, *Plant Propagation in Pictures*. Doubleday and Company, Inc., 1961.

Hottes, Alfred C., *A Little Book of Perennials*. A. T. De La Mare Company, 1923.

Jekyll, Gertrude, *On Gardening*. Charles Scribner's Sons, 1964.

Lanning, Roper, *Hardy Herbaceous Plants*. Penguin Books, 1960.

Nehrling, Arno and Irene, *The Picture Book of Perennials*. Hearthside Press, Inc., 1964.

Pettingill, Amos, *The White-Flower-Farm Garden Book*. Alfred A. Knopf, 1971.

Pirone, Pascal P., *Diseases and Pests of Ornamental Plants*. The Ronald Press Company, 1970.

Robinson, William, *The English Flower Garden*. Charles Scribner's Sons, 1933.

Rodale, J. I. and Staff, *Encyclopedia of Gardening*. Rodale Books, Inc., 1959.

Shurtleff, Malcolm C., *How to Control Plant Diseases in Home and Garden*. Iowa State University Press, 1966.

Sitwell, Sacheverell, *Old Fashioned Flowers*. Charles Scribner's Sons, 1939.

Sunset Books, *Organic Gardening*. Lane Books, 1971.

Sunset Books, *Sunset Western Garden Book*. Lane Magazine and Book Company, 1967.

Westcott, Cynthia, *The Gardener's Bug Book*. Doubleday and Company, Inc., 1964.

Wyman, Donald, *Wyman's Gardening Encyclopedia*. The Macmillan Company, 1971.

Index

Numerals in italics indicate an illustration of the subject mentioned

Lychnis, 131, chart 153. *See also*
 Catchfly, German; Maltese cross
Lythrum, 20, *21,* 25, *131, chart* 154

m *acleaya, 131-132, chart* 154. *See
 also* Plume poppy
Magnesium, 36
Maintenance, 9-10, 12
Malathion, *chart* 50, *chart* 51
Mallow. *See Malva*
Mallow, poppy. *See Callirhoë*
Mallow, prairie. *See Sidalcea*
Mallow, rose, *chart* 50. *See also
 Hibiscus*
Maltese cross, 25. *See also Lychnis*
Malva, 132, chart 154
Maneb, *chart* 52
Mantis, praying, *chart* 53
Marguerite, *18. See also
 Chrysanthemum*
Marguerite, blue. *See Felicia*
Marguerite, golden, 24. *See also
 Anthemis*
Marigold, 31
Marvel-of-Peru. *See Mirabilis*
Matricaria. See Chrysanthemum
Meadow rue, 24, *28-29. See also
 Thalictrum*
Meadowsweet, *chart* 52. *See also
 Filipendula*
Mealy bugs, *chart* 53
Measure of love, 83
Meconopsis, 132-133, chart 154
Medium-sized plants, 13, 14, 15, 24-
 25
Megasea. See Bergenia
Metaldehyde, *chart* 51
Methoxychlor, *chart* 50
Michaelmas daisy. *See Aster*
Mildew, powdery, 47, *chart* 52
Milfoil. *See Achillea*
Milkweed, 39
Milky disease, *chart* 50, *chart* 53
Mirabilis, 133, chart 154
Mistflower, 15, 25, 80. *See also
 Eupatorium*
Mites: cyclamen, *chart* 51; spider,
 chart 51; as victims, *chart* 53
Miticide, *chart* 51
Moisture: in compost making, 35;
 mulching to conserve, 45; in soil, 10,
 33, 34; in propagation, 83, 84, 89
Monarda, 11, *133, chart* 154. *See also*
 Bee balm
Mondo grass. *See Ophiopogon*
Money plant. *See Lunaria*
Moneywort. *See Lunaria*
Monkshood, *28-29;* autumn, 25;
 diseases of, *chart* 52; pests, *chart*
 51; staking, 45, *46. See also
 Aconitum*
Moonwort. *See Lunaria*
Morning glory, ground. *See
 Convolvulus*
Moss phlox, 11, 80. *See also Phlox*
Mountain bluet, 25. *See also
 Centaurea*
Mowing strip, 12
Mugwort. *See Artemisia*
Mulching: to conserve moisture, 45,
 46, 47; materials for, 46-47, 57; to
 prevent weeds, 45, 46, 47; for
 winter protection, 57

Mullein. *See Verbascum*
Mullein pink. *See Lychnis*
Myosotis, 133-134, chart 154. *See also*
 Forget-me-not
Myosotis macrophylla. See Brunnera

n ational societies, 58, 61, 65, 73
Natural controls, 51, *chart* 53
Nepeta, 134, chart 154. *See also*
 Catmint
Nierembergia, 134, chart 154. *See also*
 Cupflower
Nitrogen, 34-35, 36-37, 44
Node, 83
Nutrients, 10, 11, 33, 34, 36, 38, 80

o bedient plant. *See Physostegia*
Oenothera, 135, chart 154. *See also*
 Sundrops
Oil, *chart* 50
Ophiopogon, 135, chart 154
Organic matter, 33-35, 36, 38,
 39
Oriental poppy. *See Papaver;* Poppy,
 Oriental
Oswego tea. *See Monarda*

p *aeonia, 135-136, chart* 154. *See
 also* Peony
Painted daisy, 24. *See also
 Chrysanthemum*
Pampas grass. *See Cortaderia*
Pansy, 26, 28, *chart* 50, 88. *See also
 Viola*
Papaver, 136-137, chart 154. *See also*
 Poppy, Iceland; Poppy, Oriental
Paris daisy. *See Chrysanthemum*
Pea, perennial, 79. *See also Lathyrus*
Pearly everlasting. *See Anaphalis*
Peat moss: acidity of, 36; grades of,
 34; as mulch, 47; as soil conditioner,
 33-36, 39, 40, 81, 89
Penstemon, 24, 28, *137-138, chart* 154
Peony, 7, 9, *24, 26-27,* 28; Chinese, as
 dominant flower, *24;* for cutting, 54-
 55; disbudding, 48, *49;* diseases of,
 chart 52; dividing and planting, *44;*
 fertilizing, 57; long life of, 8, 33;
 magical past of, 57; planting, 42, 43;
 propagation of, by dividing, 44;
 propagation of, from seed, 87; rate
 of growth of, 9, 80; staking, 45-46.
 See also Paeonia
Perlite, 83, 84
Pests, *chart* 50-51
Petunia, 9, *18,* 29, *30-31*
pH factor, 36, 38, 40
Phaltan, *chart* 52
Phlox, 9, 15, 16, *17, 19,* 25, 26, *28-29,
 30-31,* 41, 44, *138-139, chart* 154;
 diseases of, *chart* 52; as indicators
 of need for watering, 47; moss, 11,
 80; pests, *chart* 51; prolonging
 bloom of, 48-54; propagation
 of, by dividing, 80, 82; propagation
 of, by root cuttings, *86;* regeneration
 from roots of, 85; reversion of
 seedlings of, 54; thinning of, for
 large blooms, 48, *49*
Phormium, 139, chart 154
Phosphoric acid, 37, 57

Phosphorus, 35, 36-37, 44
Phygon, *chart* 52
Physalis, 139-140, chart 154. *See also*
 Chinese lantern plant
Physostegia, 140, chart 154. *See also*
 False dragonhead
Pinching back, 47-48, *49*
Pincushion flower, 25. *See also
 Scabiosa*
Pink, 15, 24, *chart* 51, 83, 88. *See also
 Dianthus*
Pink, ground. *See Phlox*
Pink, moss. *See Phlox*
Pink, mullein. *See Lychnis*
Pink, sea, 80. *See also Armeria*
Pistils, 8
Planning, 11-15, 18-21, 24-31; keynote
 flowers, *24-25;* on paper, 11-12, *13,*
 14-15, *26, 28, 29, 31;* shapes and
 colors, 20; succession of bloom, 18-
 19
Plantain lily, 10, 25. *See also Hosta*
Planting, 41, 42, 43, 44; bearded iris,
 42; peonies, 44
Platycodon, 140, chart 154. *See also*
 Balloonflower
Pleurisy root. *See Asclepias*
*Plumbago larpentae. See
 Ceratostigma*
Plume poppy, 11, 28. *See also
 Macleaya*
Poker plant. *See Kniphofia*
Polemonium, 140-141, chart 154. *See
 also* Jacob's-ladder
Polygonum, 141, chart 154
Poppy, 55
Poppy, California tree. *See Romneya*
Poppy, Himalayan blue. *See
 Meconopsis*
Poppy, Iceland, 24. *See also Papaver*
Poppy, matilija. *See Romneya*
Poppy, Oriental, 7, 9, *20,* 24, 26; for
 cutting, 55; planting, 41-42, 43;
 propagation of, by root cuttings, 85-
 86. *See also Papaver*
Poppy, plume, 11, 28. *See also
 Macleaya*
Poppy, Welsh. *See Meconopsis*
Poppy mallow. *See Callirhoë*
Potash, 37
Potassium, 36-37, 44
Potting mixture, 86, 87
Powdery mildew, *chart* 52
Prairie mallow. *See Sidalcea*
Praying mantis, *chart* 53
Predators, insect, *chart* 53
Primrose, 9, *68-71,* 79, 88; auricula,
 68-69, 70, 71; categories, *68-69;*
 pests, *chart* 51; polyanthus, 25, *68-
 69;* propagation of, by dividing, 80,
 82; specialization in, 58, 70. *See
 also Primula*
Primula, 68, *141-143, 142, chart* 154.
 See also Primrose
Propagation, 79-89; biological, 79; by
 division, *44,* 80-82, 89; from root
 cuttings, *85-86, 87,* 89; by root
 division, *42;* from seed, 8, 79, 86-
 89; from stem cuttings, 82-85, *84,*
 89; vegetative, 79-86
Protective strips, *chart* 51
Public gardens, 15
Pulmonaria, 143, chart 154
Purple loosestrife. *See Lythrum*

159

PRINTED IN U.S.A.